SP Pvt. Ltd.

Management in Practice

Challenges and Strategies

Mubashir Majid Baba

2019

Studium Press (India) Pvt. Ltd.

Management in Practice
Challenges and Strategies

ISBN: 978-93-85046-50-6

Published by:

Studium Press (India) Pvt. Ltd.
4735/22, 2nd Floor, Prakash Deep Building
(Near Delhi Medical Association),
Ansari Road, Darya Ganj, New Delhi-110 002
Tel.: + 91-11-43240200-15 (15 lines); Fax: 91-11-43240215
E-mail: pubdir@studiumpress.in

Printed at India

Foreword

It is a pleasure for me to write the foreword for the book *Management in Practice: Challenges & Strategies*, edited by Dr. Mubashir Majid Baba. This book aims to improve the understanding of trends and challenges in the field of management at the Indian as well as at the global level. It helps to create a connection between business readers and academic research. The book summarizes what is contextual—each year—in the field of management, but with a focus on showing something new to professionals from an academic perspective. The book deals with different functional areas of management like Human Resource Management, Marketing, Financial Management, Economics, Entrepreneurship, and Tourism Management.

The book contains 14 chapters featuring different aspects of management. The chapters cover Diversity Management and Organizational Performance, OCTAPACE Culture, E-Loyalty, CSR Initiatives, FDI, Potential of Dark Tourism of India, Gender Disparity, Antecedents of E-Retailing on Customer Satisfaction, Workforce Diversity and Discrimination, Self-Service Technologies, Health Micro-insurance, Perceptual Factors of E-Commerce, Entrepreneurship Promotion, Swachh Bharat Abhiyan and Tourism Industry.

The contributors are from a variety of academic institutions like Ibra College of Technology, Oman; Amity University, Noida; ITM University, Gwalior; University of Kashmir; Central University of Kashmir; Lovely Professional University, Jalandhar; Cluster University Srinagar; Jaipur National University, Jaipur; National Institute of Technology (NIT), Srinagar; Jamia Millia Islamia, New Delhi.

It is a daunting task for any scholar to identify the management challenges and then outline strategies to overcome those challenges in any given year. Given this, summarizing the vast literature in management science and identifying the most cutting edge phenomena is an arduous task. I congratulate Dr. Mubashir Majid Baba for this book and look forward to seeing it soon.

Finally this book is highly topical and should be of interest to all stakeholders in the field of management. I recommend this book as a "must read" to anyone interested in issues dealing with management challenges in the current business scenario.

Prof. (Dr.) Himanshu Rai

Director

Indian Institute of Management (IIM), Indore

About the Editor

Dr. Mubashir Majid Baba is presently associated with National Institute of Technology (NIT), Srinagar Kashmir in the Department of Humanities and Social Science (Management). He has previously worked as Assistant Professor in Department of Management Studies, Cluster University Srinagar; Mittal School of Business, accredited by Accreditation Council for Business Schools and Programs (ACBSP), USA, Lovely Professional University, Jalandhar; and at Department of Management Studies (North Campus), University of Kashmir, Srinagar. Dr. Baba holds Ph.D. in Business Administration from University of Kashmir, Masters Degree in Business Administration (MBA) from Central University of Kashmir. In addition, the editor holds Post Graduate Diploma in International Business Operations (PGDIBO) and Post Graduate Diploma in Information Technology (PGDIT). Dr. Baba has one book to his credit and has published papers in journals of National/International repute and has also presented papers in National/International conferences, besides attended many workshops, seminars, conferences outside state. He has also remained associated with Indian Institute of Management, Lucknow (IIML) as Project Fellow. The editor was also selected for prestigious Stipendium Hungaricum Scholarship 2015 by Tempus Public Foundation and University Grants Commission (UGC) for Ph.D. programme in University of Kaposvar (Doctoral school for Management and Organization Science), Hungary as a Stipendium Hungaricum Scholar. The editor is columnist for various newspapers, the write ups mostly focus on education. His areas of interest include Organisational Behaviour, Human Resource Management, Leadership, Emotional Intelligence, Research Methodology, Marketing.

About the Editor

List of Contributors

Aastha Singh: Amity International Business School, Noida

Abid Suhail Nika: Department of Tourism Studies, Central University of Kashmir

Adil Amin Nazki: Department of Tourism Studies, Central University of Kashmir

Dr. Aditya Tripathi: School of Management, ITM University Gwalior, Madhya Pradesh

Dr. Bilal Ahmad Dar: School of Business and Management Jaipur National University, Jaipur

Dr. Chitra: Ibra College of Technology, Oman

Danish Mehraj: Department of Management Studies, University of Kashmir (J&K)

Prof. Fayaz Ahmad Nikka: Department of Management Studies, Central University of Kashmir, J&K

Dr. Gurinder Singh: Group Vice Chancellor, Amity University, Noida

Dr. Ishtiaq H. Qureshi: Department of Management Studies, University of Kashmir (J&K)

Prof. J.K. Tandon: School of Business and Management Jaipur National University, Jaipur

Dr. Jahangir Malik: Higher Education, Jammu and Kashmir

Prof. Keshav Kansana: School of Management, ITM University Gwalior, Madhya Pradesh

Dr. Mohd Rafiq Teli: Department of Management Studies, University of Kashmir

Dr. Mubashir Majid Baba: National Institute of Technology (NIT), Srinagar, J&K

Dr. Richa Goel: Amity International Business School, Noida, India

Prof. S. A. Mufeed: Dean, School of Business Studies, University of Kashmir (J&K)

Sadaf Mushtaq: Jamia Millia Islamia (Central University), New Delhi

Salsabeel Nazir: Department of Management Studies, Central University of Kashmir

Dr. Shahid Amin: School of Management, ITM University Gwalior, Madhya Pradesh

Dr. Sheikh Aftaab-Ul-Maroof: AAA Memorial Degree College, Bemina, Cluster University Srinagar (J&K)

Sugandh Arora: Mittal School of Business, Lovely Professional University, Jalandhar

Dr. Tahir Ahmad Wani: National Institute of Technology (NIT), Srinagar, J&K

Dr. Tawheed Nabi: Mittal School of Business, Lovely Professional University, Jalandhar

Ursil Majid Makhdoomi: Department of Management Studies, Central University of Kashmir

Waseem Jahangir: Department of Management Studies, Central University of Kashmir, J&K

Dr. Zahid H. Bhat: Department of Higher Education, Government of Jammu & Kashmir, J&K

Dr. Zia-ul-Haq: Department of Management Studies, Central University of Kashmir, J&K

Preface

Growing businesses face a range of challenges. As business grows, different problems arise which demand different solutions - what worked a year ago might now be not the best approach. Recognizing and overcoming the common pitfalls associated with growth is essential if your business is to continue to grow and thrive. Crucially, you need to ensure that the steps you take today don't themselves create additional problems for the future. Effective leadership will help you to make the most of the opportunities, thus creating sustainable growth for the future. This book is an attempt in the same direction.

The book follows the theme, *Management in Practice: Challenges & Strategies.* It deals with different functional areas of management where changes are occurring due to emergence of new business models and innovative ways to follow them.There are also many challenges facing businesses in the fast-paced globally oriented markets of today's world. One of the biggest, and also one of the hardest to solve, is how to effectively manage across the various functions of a business without micromanaging and without causing excessive delays or conflicts within these functions. Several different functions of a business may need to be integrated into a management plan, and there are numerous schools of thought on how to accomplish these challenges.

This modest effort is a result of the blessings of my mentors particularly Prof. Mushtaq Ahmad Siddiqi, Department of Management Studies, University of Kashmir. I also express gratitude to Prof. Himanshu Rai, Director, Indian Institute of Management (IIM), Indore for being a continuous source of motivation and guidance.

I also show appreciation for all the contributors of the research papers who shared their research experience with me, this book would not have been possible without them. I am also thankful to STUDIUM PRESS for publishing this book.

Last but not least, I dedicate this book to my Parents and my Sister Er. Samiya.

I am sure that the book will be a good source of reference for managers, researchers, academicians and students in issues dealing with management challenges in the current business scenario.

Dr. Mubashir Majid Baba
(Editor)

Table of Contents

1

A Study on Diversity Management and Its Impact on Organizational Performance with Special Reference to Hospitality Industry in India

CHITRA[1]*, GURINDER SINGH[2], AASTHA SINGH[3] AND RICHA GOEL[4]

ABSTRACT

The main intent of this study is to examine whether an organization benefits by investing in diversity and diversity management practices. Any investment requires a profitable gain over an extended period of time and similarly, diversity management and its practices must have an impact on the overall performance and profitability of the company. The main objectives of this paper are: to understand the effect of diversity and its factors on organizational performance in the hospitality industry and to understand the impact of Human Resource practices on organizational performance in the hospitality industry. These issues have prompted the study of diversity management in-depth and its effects on organizational performance. This research is of an exploratory nature that makes use of data collected from respondents by means of questionnaires. This study uses both qualitative and quantitative analytical techniques for data analysis. The results of this study show a positive relation existing between

[1] IBRA College of Technology, Oman.
[2] Amity University, Noida, UP, India.
[3,4] Amity International Business School, Noida, UP, India.
**Corresponding author:* E-mail: ananya.chitra@gmail.com

employee attraction, employee selection, employee inclusion, and employee retention on organizational performance. Employee selection plays maybe the higher role among the four in influencing the changes in organizational performance. Further implications of this study have also been included.

Key words: Diversity, Organizational performance, Retention, Selection.

BACKGROUND

It is evident to say that diversity is an essential tool in building business strength. If the hiring procedure is conducted through partial means improper planning, or if the selected candidates consist of people with thinking like that of the current employees, the end result would lead to a pool of candidates with less diversity. For any B2C companies, however, the main function of diversity is to access markets worldwide. A diverse workforce helps to divert management from cognitive grooves and enables it to identify opportunities others will miss (Roberts, 2017).

Despite the fact that "valuing diversity" has become a common saying, a proper study of its impact on organizational performance has not yielded the desired results. The increasing amount of diversity within companies poses as one of the most challenging human resource issues of our time. Academicians and researchers have sought to study the impact of both diversity and its management on organizational performance. A diverse workforce and diverse customers, combined with worldwide market reach and global competition is leading to an increase in amount of variety that an organization has to handle and therefore challenging current diversity management theories as well as creating new ones (counter-theories). In today's times, diversity management is under the spotlight and more and more companies are on the lookout for people who have knowledge in the area, owing to globalization and its effect on individuals and families. The process of diversity management and its alignment with the organization mission and vision is essential for the effective management of people who may come from different parts of the globe and work together in the organization. Several other studies expedite strategically different and often creative methods of problem solving and decision-making, leading to fewer errors in final implementations that thereby lead to better and sometimes more fruitful results. It also increases creativity and innovation leading to better organizational performance (Robbins, Odendaal & Roodt, 2003).

The entry of diversity into human resources occurred in the late 20th century, when the concept of globalization had bought out new opportunities for various industries across various countries. This was shortly followed by the need for movement and business expansion into other countries. This bought up the need for individuals with knowledge about the way the industry should work abroad. Over a period of time, almost every organization that had gone global refrained from having a homogeneous workforce and supported a uniquely diverse culture. This internal diversity, however bought about the need for better management for people from various cultural backgrounds. If the company is to exploit the presence of a variety of individuals for their betterment, there had to be better measures taken to ensure that the employees were treated fairly and equally. Workers will probably feel good and cheerful in a domain where inclusivity is a need. Fairness in the working environment is vital for empowering laborers from all foundations to feel certain about their capacity and accomplish their best. The higher the camaraderie, the more gainful workers are organizations having a diverse workforce are highly capable of providing quality products and services due to the expanded knowledge about the various types of customers and their requirements (Wentling & Palma-Rivas, 2000). Having a diverse human resource can aid in acquiring various niche markets. Over the past few decades, there has been an increase in diversity related practices within organizations, as people have begun to speak up against discrimination, against sexism, against suppression and various other issues. Companies have bought about various reforms, such as increasing the ratio of women to men in the workforce, equal pay on the basis of job, equal opportunities for minorities, and equal learning and development opportunities for all.

With an increased gravity of movement, comes greater diversity within a company, and with that, more complicated human resource practices and dynamic workforces. And while that can prove to be an advantage, if company strategies and work teams are planned out well, it can also cause serious backlashes from people from various backgrounds that are unable to work in unison. Diversity Management thus helps companies in stepping out of their national boundaries and going international, all while curbing unnecessary obstacles that arise due to cultural, racial or gender differences. When companies involve themselves towards leading a diverse workforce, they are likely to be more successful. High diversity companies are said to attract the talent they need, implement selection practices that do not discriminate, give employees a sense of inclusion and empowerment and retain the talent they wish to keep. All of this ultimately leads to a high return on investment.

When it comes to research about diversity, a study by (Allmark, 2004), a paradoxical situation was created wherein the author debates whether research samples should include the diversity of the population. While on one hand, the inclusion of diversity would allow for easy analysis of the population, on the other hand its representation would contradict itself. Various findings and assumptions have been made in this field of study and this study intends to add more towards the development of the subject. A diverse workforce makes your organization more grounded, which can expand development and benefits. Organization development assumes a vital part in representative development, as it gives more chances to progression. Workers who originate from an assortment of racial and ethnic gatherings and genders can give important knowledge with respect to the best promoting or client benefit strategies to expand deals and enhance consumer loyalty appraisals among their separate gatherings.

In a study conducted on the impact of workforce diversity on organizational performance in the education sector in Karachi by (Iqbal & Shah, 2015) it was found that a relation exists between gender and experience. It was also found that no relationship exists between diversity and efficiency and diversity and effectiveness in the education sector. On the other hand, education diversity, and efficiency and effectiveness have a positive relationship. This goes to prove that a variety in education level can still allow proper functioning in an organization. A study conducted on the influence of diversity management practices on performance in commercial government agencies in Kenya (Kyambi, 2015) showed that these practices, namely diversity recruitment, diversity training, diversity retention and institutionalization of diversity are important procedures for enhancing and maintaining the standard of organizational performance of non-commercial government agencies in Kenya. They also suggested that a comprehensive and suitable work environment can bring about the creation of improved diversity goals for the sector. The study on Cultural Intelligence and Openness and its effects on task performance (Duff, Tahbaz & Chan, 2012) give a view on diversity management from the emotional aspect. The results to the study were an important addition in diversity literature. They showed that the effectiveness and execution of a task by culturally diverse parties is possible when behavioral intelligence of the culturally diverse parties is taken into view. Cultural Intelligence, *i.e.,* the process and ability to accept a new cultural environment and people with higher Cultural Intelligence were seen to hold leadership and management in regards to cross-cultural encounters.

A secondary study by (Gavrea, Ilies & Stegerean, 2011) allowed the researchers to develop a model allowing Romanian manufacturing companies to find a relation between their operations and performance. They made the use of current literature and identified various factors affecting an organizations' performance. The results to the research showed only 55% of the Romanian companies considered performance enhancement procedures a priority. A large section of the industry was yet to consider the importance of performance enhancement as an important tool of progress. A study by (Chaudhary & Gupta, 2010) shows that gender biases continue to exist even in the 21st century. The study claimed the fact that women are mostly not favored in the organizational policies and there is evidence of biases in management practices. Men are often preferred for higher and authoritative positions while women, especially young employees were assigned at the front end service or other lower positions. Despite various measures and reforms taken by the government, the empowerment that women receive in the hotel industry is still relatively low. Another study, giving the holistic view of diversity management (Ollapally & Bhatnagar, 2009) gave view on the importance of diversity management in the changing times. It should be incorporate into the company strategy as it directly has an effect on the bottom line. That being said, the Human Resources department should make constant efforts and device strategies to attract and retain a good quality diverse workforce. The trend has begun its initiation phase in organizations present in India.

A study by (Choy, 2007) found that inclusion of the diversity domain is crucial as more and more companies choose to go international and multicultural. The study stressed on the importance of shaping the levels of organizational development to be more culture friendly, and thus to enhance international human resource management. The obstacles that workforce diversity and communication with multicultural individuals pose can only be overcome when managers take into account the variety of behaviors, attitudes and values of the diverse workforce that go across national and socio-cultural boundaries. In the study conducted by (Bassett-Jones, 2005) a paradox was identified. While the study proved that diversity is a driving force of creativity and innovation, that in turn drives competitiveness, it is also the reason behind several internal conflicts, miscommunication scenarios and comprehension abilities. Therefore, the companies that adopt the concept of diversity are in the midst of a paradox. While on one hand diversity creates a competition ground, on the other it may disrupt internal operations. In such a case, management of a company must strategize and implement a multi-layered structure that encapsulates effective Human Resource Policies and Practices, Quality Leadership, and Emotional Intelligence that can allow smooth flow of communication between individuals within the firm.

A case study conducted by (Kossek, Lobel & Brown, 2005) identified the need for strategies related to diversity and the responses from various organizations regarding the same. With the increasing need to better manage the variety of culture between employees, many organizations have marginally increased the limit of the budget they expend on diversity initiatives, with more focus on race and ethnicity. The study also implied further future scope of investment on diversity practices as they will hold a place of importance for the proper management of the diverse workforce. A secondary analysis on workforce diversity at IBM by (Jr., 2005) states the importance of diversity leadership and why it is necessary to interpret a foreseeable future of any company. The involvement of the Top Management, HR Management and diversity leaders is crucial because the workforce diversity cannot run smoothly without the presence of wither parties. There needs to be a proper amalgamation of the necessary parties without which, the concept is a failure.

Richard, Barnett, Dwyer and Chadwick (2004) sought to analyze the curvilinear relationships between race and gender diversity in management and organization performance. Results to their study showed that innovativeness and risk taking, both factors of firm performance had a positive and negative non-linear relationship on race and gender diversity respectively. This calls for the exploitation of existing cultural diversity to gain a competitive advantage. (Kundu, 2003) conducted a primary study on the reactions and opinions of employees about the workforce diversity status about their organizations. The results showed high levels of gender bias and gender based perceptions. While males were convinced that they more qualified and competent than their female counterparts, many of the female respondents believed that their chances of receiving monetary incentives than males. The study also took into view the opinions of minority, disabled and socially disadvantaged employees and revealed that such groups placed a lot of importance on their employer's initiatives to promote diversity.

A SWOT analysis of 63 papers was done by (Jackson, Joshi & Erhardt, 2003) to examine the impact of workforce diversity on teams and organizations. Conclusions to the study reveal that companies must actively be involved in diversity management if they are to unlock the abilities of their diverse workforce for their advantage. Many researches offer principles and strategies for companies to implement, however there is no concrete method of establishing the necessary changes for the benefit of an organization. A study by (Chatboth & Olsen, 2002) speaks about organizational leadership from a macro and micro perspective, and the analysis of a firm in the hospitality industry. The study considers diversity to be an important aspect in the development of organizational leadership. More and more companies within the industry should strive towards becoming leaders, lest they fall out of the crowd.

According to (Richard, 2000) a study was conducted to find out the relationships existing between racial diversity, business strategy and organizational performance in the banking industry. Results to the study show an increasing need for better business strategies and policies in support of culturally diverse employees. The involvement of Human Resource and the top management is crucial to ensure that these strategies have a positive impact on the company's overall performance, and not just as an initiative of corporate social responsibility. (Lorbiecki & Jack, 2000) conducted an in-depth analysis in order to analyze critical changes made in the timeline of diversity in its existing years. The study showed diversity in a positive light, and highlighted on the importance of diversity management to solve problems in the workplace related to discrimination, minorities, and most importantly, to implement successful organizational change. A study conducted by (Jehn, Northcraft & Neale, 1999) showed the impact of three types of diversity, namely social diversity, informational diversity, and value diversity and its impact on workgroup performance. The results of the study showed that different types of diversity and different consequences on performance in a group, which in turn affects other aspects related to the group like actual and perceived performance, satisfaction, motivation, and commitment. According to (Harrison, Price & Bell, 1998) there exist two levels of diversity. When these two levels were studied to analyze its impact on group cohesion, it was found that as the duration of group work persisted, the effects of surface-level diversity weakened while the effects of deep-level diversity increased. This was due to the prolonged exposure to the group activity and members that bought about such changes.

CONCEPTUAL FRAMEWORK

In this study we aim to find out the various implications of diversity in human resource practices and the impact it has on the organizational performance of a firm in the hospitality sector. The proposed model is given in Fig. 1. Further, the independent and dependent factors of our study are as follows:

***Independent Variable(s)*:**

- ***Employee attraction***
- ***Employee selection***
- ***Employee inclusion***
- ***Employee retention***

Dependent Variable(s):

- ***Organizational performance***

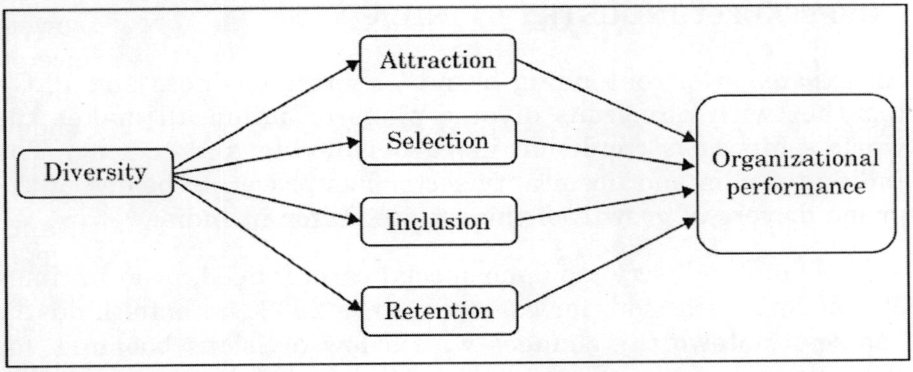

Fig. 1: Proposed model of the study.

DIVERSITY MANAGEMENT IN INDIA

India, a uniquely self-diverse geography that supports people with various cultural beliefs, norms and societies has the second largest population in the world. The youth make up the majority of the population and with the gradual increase in the retirement, more and more pressure is falling on the young minds.

Ram Nath Kovind, the newly appointed President of India, in 2017 said (Hebbar, 2017) the "key to India's success is its diversity. Our diversity is the core that makes us so unique". Nations, as he said, were "not built by governments alone", and required national pride, in the soil and water of the country, in its diversity and inclusiveness, in its culture and "in the little things we do every day".

With the changing population composition, changing norms and beliefs, organizational matters, and women empowerment, most of the Indian organizations are forced to accept the dynamic and diverse workforce. Women empowerment and the additional support from the government have led to an increase in the number of working women throughout the country. This has also led to the creation of dual-income, DINK, and DISK families. The changing scenario of the country holds many challenges as well as opportunities not just for women, but also other minority groups.

HOSPITALITY INDUSTRY IN INDIA

An expansion of contending brands, shorter business and PLC's together with numerous diverse plans of action all makes the world's business condition more perplexing and testing. The Indian tourism and hospitality sector has proven to be one of the prime drivers of growth of the service sector in India.

The hotel industry too is no special case. Indeed, even in times of economic recession, for example, since 2008 the hotel industry has seen noteworthy changes with a few divisions booming, for example, eateries, cafés and the spending lodgings areas, while others have seen a similarly sensational decay, for example, the general population house (authorized bar) area. There is also the continuing growth of boutique hotels, once the protest of energetic private lodging administrators, into critical chains inside bigger multinational chains. At the global level we likewise observe fast extension of global lodging brands, for example, Hilton, as the white collar classes develop in numerous nations including the BRIC nations to which are included some African economies.

The Indian hospitality industry is also known to be one of the main job creators, as it is able to hire people from wither rural or urban areas. India, being a famous tourist attraction supports a hue footfall in a year, and is also a contributor to the high revenue generated by hotels and resorts at tourist destinations.

OBJECTIVES OF THE RESEARCH

The main objectives of this paper are:

1. To understand the effect of diversity and its factors on organizational performance in the hospitality industry.
2. To understand the impact of Human Resource practices on organizational performance in the hospitality industry.

Research Hypotheses

In accordance to our objectives, we devise the following hypotheses:

Hypothesis 1a: There is no significant relationship between employee attraction and organizational performance.

Hypothesis 1b: There is a significant relationship between employee attraction and organizational performance.

Hypothesis 2a: There is no significant relationship between employee selection and organizational performance.

Hypothesis 2b: There is a significant relationship between employee selection and organizational performance.

Hypothesis 3a: There is no significant relationship between employee inclusion and organizational performance.

Hypothesis 3b: There is a significant relationship between employee inclusion and organizational performance.

Hypothesis 4a: There is no significant relationship between employee retention and organizational performance.

Hypothesis 4b: There is a significant relationship between employee retention and organizational performance.

Research Methodology

This paper makes use of primary research through means of exploratory research. The data for analysis was collected by means of a questionnaire and only collected from individuals employed under the hospitality industry. There were a total of 116 responses collected from various individuals working in the hotel industry. They belong to various organizations of the industry, but for research purposes, the names of the organizations was not deemed necessary, since this research does not target a specific brand or entity, but the industry as a whole. A consistent questionnaire was created that took into account all the variables required to fulfill our research objectives. The data required for both the independent as well as dependent factors was captured. The questionnaire was divided into three parts; the first part collected data related to the respondents' demography, the second part consisted of Likert Scale questions that assessed the respondents' opinion about diversity in their organization, and the third part also consists of questions in the Likert Scale format that captured the organizational performance aspect in the respondents' company.

This research makes use of the standardized questionnaire as a research instrument to collect data from the respondents. The survey was filled up by online means and no physical form of the questionnaire was distributed to any party. Respondents' received access to the questionnaire through sharing of the URL through known connections and parties. This research made use of both qualitative and quantitative techniques for data analysis. The data from the respondents was collected, codified and then tabulated accordingly. IBM's Statistical Program for Social Sciences (SPSS) [Version 23] was used for extensive and detailed analysis of the codified data. The program is well known by researchers and academicians for its friendly user interface, speed, accuracy and convenience. The demographics of the respondents' is depicted through pie charts, tables and percentages.

Research Findings

Response rate

The questionnaire for our study was only available online and accessible through ownership of the link. Through random sampling method, a total of 116 respondents, all employed in the hotel industry had filled up the questionnaire of their own accord.

Reliability analysis (Cronbach's alpha)

Cronbach's alpha reliability test is a famous measurement unit that gives the researcher the estimate of internal consistency reliability of their research data.

The result of Cronbach's alpha is generally a coefficient that can range from 0.0 to 1.0. A negative coefficient would mean negative consistency in the measurement process, which is inappropriate for further data analysis. A coefficient of 1.0 defines perfect consistency in measurement, however for the purpose of research; a score of more than 0.7 is also accepted as reliable variance. Since our Cronbach alpha coefficient is 0.95 (Table 1) we accept that our data is highly reliable for the purpose of further research and analysis.

Table 1: Cronbach's alpha

Reliability statistics	
Cronbach's alpha	***N of items***
.95	29

Source: Authors' own

KMO AND BARTLETT'S TEST OF SPHERICITY

The KMO and Bartlett's Test are conducted to find out the factors that are the most suitable for our research purposes. Our KMO factor of .88 (Table 2) indicates that our data set is well suited for factor analysis. The Bartlett's test for Sphericity indicates that our significance of .00 shows no scope of dimensionality reduction.

Table 2: KMO and Bartlett's

KMO and Bartlett's test		
Kaiser-Meyer-Olkin measure of sampling adequacy.		.880
Bartlett's Test of sphericity	Approx. Chi-Square	2539.099
	df	406
	Sig.	.000

Source: Authors' own

Inferential Analysis

Correlation analysis

This research made use of correlation analysis to understand the degree of relationship between diversity (independent variable) and organizational performance (dependent variable). According to the information prescribed in Business Research Methods by Cooper and Schindler, the coefficient of correlation (r) is a number ranging from -1 to +1. A +1 or a number higher than 0 indicates a positive relationship between the independent and dependent variables. On the contrary, a -1 or number less than 0 shows a negative correlation between the independent and dependent variables. 0 indicates that there is no correlation between the dependent and independent variable. Hence, a coefficient closer to +1 would indicate a positive linear relationship between the two variables, whereas a coefficient closer to -1 would show a negative linear relationship between the two variables.

Table 3: Correlation coefficients

		Correlations			
		Employee attraction	***Employee selection***	***Employee inclusion***	***Employee retention***
Organizational performance	Pearson correlation	.592**	.628**	.612**	.595**
	Sig. (2-tailed)	.000	.000	.000	.000
	N	116	116	116	116

Source: Authors' own

As the Table 3 depicts, there is a correlation of 0.592 between employee attraction and organizational performance, indicating that any change in attraction methods would have an impact on the organizational performance as well. Similarly (Table 4) the remaining factors also showed a positive correlation with organizational performance, highest being with employee selection and its process (0.628). This indicates that companies must have selection procedures that are pro-diversity and do not include any form of bias to ensure that the organization is able to perform well.

Regression Analysis

After correlation, this research made use of regression analysis by applying each of our independent variables to our dependent variables. According to Cooper and Schindler, the purpose of regression for this study is to analyze the degree of control each of the independent variables has on the dependent variable. It aims to examine the specific nature of relationship between each independent variable on the dependent variable.

Table 4: Correlation coefficients of all factors.

Correlations						
		EA	***ES***	***EI***	***ER***	***OP***
EA	Pearson correlation	1	.621**	.475**	.377**	.592**
	Sig. (2-tailed)		.000	.000	.000	.000
	N	116	116	116	116	116
ES	Pearson correlation	.621**	1	.590**	.538**	.628**
	Sig. (2-tailed)	.000		.000	.000	.000
	N	116	116	116	116	116
EI	Pearson correlation	.475**	.590**	1	.618**	.612**
	Sig. (2-tailed)	.000	.000		.000	.000
	N	116	116	116	116	116
ER	Pearson correlation	.377**	.538**	.618**	1	.595**
	Sig. (2-tailed)	.000	.000	.000		.000
	N	116	116	116	116	116
OP	Pearson correlation	.592**	.628**	.612**	.595**	1
	Sig. (2-tailed)	.000	.000	.000	.000	
	N	116	116	116	116	116

**. Correlation is significant at the 0.01 level (2-tailed).

Bivariate Analysis of Employee Attraction and Organizational Performance

The Table 5 showing the values of R and R^2 being positive indicate that there exists a positive relationship between employee attraction and organizational performance. The R^2 value of 0.35 indicates the explanatory power of employee attraction, *i.e.,* 35% of the variation in organizational performance was the result of variation in employee attraction. The remaining variation lies in with the other independent variables to varying degrees. This clearly proves that employee attraction influences organizational performance to a great extent.

Table 5: Regression model of employee attraction.

Model summary[b]					
Model	***R***	***R square***	***Adjusted R square***	***Std. error of the estimate***	***Durbin-Watson***
1	.592[a]	.350	.344	.41471	1.661

a. Predictors: (Constant), Employee attraction
b. Dependent variable: Organizational performance

Source: Authors' own

Table 6: ANOVA of Employee attraction and OP.

ANOVA[a]						
	Model	***Sum of squares***	***df***	***Mean square***	***F***	***Sig.***
1	Regression	10.554	1	10.554	61.362	.000[b]
	Residual	19.607	114	.172		
	Total	30.160	115			

a. Dependent variable: Organizational performance
b. Predictors: (Constant), Employee attraction

Source: Authors' own

The results of ANOVA variance in the Table 6 indicate that the p value of the F statistic was less than 0.00, highly implying that employee attraction has a huge effect on organizational performance.

Table 7: Regression coefficients of employee attraction.

Coefficients[a]					
Model	***Unstandardized coefficients***		***Standardized coefficients***		
	B	***Std. error***	***Beta***	***t***	***Sig.***
1 (Constant)	2.276	.254		8.978	.000
Employee attraction	.461	.059	.592	7.833	.000

a. Dependent variable: Organizational performance

Source: Authors' own

The Table 7 shows the beta coefficients of employee attraction, which had a value of 0.592. This along with the constant coefficient 2.276 was used to create the equation Y=2.276 + 0.592Xβ, where Y is organizational performance and Xβ is employee attraction.

Bivariate Analysis of Employee Selection and Organizational Performance

Table 8: Regression model of employee selection.

			Model summary[b]		
Model	***R***	***R square***	***Adjusted R square***	***Std. error of the estimate***	***Durbin-Watson***
1	.628[a]	.394	.389	.40035	1.897

a. Predictors: (Constant), Employee selection
b. Dependent variable: Organizational performance

Source: Authors' own

The Table 8 showing the values of R and R^2 being positive indicate that there exists a positive relationship between employee selection and organizational performance. The R^2 value of 0.394 indicates the explanatory power of employee selection, *i.e.*, 39.4% of the variation in organizational performance was the result of variation in employee selection. This clearly proves that employee selection influences organizational performance to a great extent.

Table 9: ANOVA of employee selection and OP.

			ANOVA[a]			
	Model	***Sum of squares***	***df***	***Mean square***	***F***	***Sig.***
1	Regression	11.888	1	11.888	74.169	.000[b]
	Residual	18.272	114	.160		
	Total	30.160	115			

a. Dependent variable: Organizational performance
b. Predictors: (Constant), Employee selection

Source: Authors' own

The results of ANOVA variance in the Table 9 indicate that the p value of the F statistic was less than 0.00, highly implying that employee selection has a huge effect on organizational performance.

The Table 10 shows the beta coefficients of employee selection, which had a value of 0.628. This along with the constant coefficient 1.994 was used to create the equation Y=1.994 + 0.628Xβ, where Y is organizational performance and Xβ is employee selection.

Table 10: Regression coefficients of employee selection.

	Coefficients[a]				
Model	***Unstandardized coefficients***		***Standardized coefficients***	***t***	***Sig.***
	B	***Std. error***	***Beta***		
1 (Constant)	1.994	.263		7.575	.000
Employee selection	.532	.062	.628	8.612	.000

a. Dependent variable: Organizational performance

Source: Authors' own

Bivariate Analysis of Employee Inclusion and Organizational Performance

Table 11: Regression model 3 of employee inclusion.

			Model summary[b]		
Model	***R***	***R square***	***Adjusted R square***	***Std. error of the estimate***	***Durbin-Watson***
1	.612[a]	.374	.368	.40697	1.717

a. Predictors: (Constant), Employee inclusion
b. Dependent variable: Organizational performance

Source: Authors' own

The Table 11 showing the values of R and R^2 being positive indicate that there exists a positive relationship between employee inclusion and organizational performance. The R^2 value of 0.374 indicates the explanatory power of employee inclusion, *i.e.,* 37.4% of the variation in organizational performance was the result of variation in employee inclusion. This clearly proves that employee inclusion influences organizational performance to a great extent.

The results of ANOVA variance in the Table 12 indicate that the p value of the F statistic was less than 0.00, highly implying that employee inclusion has a huge effect on organizational performance.

Table 12: ANOVA of employee inclusion and OP.

ANOVA[a]						
Model		***Sum of squares***	***df***	***Mean square***	***F***	***Sig.***
1	Regression	11.279	1	11.279	68.097	.000[b]
	Residual	18.881	114	.166		
	Total	30.160	115			

a. Dependent variable: Organizational performance
b. Predictors: (Constant), Employee inclusion

Source: Authors' own

Table 13: Regression coefficients of employee inclusion.

Coefficients[a]						
Model		***Unstandardized coefficients***		***Standardized coefficients***		
		B	***Std. error***	***Beta***	***t***	***Sig.***
1	(Constant)	2.224	.247		8.999	.000
	Employee inclusion	.476	.058	.612	8.252	.000

a. Dependent variable: Organizational performance

Source: Authors' own

The Table 13 shows the beta coefficients of employee inclusion, which had a value of 0.612. This along with the constant coefficient 2.224 was used to create the equation $Y=2.224 + 0.612X\beta$, where Y is organizational performance and $X\beta$ is employee inclusion.

Bivariate Analysis of Employee Retention and Organizational Performance

The values of R and R^2 in Table 14 being positive indicate that there exists a positive relationship between employee retention and organizational performance. The R^2 value of 0.354 indicates the explanatory power of employee retention, *i.e.,* 35.4% of the variation in organizational performance was the result of variation in employee retention. This clearly proves that employee retention influences organizational performance to a great extent.

Table 14: Regression model of employee retention.

			Model summary[b]		
Model	***R***	***R square***	***Adjusted R square***	***Std. error of the estimate***	***Durbin-Watson***
1	.595[a]	.354	.348	.41350	1.989

a. Predictors: (Constant), Employee retention
b. Dependent variable: Organizational performance

Source: Authors' own

The results of ANOVA variance in the Table 15 indicate that the p value of the F statistic was less than 0.00, highly implying that employee retention has a huge effect on organizational performance.

Table 15: ANOVA of employee retention and OP.

			ANOVA[a]			
Model		***Sum of squares***	***df***	***Mean square***	***F***	***Sig.***
1	Regression	10.668	1	10.668	62.395	.000[b]
	Residual	19.492	114	.171		
	Total	30.160	115			

a. Dependent variable: Organizational performance
b. Predictors: (Constant), Employee retention

Source: Authors' own

The Table 16 shows the beta coefficients of employee retention, which had a value of 0.595. This along with the constant coefficient 2.030 was used to create the equation $Y = 2.030 + 0.595X\beta$, where Y is organizational performance and $X\beta$ is employee retention.

Table 16: Regression coefficients of employee retention.

Model	Coefficients[a] Unstandardized coefficients B	Std. error	Standardized coefficients Beta	t	Sig.
1 (Constant)	2.030	.282		7.189	.000
Employee retention	.531	.067	.595	7.899	.000

a. Dependent variable: Organizational performance

Source: Authors' own

TESTING OF HYPOTHESES

Testing Hypothesis 1

Null hypothesis 1a (H1a): There is no significant relationship between employee attraction (Xβ) and organizational performance (Y) in the hospitality industry.

Where,

H1a: $\beta = 0$

Since in our equation $Y = 2.276 + 0.592X\beta$, the value of β is not zero, we can reject our null hypothesis and adopt the alternate hypothesis. We therefore conclude that Employee Attraction has a positive correlation and therefore an impact on organizational performance.

Hypothesis 1a: *There is no significant relationship between employee attraction and organizational performance. (REJECTED)*

Hypothesis 1b: *There is a significant relationship between employee attraction and organizational performance. (ACCEPTED)*

Testing Hypothesis 2

Null hypothesis 2a (H2a): There is no significant relationship between employee selection (Xβ) and organizational performance (Y).

Where,

H2a: = 0

Since in our equation, Y = 1.994 + 0.628Xβ, the value of β it is not zero, we can reject the null hypothesis that employee selection has no effect on organizational performance. We can therefore conclude that employee selection has a positive correlation and therefore an impact on organizational performance.

Hypothesis 2a: *There is no significant relationship between employee selection and organizational performance. (REJECTED)*

Hypothesis 2b: *There is a significant relationship between employee selection and organizational performance. (ACCEPTED)*

Testing Hypothesis 3

Null hypothesis 3a (H3a): There is no significant relationship between employee inclusion (Xβ) and organizational performance (Y).

Where,

H3a = 0

Since in our equation, Y = 2.224 + 0.612Xβ, the value of β it is not zero, we can reject the null hypothesis and adopt the alternate that employee inclusion has not effect on organizational performance. We can therefore conclude that employee selection has a positive correlation and therefore an impact on organizational performance.

Hypothesis 3a: *There is no significant relationship between employee inclusion and organizational performance. (REJECTED)*

Hypothesis 3b: *There is a significant relationship between employee inclusion and organizational performance. (ACCEPTED)*

Testing Hypothesis 4

Null hypothesis 4a (H4a): There is no significant relationship between employee retention (Xβ) and organizational performance

(Y).

Where,

H4a: = 0

Since in our equation, Y = 2.030 + 0.595Xβ, the value of β it is not zero, we can reject the null hypothesis and adopt the alternate that employee retention has not effect on organizational performance. We can therefore conclude that employee retention has a positive correlation and therefore an impact on organizational performance.

Hypothesis 4a: *There is no significant relationship between employee retention and organizational performance. (REJECTED)*

Hypothesis 4b: *There is a significant relationship between employee retention and organizational performance. (ACCEPTED)*

DISCUSSION AND CONCLUSIONS

The findings of this research may bring a certain amount of contribution into the study of diversity management and human resources. In this paper, we attempted to find out how diversity has an impact on the organizational performance of a company, namely those in the hospitality sector.

We identified that out of all the factors, employee selection plays the most important role. A well-planned and unbiased selection process can help bring in a lot of talent into the company as well as bring new ideas to the table. A fair selection procedure that can be attempted by any group of diverse people helps widen the scope of hiring a top performer. In addition to that, selection by means of geography can also provide the company with an extensive list of quality candidates.

The second most important factor influencing organizational performance was employee inclusion. A work environment where all the employees of the organization receive fair treatment and are not left out either physically or mentally is highly sought after and highly preferred by employees of the modern world. The world where any form of discrimination is shunned upon has set a standard of equal treatment in the workspace that overall leads to employee satisfaction which in turn affects organizational performance.

The third factor that plays a vital role in the organizational performance was employee retention. When the organization implements strategies to retain employees, it reduced the chances of turnover and well as of training and development. However, if an employee feels they are not compensated well or feel like they are not valued by the company, there tends to be a movement towards resignations or even demands of pay raises. It is evident to see that monetary as well as non-monetary benefits have a great impact in the work performance of an individual. Herzberg's motivation factor that connects hygiene to the motivation of an employee proves that a good work environment is needed in order for an employee to efficiently perform their duties.

REFERENCES

Allmark, P. (2004). Should research samples reflect the diversity of the population? *Journal of Medical Ethics*, pp. 185–189.

Barak, M.E. (2005). *Managing Diversity: Toward a Globally Inclusive Workplace.* Sage.

Bassett-Jones, N. (2005). The Paradox of Diversty Management, Creativity and Innovation. *Creativity and Innovation Management*, pp. 169–175.

Boehm, S.A., Kunze, F., & Bruch, H. (2014). Spotlight on age-diversity climate: The impact of age-inclusive HR practices on firm-level outcomes. *Personnel Psycology*, pp. 667–704.

Chatboth, P.K., & Olsen, M.D. (2002). Organisational Leadership and Strategy in the Hospitality Industry. *Journal of Services Research*, pp. 5–23.

Chaudhary, M., & Gupta, M. (2010). Gender inequality in Indian hotel industry - A study of perception of male and female employees. *International Journal of Hospitality & Tourism Systems*, pp. 31–41.

Choi, Y., & Dickson, D.R. (2009). A case study into the benefits of management training programs: Impacts on hotel employee turnover and satisfaction level. *Journal of Human Resources in Hospitality & Tourism*, pp. 103–116.

Choy, W.K. (2007). Globalisation and workforce diversity: HRM implications for multinational corporations in Singapore. *Singapore Management Review*, pp. 1–19.

Dobbin, K., & Kaler, P. (2007). *Diversity and Organizational Management.* CA: Sage.

Duff, A.J., Tahbaz, A., & Chan, C. (2012). The interactive effect of cultural intelligence and openness on task performance. *Research and Practice in Human Resource Management*, pp. 1–17.

Ettorre, B. (1997). How are companies keeping the employees they want? *Management Review*.

Gavrea, C., Ilies, L., & Stegerean, R. (2011). Determinants of organizational performance. *Management & Marketing Challenges for the Knowledge Society*, pp. 285–300.

Georgopoulos, B., & Tannenbaum, A. (1957). A study of organizational effectiveness. *American Sociological Review*, pp. 534–550.

Harrison, D.A., Price, K.H., & Bell, M.P. (1998). Beyond relational demography: Time and the effects of surface and deep level diversity on work group cohesion. *Academy of Management Journal*, pp. 96–107.

Harrsion, D.A., & Sin, H.P. (2006). What is diversity and how it should be measured? *In:* Konrad, A.M., Prasad, P., & Pringle, J. *Handbook of Workplace Diversity*.

Hebbar, N. (2017). Diversity is key to India's success: Kovind. *The Hindu*, p. 1.

Jackson, S.E., Joshi, A., & Erhardt, N.L. (2003). Recent research on team and organizational diversity: SWOT analysis and implications. *Journal of Management*, 29(6): 801–830.

Jehn, K.A., Northcraft, G.B., & Neale, M.A. (1999). Why differences make a difference: A field study of diversity, conflict and performance in workgroups. *Administrative Science Quarterly*, 44(4): 741–763.

Knippenberg, D.V., & Schippers, M.C. (2007). Work group diversity. *Annual Review of Psychology*, pp. 515–541.

Kossek, E.E., Lobel, S.A., & Brown, J. (2005). Human resource strategies to manage workforce diversity: Examining 'The Business Case'. Sage.

Kreitz, P.A. (2008). Best practices for managing organizational diversity. *The Journal of Academic Librarianship*, pp. 101–120.

Kundu, S.C. (2003). Workforce diversity status: A study of employees' reactions. *Industrial Management & Data Systems*, pp. 215–226.

Lorbiecki, A., & Jack, G. (2000). Critical turns in the evolution of diversity management. *British Journal of Management*, 11: S17–S31.

Quinones, M.A., Ford, J.K., & Teachout, M.S. (1995). The relationship between work experience and job performance: A conceptual and meta-analytic review. *Personnel Psychology*, pp. 887–910.

R. Roosevelt Thomas, J. (2005). Building on the promise of diversity: How we can move to the next level in our workplaces, our communities, and our society, AMACOM.

Ramirez, S.A. (2011). Diversity and the boardroom. *Stanford Journal of Law, Business and Finance*, pp. 17–19.

Richard, O.C. (2000). Racial diversity, business strategy, and firm performance: A resource-based view. *Academy of Management Journal*, pp. 164–177.

Richard, O.C., Barnett, T., Dwyer, S., & Chadwick, K. (2004). Cultural diversity in management, firm performance, and the moderating role of entrepreneurial orientation dimensions. *Academy of Management Journal*, pp. 255–266.

Robbins, S.P., Odendaal, A., & Roodt, G. (2003). Organizational behaviour: Global and South African perspectives using needs assessment to resolve controversies in diversity training design. *Group and Organization Management*, pp. 148–174.

Roberge, M.É., & Dick, R.V. (2010). Recognizing the benefits of diversity: When and how does diversity increase group performance? *Human Resource Management Review*, pp. 295–308.

Roberts, J. (2017). Diversity — Nobody does it perfectly and help is at hand. Retrieved February 26, 2018, from Financial Times: https://www.ft.com/content/a8bd4986-c3e5-11e7-b30e-a7c1c7c13aab

Saz-Carranza, A., & Ospina, S.M. (2011). The Behavioral Dimension of Governing Interorganizational Goal-Directed Networks — Managing the unity-diversity tension. *Journal of Public Administration Research and Theory*, pp. 327–365.

Svehla, T. (1994). Diversity management: Key to future success. *Frontiers of Health Services Management;* Chicago, pp. 3–33.

2

Octapace Culture: A Comparative Analysis of Higher Education Institutions

MOHD RAFIQ TELI[1]* AND S.A. MUFEED[1]

ABSTRACT

The main objective of the study is to evaluate and compare the OCTAPACE culture of the selected universities in the higher education sector. 172 responses on a 4 point scale questionnaire based on the OCTAPACE profile developed by Udai Pareek were obtained from the academicians of the two state universities of Jammu and Kashmir. The results indicate that the OCTAPACE profile of both the institutions is perceived favorably by the respective academic staff members and the overall OCTAPACE profile of the two universities is not significantly different.

Key words: OCTAPACE culture, Academicians, Higher education.

INTRODUCTION

Higher education institutions around the world are undergoing a change and are competing like business enterprises (Malhan, 2006). Unlike the many businesses that develop concrete, reproducible items, an educational institution encompasses the characteristics related to a service industry. Educational services are intangible, heterogeneous; inseparable from the person delivering it, variable, perishable, and the customer (student) participate in the process. Additionally, universities and colleges are increasingly finding

[1] Department of Management Studies, University of Kashmir, Srinagar, J&K.
**Corresponding author*: E-mail: mohammadrafiq401@yahoo.com

themselves in an environment that is conducive to understanding the role and importance of service quality; this environment is a fiercely competitive one (Shank *et al.,* 1995). The higher education institutions around the world are responding to these changes by developing the capabilities of their human resource, in order to deliver high quality educational services, to be relevant in the highly competitive market place and create a sustainable competitive advantage.

Organizations can develop the competency levels of their employees and thereby the overall organizational performance through training, education and development programmes. However, organisations cannot capture the essence and efficacy of training and development programmes without the presence of an "enabling" organisational culture. As per Pareek *et al.* (2003) when employees use their initiative, take risks, experiment, innovate and make things happen, the organization may be said to have an "enabling" culture and this is referred to as OCTAPACE Culture. A positive developmental climate can be developed and nurtured in an organisation only when it is built on eight culture characteristics namely, Openness, Confrontation, Trust, Autonomy, Proactivity, Authenticity, Collaboration and Experimentation (Rao & Abraham, 1986).

LITERATURE REVIEW

Organizational culture refers to a system of shared meaning held by members that distinguishes the organization from other organizations. This system of shared meaning is, a set of key characteristics that the organization values. It includes, among other things, the values, beliefs and behavioral norms and expectations shared by an organization's members.

OCTAPACE culture items deal with the extent to which Openness, Confrontation, Trust, Autonomy, Pro-activity, Authenticity, Collaboration and Experimentation are valued and promoted in an organization (Rao & Abraham, 1986). Studies conducted by (Kumar & Patnaik, 2002; Kumar, 1997) shows that the culture of OCTAPACE values is absorbed in the culture of the many organizations to a good or moderate degree. These values help an organization to grow by making its employees dynamic and growth-oriented and fostering a climate of continuous development of human resources.

a. Openness

The term refers to the freedom to express ideas, opinions and views (Mariyappa, 2010). It is a spontaneous expression of feelings and thoughts and receiving feedback and information without defensiveness (Pareek, 1992). Rohmetra (1998) in a study conducted on banking sector reported that the environment is less open for employees. Alphonsa (2000) surveyed HRD climate in private hospital of Hyderabad with a sample of 50 supervisors from different departments and reported a good level of openness.

b. Confrontation

Confrontation is facing but not shying away from problems; deeper analysis of interpersonal problems and taking on challenges (Pareek, 1992). Mufeed (2001) in a study of the perception of medical staff towards HRD climate found that there existed a reasonably good climate for the value of confrontation. Some research studies *e.g.*, Krishna and Rao (1997), Rohmetra (1998) and Shakeel (1999) in their studies on HRD climate found that the value of confrontation was perceived low by the employees.

c. Trust

Trust means maintaining confidentiality of information shared by others and not misusing it; a sense of assurance that others will help when needed and will honour mutual obligations and commitments (Pareek, 1992). Research studies by Patel (1999) and Rohmetra (1998) reported that a good degree of trusted existed between employees.

d. Authenticity

Authenticity refers to similarities between what one feels, says, and does; taking ownership of one's actions and mistakes; unreserved sharing of feelings. Mufeed (2001) in his empirical study of the HRD climate in hospitals found that the value of authenticity had been well developed and signified cohesion and trust exist in the employees' personal relationship. The value of authenticity was recorded average in a study conducted on middle level managers of manufacturing (Pharmaceutical) and service (Banking) companies (Mishra, Dhar & Dhar, 1999).

e. Proactivity

Proactivity refers to encouraging employees to take initiatives and risks. It is initiative, preplanning and preventive action; calculating payoffs before taking action (Pareek, 1992). Kumar (1997) conducted an investigation into the contribution of training towards the HRD climate values in a public sector organization and reported that the training has the potential to contribute to all the values of HRD climate especially the value of proactivity.

f. Autonomy

Autonomy refers to giving freedom to let people work independently with responsibility: to plan and act in one's own way; respecting and encouraging individual and role autonomy (Pareek, 1992). Research studies by Krishna and Rao (1997) and Rainayee (2002) reported that the value of autonomy is a missing factor in the organizations.

g. Collaboration

Collaboration is giving help to and asking for help from others; team sprit; working together (individuals and groups) to solve problems (Pareek, 1992). Collaboration is reflected in strong and effective team and inter-teams in the organization (Pareek & Rao, 1992).

h. Experimentation

It refers to using and encouraging innovative approaches to solve problems; using feedback for improving; taking a fresh look at things and encouraging activities (Pareek, 1992). Krishna and Rao (1997) found that value of experimentation was favorably perceived among middle and senior managers. Research studies by Rainayee (2002) and Mufeed (2001) reported that the value of experimentation has been discouraged by the organizations. Shakeel (1999) found experimentation to be perceived at a low degree in a study conducted on two Indian universities.

OBJECTIVES OF THE PRESENT STUDY

Based on the preceding discussion, the study was undertaken to;

1. To examine the health of OCTAPACE Culture in the sample higher education institutions.
2. To compare the prevalent OCTAPACE Culture of the selected higher education institutions.

METHODS

Sample and Procedure

Two hundred full-time academicians belonging to two state universities (*i.e.,* University of Kashmir & University of Jammu) located in the state of Jammu and Kashmir were surveyed. The elements included professors, associate professors and assistant professors of the aforementioned institutions. The academicians completed the survey of their own accord during their regular scheduled work hours at their respective work sites. To encourage respondents to share free and frank opinion, we assured them of anonymity through both verbal and written means. We further guaranteed that only group data will be communicated to the organizations. Survey questionnaires were distributed and retrieved by the researchers in sealed envelopes. Eighty-six percent (N=172) of the participants returned the questionnaires.

Scale

The four point scale developed by Pareek (2003) has been used for the present study. The OCTAPACE profile is a 40 item instrument that gives the profile of the organization's ethos in eight values. These values are Openness, Confrontation, Trust, Authenticity, Proaction, Autonomy, Collaboration and Experimentation.

Reliability of the questionnaire was checked through Cronbach's alpha, which was computed to be .87, indicating a good internal consistency.

RESULTS

Descriptive Statistics

The perception of the employees of the sample universities regarding the eight components of OCTAPACE namely, Openness, Confrontation, Trust, Autonomy, Proactivity, Authenticity, Collaboration and Experimentation, is given in Table 1.

Table 1: Components of OCTAPACE culture.

Component	*Mean score*	*Standard deviation*	*Percentage score*
Openness	3.38	0.432	84.50
Confrontation	3.28	0.466	82.00
Trust	3.25	0.354	81.25
Authenticity	3.19	0.412	79.75
Proactivity	3.14	0.299	78.50
Autonomy	3.39	0.503	84.75
Collaboration	3.43	0.376	85.75
Experimentation	3.22	0.309	80.50
OCTAPACE	3.29		82.13

Source: Authors' own

Among the eight components of OCTAPACE, *Collaboration* is perceived most favorably (mean score=3.43) by the employees of the sample universities, whereas the *Proactivity* component (mean score=3.14) of the OCTAPACE is perceived relatively less favorable. The results indicate that the employees show interdependence and work as a team, whereas the employees perceive the environment present in universities relatively less favorable for learning, skill enhancement and acquiring new knowledge in consonance with the future requirements.

The overall perception of the academic and administrative staff of the sample universities with respect to the level of OCTAPACE culture existing in their respective institutions is recorded in the present study at a mean score of 3.29, which signifies that the culture present in the two institutions under study is fairly supportive of the OCTAPACE values.

From a comparative viewpoint, the academicians of *University of Jammu* have reported higher values for overall OCTAPACE culture as well as for all the eight components of OCTAPACE culture as compared to the respondent academicians from the *University of Kashmir* (Table 2).

Table 2: Comparison of employee perception regarding components of OCTAPACE.

Component	***University of Kashmir*** **Mean score** ***(N=93)***	***University of Jammu Mean score (N=79)***	***Total mean score (N=172)***	***Z Value****
Openness	3.32	3.44	3.38	.27ns
Confrontation	3.25	3.31	3.28	.32ns
Trust	3.24	3.26	3.25	.29 ns
Authenticity	3.15	3.23	3.19	.18 ns
Proactivity	3.13	3.15	3.14	.22 ns
Autonomy	3.37	3.41	3.39	.23 ns
Collaboration	3.40	3.46	3.43	.08 ns
Experimentation	3.19	3.25	3.22	.12 ns
OCTAPACE culture	3.26	3.31	3.29	.64 ns

Source: Authors' own; *Note*: *p<.05; ns = not significant

However, the results of *z* test, administered to ascertain whether the difference in the mean scores reported by the academic staff of the two sample universities is significant or merely an outcome of chance factor, indicated that the difference in the mean scores is statistically insignificant as $p > .05$ in all the cases, indicating that the perception of the sample academic staff of the two universities regarding the existing OCTAPACE culture in their respective institutions is more or less the same (Table 2).

CONCLUSIONS

The objective of this study was to evaluate and compare the health of OCTAPACE Culture prevalent in the two state universities *i.e.,* University of Kashmir and University of Jammu. Findings revealed that the culture prevalent in the two sample universities fairly values the components of OCTAPACE namely, Openness, Confrontation, Trust, Autonomy, Proactivity, Authenticity, Collaboration and Experimentation. Further, a comparative analysis of the two sample institutions revealed that the mean score (M =3.31) of OCTAPACE profile of *University of Jammu* is slightly better than the mean score (M =3.26) of the *University of Kashmir*. The result shows that the mean scores of eight important values relevant to the developing culture *i.e.,* openness, proaction, collaboration, authenticity, experimentation, autonomy, trust, and experimentation are slightly more for the *University of Jammu*. However, the results of the independent samples test (*z*-test) utilized to examine whether there are any significant differences in the OCTAPACE culture of the two organizations, revealed that the level of the OCTAPACE culture is not significantly different in the two higher education institutions.

REFERENCES

Alphonsa, Y.K. (2000). "HRD Climate in a Private Hospital in Hyderabad: An Empirical Study". *Indian Journal of Training and Development,* pp. 30(4).

Krishna, P.M., & Rao, P.S. (1997). Organisational and HRD climate in BHEL — An Empirical Study. *Indian Journal of Public Administration*, 43(2): 209–216.

Kumar, N.R. (1997). An investigation into the contribution of training towards HRD climate values in a public sector organisations. *IJTD*, XXVII(3).

Kumar, S., & Patnaik, S. (2002). HRD climate and attributes of teachers in JNVS. *Indian Journal of Training and Development*, 32(2): 31–37.

Malhan, I.V. (2006). Strategic planning for developing Indian university libraries into knowledge resource and service centres.

Mariyappa, S. (2010). "OCTAPACE Culture: A Case Study of Rourkela Steel Plant". *The Business Review,* 5(1&2): 203–210.

Mishra, M., Dhar, U., & Dhar, S. (1999). Job satisfaction as a correlate of HRD climate (An empirical study). *Indian Journal of Training and Development*, 29(2): 5.

Mufeed, S.A. (2001). The need for a focus on key elements of HRD climate in hospitals: An empirical study. *Management and Labour Studies, XLRI Jamshedpur*, 31(1): 57–69.

Pareek, U. (1992). Challenges for HRD in the Nineties. *In:* Pareek, U., Padaki, R., & Nair, R.R. *(eds.),* Managing Transition: The HRD Response Tata McGraw-Hill, pp. 3–8.

Pareek, U. (2003). Training instruments in HRD and OD. 2nd ed. Tata Mcgraw-hill Publishing Company Limited, New Delhi.

Pareek, U., & Rao, T.V. (1992). *First Handbook of Psychological and Social Instruments* (Vol. 25). Concept Publishing Company.

Patel, M.K. (1999). HRD climate: A comparative study among two ends of performance. The *Journal of Indian Management and Strategy*, 4(3).

Rainayee, R. (2002). HRD climate in commercial banks: An empirical study. *The Business Review*, 9(1).

Rao, T.V., & Abraham, E. (1986). HRD climate in organizations. *Readings in Human Resource Development*, pp. 36–45.

Rohmetra, N. (1998). Towards creating a learning organization: The HRD climate focus. *Paradigm*, 2: 56–63.

Shakeel, A. (1999). HRD in universities. New Delhi: ABH Publishing House.

Shank, M.D., Walker, M., & Hayes, T. (1995). "Understanding professional service expectations: Do we know what our students expect in a quality education?". *Journal of Professional Services Marketing*, 13(1): 71–83.

3

Antecedents of E-Loyalty: Empirical Evidence from Indian E-Commerce Users

Tahir Ahmad Wani[1]* and Sadaf Mushtaq[2]

ABSTRACT

E-commerce is one of the booming industries in India. Customer engagement in this sector is very high. Organizations rely on loyalty of customers to gain market share and have a strong position in the market place as getting new customers is costly compared to retaining existing ones. Loyalty is one of the foundations of relationship marketing. E-commerce companies rely mostly on repurchase orders from the same customers and hence loyalty and relationship with the customers is important. There have been many studies around the world that determine what causes customers loyal to a particular firm. However, e-loyalty is a bit different because there is no face-to-face communication between the seller and the buyer nor is there any physical evidence linked. Huge expenses are involved in getting new customer over the internet unless they stay and make repeated purchases throughout the year. This makes it hard to find the determinants of e-loyalty. The focus of the current study is on identifying the antecedents of e-loyalty with respect to Indian e-commerce industry. A sample of 290 respondents is taken to determine the relationship between various determinants of e-loyalty. Measurement and structural modeling has been performed on the data to obtain the results. The results indicate that the factors – Brand Image, Trust and Security and Value Proposition have significant impact on satisfaction and ultimately e-loyalty.

[1] National Institute of Technology, Srinagar (NIT), J&K.
[2] Jamia Millia Islamia (Central University), New Delhi.
**Corresponding author:* E-mail: taha.*wani@gmail*.com

Key words: E-loyalty, E-commerce, Customer engagement.

INTRODUCTION

Electronic-commerce in modern day world is one of the primary platforms of conducting business. In fact, it has cut through the traditional ways of doing business and commerce in most of the industries. The changing technology or one can say that the improving technology particularly in the field of communications is giving an exponential boom to this industry. Introduction of technologies like 4G, smartphones, user-friendly operating systems, e-commerce apps, digital wallets, online banking, high speed Wifi and tethering etc., has given this industry tremendous push. Not only this platform provides variety and low cost to the customers but comes with bunch of other features which makes it more attractive to the customers. Users can shop millions of products sitting at their native places from any corner of the world. They can pay online, return the products easily, get discounts, read reviews, and post comments. These features of e-commerce not only separate it from traditional ways of conducting commerce but give it an edge in terms of customer satisfaction and profitability. Past one decade is witness to the rise of multi-million-dollar companies both in developed and developing nations. According to Statista.com1 the global e-commerce business (retail) grew up to $2.3 trillion and the same is expected to reach $4.88 trillion in 2021. These are very huge numbers and talk about the volume of business conducted by e-commerce sites. According to Turban *et al.* (2002) e-commerce is the future of conducting business and will cover most of the supply chain of the products and services. Delone and Mclean (2004) argue that the more IT & Communications field will improve and grow the more will be investments and profitability in e-commerce industry.

While on one side we see tremendous growth and opportunities in e-commerce industry we have also seen incremental cases of fraud and deception. Newspapers are flooded so are the sites with bad review about products and services offered by e-commerce sites. We have examples of customers receiving fakes, duplicates, sub-standard products, and late deliveries causing deep inconvenience and trauma to the customers. According to Gefen

(2000) there is heightened importance of familiarity and trust in e-commerce industry. If customers loose trust towards an e-commerce company it is very hard to regain that trust. McKnight *et al.* (2002) thus impress upon the need of building trust and eventually loyalty to remove hesitations, fear and uncertainty of buying from the e-commerce portals. Companies shall that focus on every aspect of their websites, logistics and support services (Klopping & McKinney, 2004) to remain relevant, reliable, profitable and build as base of loyal customers to gain competitive edge. Srinivasan *et al.* (2002) highlight the importance of customer loyalty in a competitive market structure. In a country like India were there are thousands of e-commerce sites there is a growing need for companies to understand the concept of e-loyalty in order to remain profitable in a lucrative but rapidly changing online market. The decisions and policies of government to allow FDIs further support the cause of e-loyalty of e-commerce sites in India.

REVIEW OF LITERATURE

According to Jacoby and Chestnut (1978) successful brands don't boast the number of one- time customers but a base of customers who are regular's buyers of the particular brand. These customers with repurchase behavior towards a particular brand are called 'loyal's' and are in fact the real assets of an organization. Customer loyalty has been defined as "a deeply held commitment to rebuy or re-patronize a preferred product/service consistently in the future, thereby causing repetitive same-brand or same brand-set purchasing, despite situational influences and marketing efforts having the potential to cause switching behavior" (Oliver, 1999). Brand loyalty as per Engel *et al.* (1982) is "the preferential, attitudinal and behavioral response toward one or more brands in a product category expressed over a period by a consumer". Two contrasting streams of research define the literature on the concept of loyalty: the stochastic approach and the deterministic approach. The former approach defines loyalty as a 'behavior' making it complex to measure and find causes of its happening (Bass, 1974; McAlister & Pessemier, 1982). The later approach treats loyalty more as an 'attitude'. This approach only considers the psychographics of the customers without considering the environmental sand situational factors (*e.g.*, Jacoby, 1969, 1971;

Jacoby & Olson, 1970; Jarvis & Wilcox, 1976). In contemporary research in the field of customer loyalty relational approach has been advocated over behavioral and attitudinal approaches. This approach focuses on empathy and emotional connect between the buyer and the seller and supports a continuing relationship. It not only focuses on the behavior of the customer but on the efforts of the seller to make the customer to make repeated purchases from the same brand. This approach translates the idea of loyalty from theory into action and behaviors and thus makes it easy for the sellers to build a loyal customer base by understanding the underlying antecedents of loyalty (N'goala, 2007).

CONCEPT OF E-LOYALTY

Retail quality, e-satisfaction and e-trust are the factors that lead to e-loyalty in the e-markets (Kim *et al.,* 2009). Not only is loyalty building more important in e-commerce but the rules and underlying factors are also different (Anderson & Srinivasan, 2003). Chang *et al.* (2009) argue that is very difficult to create a loyal customer base in the e-commerce industry given the competitors are just a click away. Reichheld and Schefter (2000) advocate the importance of e-loyalty for successful business operations online but caution the marketers not to rely only on technology but on continued and consistent superior customer experience. Conceptually e-loyalty is similar to the traditional view of customer loyalty but mediated by technology (Corstjens & Lal, 2000). E-loyalty is "intention to revisit a website" (Gommans *et al.,* 2001; Corstjens & Lal, 2000). The current study looks at e-loyalty as the perceived loyalty towards an online website, with intentions of customers to revisit and repurchase from the site.

In classical sense, loyalty has always been seen as a concept driven by the marketers through better products and differentiated services (Schultz & Bailey, 2000). On the other hand, e-loyalty is seen as a consumer driven concept facilitated by technology supported by the effective distribution networks. One can differentiate between loyalty in physical markets and e-markets simply by saying e-loyalty is driven by technology particularly the internet. While traditional loyalty research has shown relationship between satisfaction and loyalty (Oliver, 1999) many of the researchers in the e-loyalty domain have established similar linkage in e-platforms. Satisfaction is customers is therefore pivotal to create an e-loyalty among the existing customers and alluring the new buyers. Although satisfaction has been always seen as a precursor of e-loyalty but satisfaction in itself is driven by many factors particularly in online market space (Gommans *et al.,* 2001). Valvi and Fragkos (2012) while reviewing previous literature have found that website design, assurance, privacy concerns, perceived value, convenience, web usability, trust, care, empathy, responsiveness, reliability, interactivity, customization, choice and quality etc. are some of the important factors that have been seen to have an impact on satisfaction and e-loyalty of the customers. While much of the literature talks about the design of the websites, many focus on the products or services being offered by the e-commerce sites. This study will try to simplify the complex models given by previous researchers and try to test it on Indian e-commerce users to see what factors can lead to e-loyalty in Indian e-commerce industry.

Research Gap

This study refers to the model given by Gommans *et al.* (2001). The antecedents given in the model seem to be compiled after an extensive literature survey and encompass most of the underlying factors given by other researchers. Also, there is no significant research contribution to see the effect of the variables suggested on satisfaction and ultimately on e- loyalty. In addition, not much of the study has been carried out in India on the subject matter of e-loyalty. The framework of the study is given in Fig. 1.

Further, the focus of studies carried in this area has not specifically been on young users who now hold the largest share in terms of the e-commerce users in India.

Research Questions

- Do Website & Technology influence satisfaction towards e-commerce websites?
- Does Value Proposition influence satisfaction towards e-commerce websites?

- Does Customer Service influence satisfaction towards e-commerce websites?
- Does Brand Image influence satisfaction towards e-commerce websites?
- Do Trust & Security influence satisfaction towards e-commerce websites?
- Does Satisfaction influence e-loyalty?

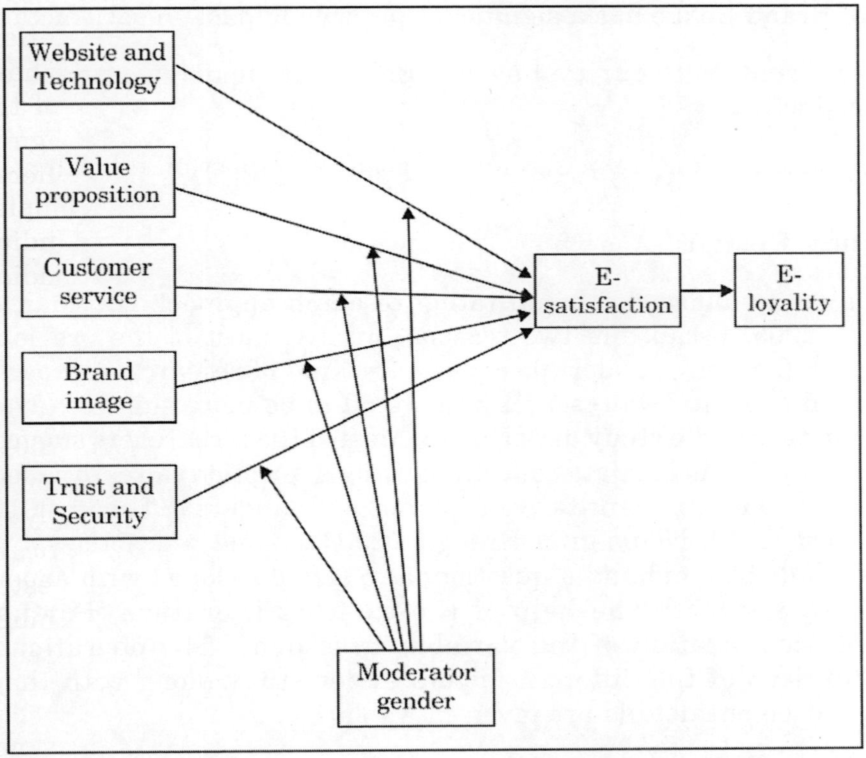

Fig. 1: Theoretical framework

Hypotheses

Since the previous literature mostly indicates a positive relationship between each of the proposed antecedents only directional hypotheses were given.

H1: Website & Technology has a significant positive impact on satisfaction.

H2: Value Proposition has a significant positive impact on satisfaction.

H3: Customer Service has a significant positive impact on satisfaction.

H3: Brand Image has a significant positive impact on satisfaction.

H4: Trust & Security has a significant positive impact on satisfaction.

H5: Satisfaction has a significant positive impact on e-loyalty.

Study Design

The study followed a quantitative research approach (Bryman & Bell, 2005) because of two reasons. Firstly, most of the previous researchers have undertaken a similar kind of research approach, second quantitative research was found to be more suitable given the nature of the study undertaken. Most of the researchers suggest a survey method of data collection, using a questionnaire, to collect primary data in quantitative researches (Saunders & Lewis, 2012; Gorard, 2010; Neuman & Kreuger, 2003). Same was followed in the study at hand and a questionnaire was developed with expert advice and with the help of the existing literature. Further operationalization of the variables was done. The operational definitions of the different factors under study along with their measurement details are given in Table 1.

The convenience sampling method was used (Sekaran, 2006) and a sample of 290 was estimated for the study using estimates given by Guilford (1954), Cattell (1978), Comrey and Lee (1992) and Bentler and Chou (1987). All the respondents were in the age group of 18-36 representing the young e-commerce users. Data collection was done using both online as well as offline questionnaire mostly in the Delhi-NCR region. However, online responses were received from parts of J&K, Gujarat, Maharashtra and Madhya Pradesh, Punjab and Haryana giving some sort of diversity to the sample.

Table 1: Operationalization

Factor	*Operational definition*	*Measurement details / questions*
E-loyalty	"The chance of a customer returning, providing positive word-of-mouth as well as providing references and pubilcity for the business".	LOY1-LOY7 (Based on Zeithaml *et al.,* 1996; Gremler, 1995).
E-satisfaction	"Post-consumption evaluation of how well a store or product meets or exceeds customer expectations".	SAT1-SAT6 (Based on Evrard & Aurier, 1996; Hsin Chang, Yao-Hua Wang & Wen-Ying Yang, 2009).
Website & Technology	"The first impression that a visitor experience when visit a site. The design of the Website is also important in-service quality to create customer satisfaction".	W&T1-W&T8 (Based on Gommans *et al.,* 2001).
Value Proposition	"The extent to which an e-retailer's Website can recognize a customer and then tailor the choice of products, services, and shopping experience for that customer".	VP1-VP6 (Based on Gommans *et al.,* 2001).
Customer service	"The ability of e-retailers to provide appropriate information to customers when a problem occurs, having mechanism for handling returns, and providing online guarantees".	CS1-CS7 (Based on Gommans *et al.,* 2001).
Brand image	"The current view of the customers about a brand. It can be defined as a unique bundle of associations within the minds of target customers. It signifies what the brand presently stands for. It is a set of beliefs held about a specific brand".	BI1-BI6 (Based on Eunjoo Cho, 2011).
Trust & Security	"A psychological state composing the intention to accept vulnerability based on expectations of the intentions or behavior of another".	T&S1-T&S6 (Based on Gommans *et al.,* 2001).

Data Analysis

Data was collected and regularly cleaned until the saturation point of sample size was achieved. Since the only intention of using demographics in the study was to check the moderation effect of gender. Segregation of the respondents was done only on that demographic factor. The demographic characteristics based on gender are given in Table 2.

Table 2: Profile of the respondents

Variables		*N*
Gender	Male	187
	Female	103

Source: Authors' own

After cleaning and imputing missing values, the data was checked for normality. However, using both univariate and multivariate tests the data was not found to be normal. Hence, the researchers went ahead with the usage of Mplus software package which can handle non-normal data for the structural equation modelling (Muthén & Muthén, 1998-2015). The instrument was found to be valid as well as reliable hence prompting the researchers to do a measurement modelling on the data (Table 3).

Table 3: Reliability and Validity analysis.

	CR	*AVE*	*MSV*	*ASV*	*SAT*	*W&T*	*VP*	*CS*	*T&S*	*BI*	*LOY*
SAT	0.946	0.747	0.162	0.115	0.864						
W&T	0.898	0.526	0.217	0.113	0.298	0.725					
VP	0.860	0.508	0.276	0.182	0.323	0.466	0.713				
CS	0.832	0.452	0.276	0.160	0.284	0.312	0.525	0.672			
T&S	0.920	0.657	0.285	0.190	0.353	0.286	0.443	0.494	0.810		
BI	0.842	0.519	0.424	0.219	0.363	0.337	0.370	0.470	0.534	0.720	
LOY	0.910	0.593	0.424	0.179	0.403	0.279	0.403	0.205	0.455	0.651	0.770

Source: Authors' own

There was one issue with Convergent Validity as AVE < 0.5 for customer service. No issues were with Discriminant Validity as

MSV < AVE, ASV < AVE and Square root of AVE was greater than inter-construct correlations (Black, Babin & Anderson, 2010), (Bagozzi & Yi, 1988). The data was found reliable with composite reliability (CR) > 0.7 proving scale reliability (Churchill, 1979).

The results of the confirmatory factor analysis are given in Table 4 and Fig. 2.

Table 4: Loadings of items after CFA.

	Estimate	*S.E.*	*Est./S.E.*	*P-value*
WT	BY	–	–	–
WT1	0.88	0.017	52.714	0.00
WT2	0.875	0.016	54.981	0.00
WT3	0.888	0.013	68.543	0.00
WT4	0.872	0.017	51.632	0.00
WT5	0.903	0.014	64.992	0.00
WT6	0.811	0.03	27.133	0.00
WT7	0.855	0.018	46.305	0.00
WT8	0.839	0.02	42.601	0.00
VP	BY	–	–	–
VP1	0.839	0.019	44.683	0.00
VP2	0.867	0.017	51.255	0.00
VP3	0.834	0.021	39.448	0.00
VP4	0.864	0.016	54.375	0.00
VP5	0.87	0.017	51.999	0.00
VP6	0.846	0.018	47.265	0.00
CS	BY	–	–	–
CS1	0.837	0.021	39.96	0.00
CS2	0.816	0.023	35.591	0.00
CS3	0.836	0.022	37.293	0.00
CS4	0.876	0.014	61.811	0.00
CS5	0.844	0.018	46.36	0.00
CS6	0.798	0.024	33.787	0.00
CS7	0.836	0.021	39.696	0.00
TS	BY	–	–	–
TS1	0.874	0.016	53.247	0.00
TS2	0.838	0.019	43.77	0.00
TS3	0.847	0.025	33.263	0.00
TS4	0.298	0.074	3.999	0.00
TS5	0.811	0.022	37.525	0.00
TS6	0.841	0.029	29.397	0.00

Table 4: *Contd...*

	Estimate	*S.E.*	*Est./S.E.*	*P-value*
LOY	BY	–	–	–
LOY1	0.717	0.029	25.143	0.00
LOY2	0.739	0.028	26.026	0.00
LOY3	0.88	0.018	50.155	0.00
LOY4	0.815	0.031	26.625	0.00
LOY5	0.841	0.022	38.773	0.00
LOY6	0.712	0.036	19.791	0.00
LOY7	0.709	0.044	16.141	0.00
SAT	BY	–	–	–
SAT1	0.908	0.012	73.456	0.00
SAT2	0.882	0.014	61.014	0.00
SAT3	0.89	0.014	65.35	0.00
SAT4	0.894	0.014	62.338	0.00
SAT5	0.869	0.016	52.925	0.00
SAT6	0.873	0.017	50.555	0.00
BI	BY	–	–	–
BI1	0.798	0.03	26.496	0.00
BI2	0.755	0.028	27.303	0.00
BI3	0.772	0.028	27.231	0.00
BI4	0.745	0.029	25.56	0.00
BI5	0.751	0.026	29.248	0.00
BI6	0.803	0.022	35.753	0.00

Model fit information: RMSEA: 0.046; *CFI:* 0.949; *TLI:* 0.946; *Chi-Square Test of Model Fit:* 1.1059; *SRMR: 0.042; WRMR: 0.733. Source:* Authors' own.

Since all the loadings were above the least threshold level and a model fit was achieved in the measurement model (Hair *et al.*, 2010) structural modelling was performed on the data to test the proposed hypotheses. The results of structural equation modelling using Maximum Likelihood Robust estimation method is given in Tables 5 and 6.

Based on the results obtained after the structural equation modeling the hypotheses as proposed were accepted or rejected based on the 0.05 level of significance of the loadings as shown in Table 7.

Table 5: R _square values

Latent variable	*Estimate*	*S.E.*	*Est./S.E.*	*Two-tailed P-value*
LOY	0.232	0.058	4.006	0
SAT	0.869	0.041	21.388	0

Source: Authors' own

Table 6: Loadings of items after SEM.

	Estimate	*S.E.*	*Est./S.E.*	*P-value*
SAT	ON			
WT	0.175	0.164	1.07	0.285
VP	0.239*	0.115	2.08	0.038
CS	-0.245	0.249	-0.985	0.324
TS	0.747*	0.313	2.385	0.017
BI	0.061*	0.027	2.228	0.026
LOY	ON			
SAT	0.482*	0.06	8.012	0

Source: Authors' own

Table 7: SEM results

Hypothesis	*Structural paths*	*Standardized estimate*	*Hypothesis acceptance*
H1	Website & Technology → Satisfaction	0.164^{ns}	Rejected
H2	Value Proposition → Satisfaction	0.115*	Accepted
H3	Customer Service → Satisfaction	0.249^{ns}	Rejected
H4	Trust & Security → Satisfaction	0.313*	Accepted
H5	Brand Image → Satisfaction	0.027*	Accepted
H6	Satisfaction → e-loyalty	0.06*	Accepted

Source: Authors' own

MODERATION EFFECT OF GENDER

The researchers had proposed to check the moderation effect of gender on the designated paths. Therefore, before checking moderation, we performed an "invariance test" between male and female groups using 'Configural Invariance Test'. "A measure is invariant when members of different populations who have the same standing on the construct being measured, receive the same observed score on the test. A test violates invariance when two individuals from different populations who are identical on the construct score differently on it" (Schmitt & Kuljanin, 2008). The invariance test revealed that the groups aren't invariant meaning that the moderation effect can`t be determined.

RMSEA (Root Mean Square Error of Approximation)		
Estimate	0.046	
90 percent C.I.	0.040	0.051
Probability RMSEA < = .05	0.915	
CFI/TLI		
CFI	0.949	
TLI	0.946	
Chi-square test of model fit for the baseline model		
Value	9135.307	
Degrees of freedom	1035	
P- value	0.0000	
SRMR (Standardized Root Mean Square Residual)		
Value	0.069	

Fig. 2: SEM model fit information.

DISCUSSION

E-commerce in India is growing at an exponential rate particularly with investments from local and international players. The e-commerce industry has its own challenges but there is a potential for tremendous growth because of the rise in internet users and advancements in the communications technology. It is no hidden fact that each year more and more companies will try to be on e-commerce platform making it harder to the existing companies to secure a substantial market share. Loyalty of customers will be one of the ways to stay competitive in this growing market. This study was an effort to help identify the factors that lead to the loyalty in e-commerce space.

The study confirms that Trust, Value Proposition, Brand Image and Security have a significant impact on satisfaction, as the precursor of e-loyalty. Transaction security and Customer privacy are also important in online shopping. Transaction security ensures that consumers will make a secured complete transaction which augments that they are dealing with a real seller, to buy a real product, to pay securely for that product and to get the product as advertised this in turn leads to higher brand trust (Gefen, 2000). Customer privacy and security guarantees to keep confidential all the personal information of the customer related to the transaction with other parties which includes information related to the profile of the customer and payment. Customer satisfaction and e-loyalty is expected to be enhanced if the web stores are able to manage the transaction security and privacy of customer and enhance the sense of trust among them (Shin *et al.*, 2013; Nugroho *et al.,* 2015).

The Value Proposition is attributed to convenience, customization etc. Convenience is an essential feature of web store service to support and help the online consumer in their buying decision process. It tends to make the process faster and easier. The crucial value expected by the consumer is customization. In the context of online shopping, customization gives consumers the flexibility to manage their profile and transact information. Information like official identity, home and contact addresses, mode of payment, delivery option, and all other mandatory personal data is included in consumer profile.

Thirdly, Brand Image as we know is the perception of a brand in the minds of the customers. In case of websites, difference the customer perceives as compared to the competitors website can be associated with the brand image, in case of websites. Customer's expectations from a certain website service are based on the attributes like reminiscence (positive memories from present experience, positive memories from past experience), sensuality (attractive advertisements, pleasant design) and intimacy (the firm's empathy, consumer's enjoyment).

The study found that no impact on satisfaction of the other two assumed variables *i.e.,* Website & Technology and Customer Service. Customers perceive that the Website & Technology of all the websites are similar, on the basis of features they provide like ease to load, navigations, application options etc. Whereas the Customer Service is no longer treated as a differentiated benefit. In current market scenario it is expected of an e-commerce portal to provide customer service to its customers as a basic function of business operations.

Finally, the study attempts to find the relationship between satisfaction and e-loyalty. The results provided evidence to our proposition that satisfaction leads to e-loyalty. The relationship between customer satisfaction and customer loyalty tends to be a classical phenomenon. Satisfied customers will mostly buy more products again and again from the same brand. Several studies confirmed that those constructs are positively correlated (Casalo *et al.*, 2008; Chang & Chen, 2008; Sahadev & Purani, 2008; Chiou & Pan, 2009; Jamal & Anastasiadou, 2009; Kim *et al.*, 2009; Akbar & Parvez, 2009).

IMPLICATIONS

The behavior of consumers in the e-commerce seems to be a very complex issue given there is a change in the expectations of the consumer, as they challenge the traditional patterns of supply of commercial websites. To merchant website, the concepts of satisfaction and loyalty are a central concern. In the era of relationship marketing it is very important for companies to understand that to build a brand equity they first need to focus on brand loyalty. Some significant implications and findings elicited from the current study are as follows:

- Strong emphasis must be laid on maintaining strong value proposition by the marketers. They should try to provide customized services, convenience, quality products, variety etc. Focusing on these factors will lead to satisfaction in a customer and will result in making them frequent re-buyers.
- It is pivotal for the marketers to maintain trust and security of the customer so that the customer feels free and secure while making a purchase. This sense of security and protection will enhance satisfaction in the customer.

- Prime focus should be on creating a strong brand image in the mind of the customer by exhibiting the characteristics of a strong and trustworthy brand. A service provider should ensure that the customers still be satisfied and stick to their service by providing them attributes like intimacy, empathy and responsiveness etc.
- Recent developments in the FDI of retail and boom in the retail sector have increased the challenges for the marketers. So in order to get hold of their strong position in the market, they have to turn their shortcomings into their strengths. The service providers can take advantage of their websites & information and communication technologies in an innovative and transformative manner. They can also focus on providing a premium customer service, which should be exclusive to their brand and should be highly differentiated. The service provider must do more than what others (competitors) are doing and do it right. To conclude, focusing on above-mentioned factors, a marketer can ensure the satisfaction of the customer, which will lead to a stronger brand loyalty.

LIMITATIONS

Due to the paucity of time, a higher sample size couldn't be selected so the greater generalization of the results is not possible. The sample was geographically limited so the data from other cities may produce different results. Since the data collected was quantitative in nature, the limitations of the research will also apply. The study revealed that other than satisfaction there are other factors that influence loyalty but are not included in this research. Due to variance in groups of male and female, the researchers were unable to check the moderation effect of Gender.

CONCLUSIONS

In modern day marketing customer relationship and loyalty are two such phenomenons which not only lead to profitability but long term competitive advantage to companies. In e-commerce the importance of e-loyalty is heightened due of increasing competition and lack of face-to face communication. As such it is very important for both academicians and practitioners to understand the concept of e-loyalty and the factors that cause it. It's only by understanding the antecedents of e-loyalty one can build a loyal customer base to remain relevant in the fast-changing e-markets.

REFERENCES

Akbar, M.M., & Parvez, N. (2009). Impact of service quality, trust and customer satisfaction on customers loyalty. *ABAC Journal*, 29(1).

Anderson, R.E., & Srinivasan, S.S. (2003). E-satisfaction and e-loyalty: A contingency framework. *Psychology & Marketing*, 20(2): 123–138.

Bass, F.M. (1974). The theory of stochastic preference and brand switching. *Journal of Marketing Research*, pp. 1–20.

Bentler, P M., & Chou, C.P. (1987) Practical issues in structural modeling. *Sociological Methods & Research*, 16: 78–117.

Bryman, A., & Bell, E. (2015). *Business Research Methods*. Oxford University Press, USA.

Casaló, L.V., Flavián, C., & Guinalíu, M. (2008). The role of satisfaction and website usability in developing customer loyalty and positive word-of-mouth in the e-banking services. *International Journal of Bank Marketing*, 26(6): 399–417.

Cattell, R.B. (1978). The scientific use of factor analysis. New York: *Plenum*.

Chang, H.H., & Chen, S.W. (2008). The impact of customer interface quality, satisfaction and switching costs on e-loyalty: Internet experience as a moderator. *Computers in Human Behavior*, 24(6): 2927–2944.

Chang, H.H., Wang, Y.H., & Yang, W.Y. (2009). The impact of e-service quality, customer satisfaction and loyalty on e-marketing: Moderating effect of perceived value. *Total Quality Management*, 20(4): 423–443.

Chiou, J.S., & Pan, L.Y. (2009). Antecedents of internet retailing loyalty: Differences between heavy *versus* light shoppers. *Journal of Business and Psychology*, 24(3): 327.

Cho, E. (2011). Development of a brand image scale and the impact of love marks on brand equity.

Comrey, A.L., & Lee, H.B. (1992). A first course in factor analysis. Hillsdale, NJ: *Erlbaum.*

Corstjens, M., & Lal, R. (2000). Building store loyalty through store brands. *Journal of Marketing Research*, 37(3): 281–291.

Delone, W.H., & Mclean, E.R. (2004). Measuring e-commerce success: Applying the DeLone & McLean information systems success model. *International Journal of Electronic Commerce*, 9(1): 31–47.

Engel, J.F., Kollat, D.T., & Roger, D. (1982). Blackwell (1973), Consumer Behavior. New York: Holt, Rinehart and Winston.

Evrard, Y., & Aurier, P. (1996). Identification and validation of the components of the person-object relationship. *Journal of Business Research*, 37(2): 127–134.

Gefen, D. (2000). E-commerce: The role of familiarity and trust. *Omega*, 28(6): 725–737.

Gommans, M., Krishman, K.S., & Scheffold, K.B. (2001). From brand loyalty to e-loyalty: A conceptual framework. *Journal of Economic & Social Research*, 3(1).

Gorard, S. (2010). Research design, as independent of methods.

Gremler, D.D. (1995). The effect of satisfaction, switching costs, and interpersonal bonds on service loyalty (Doctoral dissertation, Arizona State University).

Guilford, J.P. (1954). *Psychometric Methods*, 2 Edt. New York: *McGraw-Hill*.

Hair, J., Black, W., Babin, B., & Anderson, R. (2010). Multivariate data analysis (7th ed.)
:Prentice-Hall, Inc. Upper Saddle River, NJ, USA.

Jacoby, J. (1969). Toward a multi-brand model of brand loyalty. *Purdue Papers in Consumer Psychology, Paper*, (105).

Jacoby, J. (1971). Model of multi-brand loyalty. *Journal of Advertising Research*, 11(3): 25–31.

Jacoby, J., & Chestnut, R.W. (1978). Brand loyalty: Measurement and management. John Wiley & Sons Incorporated.

Jacoby, J., & Olson, J.C. (1970). An attitudinal model of brand loyalty: Conceptual underpinnings and instrumentation research. *Purdue Papers in Consumer Psychology*, 159: 14–20.

Jamal, A., & Anastasiadou, K. (2009). Investigating the effects of service quality dimensions and expertise on loyalty. *European Journal of Marketing*, 43(3/4): 398–420.

Jarvis, L.P., & Wilcox, J.B. (1976). Repeat purchasing behavior and attitudinal brand loyalty: Additional evidence. Marketing, pp. 151–152.

Kim, J., Jin, B., & Swinney, J.L. (2009). The role of etail quality, e-satisfaction and e-trust in online loyalty development process. *Journal of retailing and Consumer services*, 16(4): 239–247.

Klopping, I.M., & McKinney, E. (2004). Extending the technology acceptance model and the task-technology fit model to consumer e-commerce. *Information Technology, Learning and Performance Journal*, 22(1): 35.

McAlister, L., & Pessemier, E. (1982). Variety seeking behavior: An interdisciplinary review. *Journal of Consumer research*, 9(3): 311–322.

McKnight, D.H., Choudhury, V., & Kacmar, C. (2002). Developing and validating trust measures for e-commerce: An integrative typology. *Information Systems Research*, 13(3): 334–359.

Muthén, L.K., & Muthén, B.O. (1998-2012). Mplus User's Guide. 7th Eds. *Los Angeles, CA: Muthén & Muthén.*

Neuman, W.L., & Kreuger, L. (2003). Social work research methods: Qualitative and quantitative approaches. Allyn and Bacon.

N'Goala, G. (2007). Customer Switching Resistance (CSR), The effects of perceived equity, trust and relationship commitment. *International Journal of Service Industry Management*, 18(5): 510–533.

Nugroho, S., Dharmesti, M., Septiari, E., & Gitosudarmo, I. (2015). The Impact of E- satisfaction on E-loyalty Moderated by Consumer Perceived Risk and Expertise.

Oliver, R.L. (1999). Whence consumer loyalty? *The Journal of Marketing*, pp. 33–44.

Reichheld, F.F., & Schefter, P. (2000). E-loyalty: Your secret weapon on the web. *Harvard Business Review*, 78(4): 105–113.

Sahadev, S., & Purani, K. (2008). Modelling the consequences of e-service quality. *Marketing Intelligence & Planning*, 26(6): 605–620.

Saunders, M.N., & Lewis, P. (2012). Doing research in business and management: An essential guide to planning your project. Pearson.

Schmitt, N., & Kuljanin, G. (2008). Measurement invariance: Review of practice and implications. *Human Resource Management Review*, 18(4): 210–222.

Schultz, D.E., & Bailey, S.E. (2000). Customer/brand loyalty in an interactive marketplace. *Journal of Advertising Research*, 40(3): 41–52.

Sekaran, U. (2006). Research methods for business: A skill building approach. *John Wiley & Sons.*

Shin, J.I., Chung, K.H., Oh, J.S., & Lee, C.W. (2013). The effect of site quality on repurchase intention in internet shopping through mediating variables: The case of university students in South Korea. *International Journal of Information Management*, 33(3): 453–463.

Srinivasan, S.S., Anderson, R., & Ponnavolu, K. (2002). Customer loyalty in e-commerce: An exploration of its antecedents and consequences. *Journal of Retailing*, 78(1): 41–50.

Turban, E., King, D., Lee, J., & Viehland, D. (2002). Electronic commerce: A managerial perspective. Prentice Hall: ISBN 0, 13(975285), 4.

Valvi, A.C., & Fragkos, K.C. (2012). Critical review of the e-loyalty literature: A purchase centred framework. *Electronic Commerce Research*, 12(3): 331–378.

Zeithaml, V.A., Berry, L.L., & Parasuraman, A. (1996). The behavioral consequences of service quality. *The Journal of Marketing*, pp. 31–4.

4

CSR Initiatives: A Strategic Response of Companies Operating in India Towards New CSR Regulations

WASEEM JAHANGIR[1]* AND ZIA-UL-HAQ[2]

ABSTRACT

Organizations compete with each other on the basis of the CSR initiatives they take; the type of initiatives a company takes up to make an impression in the minds of the customers. Corporate Social Responsibility (CSR) nowadays does not continue to exist as a philanthropic activity only; it has gained a strategic importance and its decisions are being taken in association with other operational decisions. Since India has made spending a portion of profits on CSR activities compulsory for all eligible companies, it becomes important to divulge companies' strategic response by finding out whether the companies are continuing with the same initiatives or looking for new and unique initiatives in order to get competitive advantage. The current study has employed quota sampling technique in order to select a sample from all listed companies from different sectors as identified by National Stock Exchange of India. In this study, secondary data from Director's reports and Business Responsibility Reports (BRR) was used and analyzed using statistical package like SPSS 20. The study revealed that companies are taking time in order to choose new initiatives. The study proved that selecting a CSR initiative after the new law was mandated is a decision of strategic importance and hence must be taken cautiously.

[1,2] Department of Management Studies, Central University of Kashmir, J&K.
**Corresponding author:* E-mail: Waseemjahangir@ymail.com

Key words: Corporate Social Responsibility (CSR), CSR initiatives, CSR regulations, Section 135 of Companies Act, 2013, Strategic response.

INTRODUCTION

Corporate Social Responsibility (CSR) has a long and an impressive history as to how it was taken in its early stage and how CSR is being perceived in today's time. Based on this changing perception towards CSR, organizations have been behaving differently at different times. The concept of CSR has changed drastically in past 60 years throughout the world (Madrakhimova, 2013). Same is the case with a developing country like India where the concept of CSR was prevalent even in ancient times but the concept got its name and shape only in twentieth century. In early times the kings or Rajas would help society in different ways be it construction of roads, wells, Sarai (a resting place for travelers), plantation of trees along roadsides etc; also other wealthy people would help needy in times of droughts, famines, floods etc. but all these things were linked with Karma rather than considering these acts as something of strategic importance. Nowadays when the concept of CSR has evolved so much, taking up a CSR initiative is not only a philanthropic activity, rather it has gained a strategic importance. It is a proven fact that a company which takes up an initiative would get a competitive advantage over another company (which does not go for any CSR activity). But in a situation where all companies in the same league do spend a portion of their profits for the betterment of the society which company will get a competitive advantage? This situation prevails in India which has mandated a separate law (Section 135 of Companies Act, 2013) making it necessary for all eligible companies to take up a CSR initiative within the territory of India and spend a portion of their profits on it. Thus, India has taken the competition among the companies to the next level. If a company has to survive in today's cut-throat competition it has to think and respond strategically. Thus taking up an initiative and liking it with karma is not going to work in today's times. Companies have to think and rethink while choosing that CSR initiative which people think is of utmost importance, only then a company may get a competitive advantage in terms of sales turnover, increased profits, brand loyal customers, good brand image etc.

The Trend of Choosing New Initiatives

Companies have been looking for new initiatives lately not only in India but throughout the world. Working for anti-corruption and bribery or passing of The Modern Slavery Act 2015 in the UK is one such example of that, wherein an attempt is being made by preventing the modern slavery which includes forced and compulsory labour, human trafficking, servitude etc. This law requires companies to publish an anti-trafficking statement duly signed by the Director of the company. All this shows that companies are on a look out for new initiatives. Likewise working for climate change was always one of the favourite CSR options for every company but nowadays just planting for trees is not going to achieve this objective. Reducing the carbon emissions is most important for every company as customers look for low carbon goods and services. There is a world market worth more than US$5.5 trillion and is growing at a decent rate (BITCI NEWS, 2016). In India, there are companies like Unilever whose carbon emissions per ton have gone 65% below than the level recorded in 1995. Other companies are looking for a new trend which is the sustainable procurement of raw materials which ultimately has a lesser impact on resources and environment (BITCI NEWS, 2016).

Schedule VI of Companies Act, 2013

In India, new CSR regulations come under Section (135) of the Companies Act, 2013. Schedule VI of the same section provides the indicators or sectors where in the companies can invest their money kept for CSR activities. These initiatives can be implemented by companies by taking into consideration the local conditions after seeking the board approval.

In schedule VII, for items (i) to (x) and the entries relating thereto, the following items and entries shall be substituted, namely:-

i. Eradicating hunger, poverty and malnutrition, promoting preventive health care and sanitation and making available safe drinking water;

ii. Promoting education, including special education and employment enhancing vocation skills especially among children, women, elderly, and the differently abled and livelihood enhancement projects;

iii. Promoting gender equality, empowering women, setting up homes and hostels for women and orphans; setting up old age homes, day care centres and such other facilities for senior citizens and measures for reducing inequalities faced by socially and economically backward groups;

iv. Ensuring environmental sustainability, ecological balance, protection of flora and fauna, animal welfare, agro forestry, conservation of natural resources and maintaining the quality of soil, air and water;

v. Protection of National heritage, art and culture including restoration of buildings and sites of historical importance and works of art; setting up public libraries; promotion and development of traditional arts and handicrafts;

vi. Measures for the benefit of armed forces veterans, war widows and their dependents;

vii. Training to promote rural sports, nationally recognised sports, paralympics sports and Olympic sports;

viii. Contribution to the Prime Minister's National Relief Fund or any other fund set up by the Central Government for socio-economic development, relief and welfare of the scheduled caste, the scheduled tribes, other backward classes, minorities and women;

ix. Contributions or funds provided to technology incubators located within academic institutions which are approved by the Central Government;

x. Rural development projects".

The Ministry of Corporate Affairs (MCA) has made it clear that the above list is only prescriptive and not exhaustive. The companies are given full freedom to explore different socio-economic avenues for their own CSR activities. As per the section 135 of Companies Act 2013 and the rules and regulations, the companies have an obligation for making a budget or creation of a fund but no obligation is on them to incur the expenditures. The companies are supposed to report their budgets or expenditures in the Director's report or BRR (Business Responsibility Report as prescribed by SEBI Act). Also, there should be an explanation given as to why expenditures were not incurred. So in case companies do not incur the expenditure officers will not be prosecuted or penalized for that but any default on the reporting provision could be subject to a fine as well as imprisonment.

In this study, an attempt has been made in order to know whether the companies continued with the same initiatives which they had taken up before the new law was mandated or they chose to look for new initiatives. Also, an attempt has been made in order to find out if the importance of CSR related decisions has changed in India after the implementation of section 135 in Companies Act, 2013.

LITERATURE REVIEW

As per the modern concept of CSR the responsibility of organizations to frame policies, take decisions and follow the rules in order to fulfill the objectives which are approved as desirable by the society (Bowen, 1953). Same idea was given by the Inyang *et al.*, in their definition of CSR as *"obligation of businessmen to pursue those policies, to make those decisions to follow those lines of action, which are desirable in terms of objectives and values to the society of their location"* (Inyang, 2013). But while choosing a CSR activity an organization must go for a "Total Social Responsibility" approach which means expects an organization to meet economic, legal, ethical and discretionary objectives simultaneously (Carroll, 1979). In comparison to large companies which attract huge volume of literature in CSR activities this study focused on small and medium enterprises too. SMEs find it an uphill task to go for a CSR activity and yet consider providing employment and supporting the local economy as important responsibility of their business (Jenkins, 2006). There are a number of studies where in an attempt has been made in order to explore the sectors or initiatives which companies take up mostly. Studies prove that companies choose an initiative based on values and the possible competitive benefits from CSR (Nair & Sodhi, 2012). Contrary to that there are certain organizations which don't look for any kind of benefits rather initiatives are taken up because of religious sentiments (Piumali & Kumari, 2015). These companies mostly choose those initiatives which are associated with Karma for example helping a cancer patient etc. The belief of managers behind this kind of CSR practice is that returns would be given in the life hereafter. This is a type of sunken or silent CSR where in organizations unknowingly contribute a lot by sacrificing a portion of their profits and taking up different type of initiatives for the betterment of the society (Azmat & Samaratunge, 2009). One of the studies of Small and medium enterprises of Australia show that SMEs take up their initiatives very wisely. They analyze whether the initiative will be beneficial for the organization or not for example the initiatives they took were providing water to the community because the organization also needed it, or helping an employee's child who was an elite swimmer. Thus SMEs too select an activity in order to enhance their competitiveness (Moyeen & Courvisanos, 2012).

For companies in India the main objective of selecting a CSR activity has changed dramatically. It no longer has anything to do with karma; it is of strategic importance nowadays. It has an impact on the financial performance which is shown as under.

CSR and Corporate Financial Performance (CFP)

In India when CSR has been made mandatory for all companies (meeting certain criterion as per section 135) it becomes very much necessary to find out the association between CSR and CFP. It was being emphasized time and again by several authors even from times when there was no concept of making CSR a mandatory thing for companies. Hillman and Kiem (2012) also had emphasized to find out the association between CSR and CFP. Since then this area has been studied meticulously but results are still unconvincing. When attempts were made to find out this association, CSR and profitability showed different results in different countries in different contexts. Studies have shown negative as well as positive association between CSR and profitability. Even some studies have shown insignificant relation too between the two variables. Taking about the positive relation there is a study wherein profitability was measured through

Economic Value Added and respondents measured through personal interviews, CSR and profitability showed less positive correlation (Emilsson, Classon & Bredmar, 2012). While in another study conducted on Malaysian Islamic Banks, it was found that CSR and the performance of banks have strong positive correlation (Arshad, Othman & Othman, 2012). But in this study the performance was measured using ROA and ROE. The fact has further being strengthen by PWC Survey wherein 33 CEOs from different countries were surveyed and 70% of them responded by saying that CSR has an impact on profitability. As mentioned earlier there are studies which revealed negative relationship between company performance and corporate social responsibility (McWilliams, Siegel & Wright, 2006; Wright & Ferris, 1997; Teoh, Welch & Wazzan, 1999). While some studies found no significant association between CSR and firm performance (Aupperle, Carroll & Hatfield, 1985).

Through a rigorous literature review, it can be understood that even though measuring company performance may be an easy task but there are certain complications also associated with it. The reason being different types of measures used by different authors. There are studies wherein market measures have been used to find the relation between performance and CSR (Alexander & Buchholz, 1978; Vance, 1975) while in other studies accounting measures were employed to find the relation (Graves & Waddock, 1994; Cochran & Wood, 1984). In addition to that, some studies have gone further and employed both measures to understand the relation between CSR and company performance in a better manner (Mcguire, Sundgreen & Schneeweis, 1988).

Above literature shows that earlier CSR was understood as a philanthropic activity but now the time has changed and it is a concept which is perceived as having a strategic importance. In India where a separate law has been mandated related to CSR, there is a need to understand whether companies are continuing with same initiatives or companies took time in choosing new initiatives after the law was mandated hence proving the strategic importance of CSR.

METHODOLOGY

Objectives of the Study

- To identify the changes in CSR initiatives taken up by companies before and after the enactment of this Law.

Hypothesis (H0): There is no significant difference in pre and post period in initiatives taken up by companies under reference.

The current study is descriptive cum exploratory study. The data for the study has been gathered using secondary data like Director's Report and Business Responsibility Reports etc. A sample of 33 companies has been selected using quota sampling from the different sectors as identified by NSE. For analysis purposes statistical package like SPSS 20 was used.

Data Analysis and Interpretation

Cross tabulations and Z-proportions test

Companies mostly seem to take up more than one initiative at a time. The notion behind it being that taking up initiatives in different domains is a rewarding strategy and it gives a competitive edge to the business organizations. But the objective here is to check if there has been any change in the type of initiatives companies used to take up in pre-2013 and post-2013 periods. For that, the cross tabulation analysis was performed and the results are represented in Table 1.

Based on the study, Table 1 shows that in pre-2013 period the initiatives which were mostly dominating and were taken up by most of the companies were Environmental care with 61.8% followed by Charity and Relief funds with 61.3% of total companies choosing this initiative. Other initiatives like Health and safety (59.3%), Education (59.2%), Nutrition (57.4%), Livelihood generation (57.1%), Community development (57%) and Women empowerment or Gender equality (53.8%) were also popular among the companies. Corresponding to that in post-2013 period there has been a decrease in the number of companies taking up these as CSR initiatives.

The initiatives which were not much popular in pre-2013 but have become favorite among the companies in India are Art & Culture or National heritage with corresponding percentages for pre and post period as 42.9% to 57.1%, Sports with percentages for two periods as 47.2% and 52.8%, Rural Development with percentages as 48.8% and 51.2%.

Table 1: Initiatives-cross tabulations.

		Custom table			
		Period			
		Pre 2013		***Post 2013***	
		Count	***Row N %***	***Count***	***Row N %***
Initiatives	Education	84	59.2%	58	40.8%
	Women empowerment or gender equality	42	53.8%	36	46.2%
	Nutrition	35	57.4%	26	42.6%
	Infra or community development or social business initiative	49	57.0%	37	43.0%
	Livelihood generation	52	57.1%	39	42.9%
	Rural development	39	48.8%	41	51.2%
	Art & Culture or National heritage	15	42.9%	20	57.1%
	Sports	17	47.2%	19	52.8%
	Environmental care	84	61.8%	52	38.2%
	Health and safety	86	59.3%	59	40.7%
	Charity and relief funds	49	61.3%	31	38.8%

In order to check whether the difference in the two periods is significant or not "Z" proportion significance test was used. Table 2 shows that there is a significant difference in the initiatives like Education, Nutrition, Infrastructure or Community development or Social Business Initiative, Livelihood generation, Art & Culture or National heritage, Environmental care, Health and Safety, and Charity and Relief funds. For other initiatives the difference was not significant.

DISCUSSION, CONCLUSIONS AND SUGGESTIONS

As we can see in the Table 1 that there are many initiatives like education, Women Empowerment or gender equality, Nutrition,

Infrastructure or Community development, Livelihood Generation, Environmental care, Health and Safety, and Charity & relief funds which are taken as initiatives by less number of companies. While the initiatives which are mostly taken up by companies post-2013 are like Rural development, Art & Culture or National heritage; and Sports, the reason for such a dramatic change in the choice of companies is due to the fact that companies are looking for new initiatives to invest their CSR funds in. As per the Director's report of these companies, they are looking for new initiatives and do not want to continue with old initiatives because having a unique initiative gives a competitive edge that too when there will be more companies taking CSR initiatives due to passing of new regulations (Section 135 of Companies Act, 2013) in India.

Table 2: Z proportions with Bonferroni correction.

	Comparisons of column proportions[a]	***Period***	
		Pre-2013 (A)	***Post-2013 (B)***
Initiatives	Education		A
	Women empowerment or gender equality		
	Nutrition		A
	Infrastructure or community development or social business initiative		A
	Livelihood generation		A
	Rural development		
	Art & Culture or National heritage		A
	Sports		
	Environmental care		A
	Health and safety		A
	Charity and relief funds		A

Results are based on two-sided tests with significance level .05. For each significant pair, the key of the category with the smaller column proportion appears under the category with the larger column proportion.

a. Tests are adjusted for all pair wise comparisons within a row of each innermost sub table using the Bonferroni correction.

The suggestion of the present study is that companies must select a unique initiative as quickly as possible so that opportunities will not be grabbed by competitors. Another suggestion is for the government authorities that companies must be given a time limit within which an initiative must be selected so that there should be no more delays in the name of saying that companies are taking time for selecting an initiative.

REFERENCES

Alexander, G.J., & Buchholz, R.A. (1978). Corporate social responsibility and stock market performance. *Academy of Management Journal*, 21(3): 479–486.

Arshad, R., Othman, S., & Othman, R. (2012). Islamic corporate social responsibility, corporate reputation and performance. *World Academy of Science, Engineering and Technology*, 64(4): 1070–1074.

Aupperle, K.E., Carroll, A.B., & Hatfield, J.D. (1985). An empirical examination of the relationship between corporate social responsibility and profitability. *Academy of Management Journal*, 28(2): 446–463.

Azmat, F., & Samaratunge, R. (2009). Responsible entrepreneurship in developing countries: Understanding the realities and complexities. *Journal of Business Ethics*, 90(3): 437–452.

Bowen, H.R., & Johnson, F.E. (1953). *Social Responsibility of the Businessman*, Harper.

Carroll, A.B. (1979). A three-dimensional conceptual model of corporate performance. *Academy of Management Review*, 4(4): 497–505.

Cochran, P., & Wood, Robert A. (1984). 'Corporate Social Responsibility and Financial Performance'. *Academy of Management Journal,* Vol. 27.

Emilsson, L.M., Classon, M., & Bredmar, K. (2012). CSR and the quest for profitability: Using economic value added to trace profitability. *International Journal of Economics and Management Sciences*, 2(3): 43–54.

Graves, S.B., & Waddock, S.A. (1994). Institutional owners and corporate social performance. *Academy of Management Journal*, 37(4): 1034–1046.

Hillman, A.J., & Keim, G.D. (2001). Shareholder value, stakeholder management, and social issues: What's the bottom line? *Strategic Management Journal*, 22(2): 125–139

Inyang, B.J. (2013). Small and medium-sized enterprises engagement in CSR. *In: Encyclopedia of Corporate Social Responsibility*. Springer, Berlin, Heidelberg, pp. 2160–2167.

Jenkins, H. (2006). Small business champions for corporate social responsibility. *Journal of Business Ethics*, 67(3): 241–256.

Madrakhimova, F. (2013). History of development of corporate social responsibility. *Journal of Business and Economics*, 4(6): 509–520.

Bartlett, N., Whittington, E., Reuvers, S., & Thoday, K. (2016). "Driving Low-Carbon Growth through Business and Investor Action".

Mcguire, J.B., Sundgren, A., & Schneeweis, T. (1988). "Corporate Social Responsibility and Firm Financial Performance". *Academy of Management Journal*, 31(4): 854–870.

McWilliams, A., Siegel, D.S., & Wright, P.M. (2006). Corporate social responsibility: Strategic implications. *Journal of Management Studies*, 43(1): 1–18.

Moyeen, A., & Courvisanos, J. (2012). Corporate social responsibility in regional small and medium-sized enterprises in Australia. *The Australasian Journal of Regional Studies*, 18(3): 364

Nair, N.K., & Sodhi, J.S. (2012). CSR practices by SMEs in India: Lessons from five case studies. *Indian Journal of Industrial Relations*, pp. 583–597.

Piumali, W.M.H., & Kumari, R.M.C. (2015). Corporate Social Responsibility Practices among Small and Medium Enterprises in Sri Lanka.

Teoh, S.H., Welch, I., & Wazzan, C.P. (1999). The effect of socially activist investment policies on the financial markets: Evidence from the South African boycott. *The Journal of Business*, 72(1): 35–89.

Vance, S.C. (1975). "Are socially responsible corporations good investment risks?" *Management Review,* 64: 18–24

Wright, P., & Ferris, S.P. (1997). Agency conflict and corporate strategy: The effect of divestment on corporate value. *Strategic Management Journal*, 18(1): 77–83.

Webliography

BITCI NEWS (2016). "CSR Trends 2016 Part 1 What Should Businesses look out for?" retrieved from *www.bitc.ie/newsroom/news/csr-trends-2016-part-1-what-should-businesses-look-out-for/*. assessed on 25/02/2018

5

The Opportunities and Challenges of FDI in Service Sector - A Study of Punjab

SUGANDH ARORA[1] AND TAWHEED NABI[2*]

ABSTRACT

FDI is a main key for economic growth, through its accelerating domestic capital, productivity, employment and also plays an important role for the up gradation of technology, skills and managerial capabilities in various sectors of the economy. The FDI inflows in the services sector have been pulling up the overall growth of the economy. The services sector in Punjab has the most vibrant sector in terms of contribution incomes, trade and FDI inflows and employment. In Punjab, it has highest efficiency in agro productivity, and projected to continue to grow at a fast pace. However, there are some concerns viz; Growth in employment in services has not been proportionate with the share of the sector in GDP. A large part of the employment is in the non-corporate or in the unorganized sector, with limited job security. The paper identifies number of opportunities and barriers faced by the services sectors and suggest policy measures, which, if implemented, will lead to inclusive growth, increased productivity, generate quality employment, increase trade and investment, and global competitiveness in services.

Key words: FDI, DIPP, IMF, UNCTAD, Services.

Mittal School of Business, Lovely Professional University, Phagwara, Punjab.
*Corresponding author: E-mail:tawheed1990@gmail.com

INTRODUCTION

Foreign direct investment is the form of managing and controlling ownership of a business in one country by entirely based in another country. It can accelerate growth, increase supply of funds, exports and foreign exchange earnings of the country. By FDI employment generates and technology gets upgraded and then it helps in upgradation and increase the overall growth of a country's economic condition. The nature of FDI, it can create a stable environment and economic growth and job creation. Countries are developing because they are having knowledge about FDI flow to their economies. International Monetary Fund (IMF) has defined FDI as "an investment which is made to attain long term interest in an enterprise operating in an economy other than that of the investor". The investor's purpose is to have an effective voice in the management of the enterprise. UNCTAD's World Investment Report defined Foreign Direct Investment (FDI) as "International investment that reflects the objective of a resident entity in one economy obtaining a 'Lasting Interest' and control in an enterprise resident in an economy other than that of the foreign direct investor. 'Lasting Interest' implies there is existence of a long-term relationship between a direct investor and the enterprise and a significant degree of influence on the management of the enterprise.

Services sector is most important module of the Indian economy. In service sector FDI is used as tool for growth prospective which strengthening of domestic capital productivity and employment. In developing countries like India, the service sector can lead to constant growth with both backward and forward links (Banga, 2005) by ensure reasonable access to acquire basic services available at low prices (Deloitte, 2011) by creating employment opportunities, and by developing human capital. India's services sector has various varieties such as trade, hotel and restaurants, banking, tourism, transport, communication, insurance and real estate, business services, infrastructure, community, social and personal services, and services associated with construction. India is among the world's rapidly growing economies. In another country economic growth has shifted from agriculture to industries whereas India there has been a shift from agriculture to other service sector. India had considered as an outlier among South Asia and another emerging country (Ansari, 1995). The study analyzed that with the increase in per capita income, the share of services in GDP rises (Gordan & Gupta, 2003; Jain & Ninan, 2010). The service sector has been contribute 55.65 percent of India's Gross Value Added at current price in 2018-19 and employed 28.6 percent of the total population.

As far as the state of Punjab is considered, it is a smallest recipient of FDI inflows in Punjab which was US$416 mn. The state has offered incentives under its IT industry policy. Punjab Agro Industries Corporation has been encouraging both the private and foreign investment to identify technically feasible and economically feasible projects with the help of financial collaborations for implementation in the joint sector (India Brand Equity Foundation). According to the Department of Industrial Policy and Promotion (DIPP), cumulative FDI inflows to Punjab amounted to US$ 1.472 billion. The state government signed Memorandum of Understandings (MoUs) in Ludhiana region with 21 industrial as worth US$ 207.43 million.

OBJECTIVES OF THE STUDY

The main aim of the study is to examine the different opportunities for FDI in service sector in Punjab (India) and the factors which are the challenging its path. Further the various policies of government on FDI in service sector will be analyzed thoroughly.

FDI in Service Sector

According to the Department of Industrial Policy and Promotion (DIPP), the services sector includes banking, insurance, real estates, research and development, courier and technology testing, which had acknowledged foreign direct investment (FDI) worth $6.89 billion in 2015-16. The detailed classification of service sector is shown in Fig. 1. Continues flow of FDI in the services sector assume significance as it contributes over 60% to India's gross domestic product. The 18% of total India FDI invested in computer software and hardware, construction development and telecommunications.

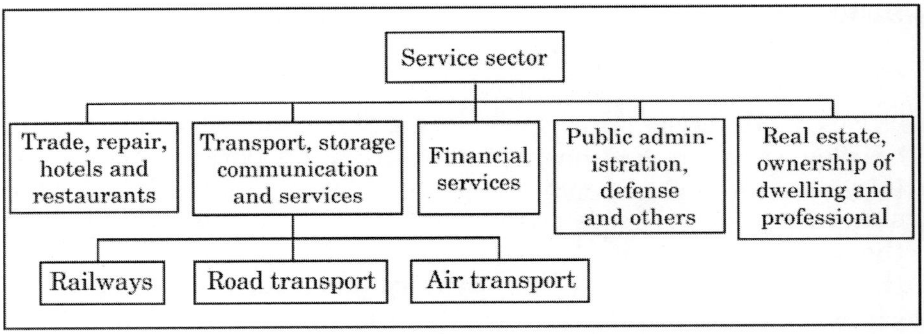

Fig. 1: Classification of service sector.

Source: Union India Budget (2018).

High FDI inflows into the sector

Government of India has brought number of reforms such as the abolition of the Foreign Investment Promotion Board and introduces the composite caps in the FDI policy which allow 100 percent of FDI under automatic route for various financial sector activities which is regulated by financial sector regulator. The services sector is the highest recipient (Fig. 2) of FDI Inflows in India with total inflow of US$ 68,617.41 million during 2000-2018.

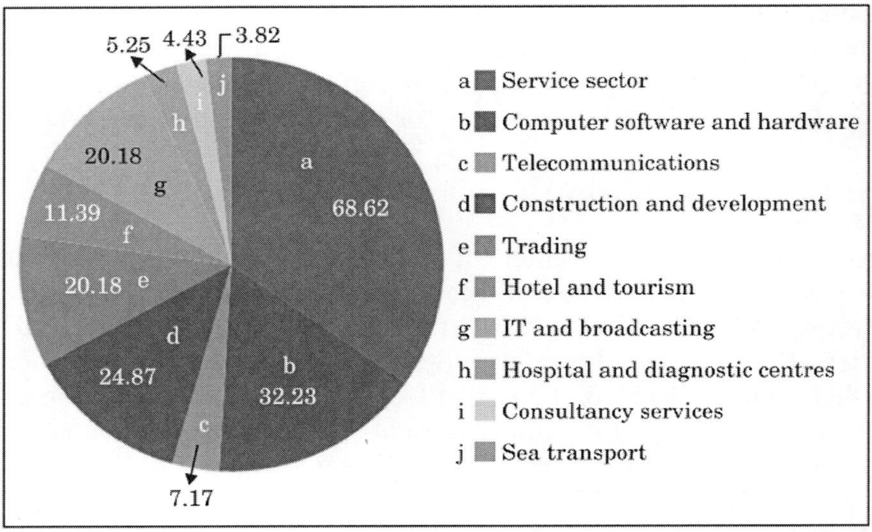

Fig. 2: FDI inflows in India [April 2000-June 2018 (US$ billions)]. *Source:* Department of Industrial Policy and Promotion.

REVIEW OF LITERATURE

Chandrasekhar and Ghosh (2012) focused on an important objective of promoting FDI has been promoted efficiency in production and increase exports. However increase in the equity stake of the foreign investors with existing joint ventures and purchase of a share by them in domestic firms would not be repeatedly change the working course of the firm. Badade and Katkar (2011) examined those India required increasing inflows of FDI with liberal policy since 1991 after decade cautious attitude. After 1990's there is sustained growth in annual FDI inflows to India. PHD Chamber (2011) analyzes that the economic analysis of Indian states and study concludes that most of the population in the northern and central states depends on agriculture. So, these states must focus towards improving the productivity of farm sector so as to make sure the sustained livelihood of the people. The states must lay emphasis on attracting private and foreign investment in manufacturing sector in particular and industries in general to lay the solid foundation to economic growth of the state. Saini, A., Law, S.H. and Ahmad, A.H. (2010) study proves that positive impact of FDI on economic growth and the financial market development which exceeds a threshold level which results the benefit of FDI is non-existent. Chee, Y.L. and Nair, M. (2010) the empirical studied focused on the financial sector development which increase the contribution of FDI inflows and economic growth of region also showed that the complementary role of FDI and financial sector development on economic growth, which plays the crucial role for least developed economies in the region. Chakravarti (2009) study the critical factors which drive investment inflows across Indian states. The empirical findings suggest that both political stability and fiscal reforms are the most essential determinants which determine the investment FDI inflows across states. The study showed that investors must firstly select states as investment destinations principally on the basis of their existing socio economic performance as divergent to their past performance as investment destinations. Veeramani and Goldar (2004) discuss the effects of investment climate on total factor of productivity in the manufacturing sector. Both these studies select a number of variables which together constitute the investment climate of a state and test their effect on total factor productivity using firm level data. Dollar, Iarossi and Mengistae (2002) analysed a good investment climate with facilitate of higher volume of investment FDI inflows focusing on high productivity manufacturing and services sectors, employment creation, income growth and, ultimately, poverty reduction and the pillars of poverty alleviation, Lipsey (2001) and Warsi *et al.* (2013). FDI is also a source of high wages in recipient countries. Academic work on FDI-wage relationship showed that Multinational Enterprises (MNEs) had a higher wages structure as compare to domestic firms. And this structure of multinational even pushed up the overall wages rate.

RESEARCH METHODOLOGY

This study is based on descriptive research. This study is based on secondary data from various sources such as Journals and Articles, IMF reports, Ministry of Finance International Journal of Commerce and Management Research Publications, Economic Survey, RBI Bulletin, Punjab Bureau of Statistics, IBEF, Trading Economics and World Bank, Department of Industrial Policy and Promotion publications, SIA Newsletter, Online database of FDI and Newspapers etc.

With the help of secondary data the challenges and opportunities on FDI in service sector has been analyzed thoroughly with the help of past studies and a review based study has been made. The study has been studied in context of objectives mentioned. The opportunities, challenges and government policies has been studied separately to reach a well defined end and to suggest the policy implications.

Opportunities in Service Sector in Punjab

Focus on agriculture sector

Among all the sector agriculture are most significant sectors for the growth of Punjab's economy. It is providing livelihoods utmost 60 percent of the state's population and is known as the 'Bread Basket of India' leading to the first Green Revolution in the country. By 2025, it is forecast that the state will be the leading producers of non food grains and exporter of various agriculture products and total food production during 2017-18 would be estimated at 31.38 million metric tons (state's economic survey) 2017-18 whereas production of horticulture in Punjab reached 6,956 thousand metric tonnes in 2017-18. There are 33 mega agriculture processing projects and 12 cold storage chains in the state.

Improvement in housing and real estate's

In the recent coming period, Punjab has make strategy provide all its 147 cities and towns with planned development including full time availability of quality power with 100% coverage for sewerage system, solid waste management facilities and projects focused on traffic issues.

Advancement in infrastructure and renewable energy

Bus Rapid Transit Systems (BRTS) have been planned in the major cities of the state to augment the urban infrastructure and State has plans to interconnectivity of road with four and six lane expressways which help to interlink the towns and rural areas of Punjab (India Brand Equity Foundation). Government has provided area of 1,700 for development and maintains infrastructure in the vicinity of the Sri Guru Ram Dass Jee International Airport (Amritsar) and the railway station and 40 acres for IT City which has been earmarked especially for electronics and hardware companies. Punjab is well linked with four neighboring states and other states through 15 national highways. Pradhan Mantri Gram Sadak Yojana (PMGSY) has provided funds US$ 36.46 million for allocated rural roads under and US$ 46.55 million for the Central Road Funds scheme. In 2017, Ministry of Civil Aviation (Government of India) announced for proper site of a Greenfield Airport will be undertaken in Machhiwara (city Ludhiana).

Power generation

The government of Punjab has mainly focused on usage of renewable Sources of energy. For the contribution of renewable energy the total installed capacity is increased from 503.42 MW to 1,282.42 MW in 2018 (India Brand Equity Foundation).

Government of Punjab has projected investment target for renewable energy generation capacity of 5,400 MW US$ 6 billion by 2022 (Punjab State Power Corporation Limited)

Improvement in telecom infrastructure

According to the Telecom Regulatory Authority of India (TRAI), Punjab had 38.49 million wireless subscribers and 837,445 wire-line subscribers' in 2018. In Punjab state, 7,512 gram panchayats were used service ready under the Bharat Net programmed. As of August 2018, Airtel was the leading telecom operator in Punjab with more than 10 million customers (India Brand Equity Foundation).

Creation of more and better employment opportunities

The entry of foreign companies into Indian services will not only creates many employment opportunities but, will also ensure quality in them. This helps the Indian human resource to find better quality jobs and to improve their standard of living and life styles on par with that of the citizens of developed nations.

Declining poverty

Punjab has done sensibly well to reduce its poverty, with only 8.4% (Ministry of Social Justice, GOI) of the population living below the poverty line (BPL) as national average is 27.5%. Declining the poverty from the economy means increase in the income level of the people which will ultimate result in increase in the domestic income and increase in consumption which indicates positive impact on service sector.

Living standard

Living standard is also another part of Punjab culture like to maintain high standard in the society even if they have to go for credit. Dining in restaurants, having all necessary comforts of life, habit of having relish food etc. it can also consider an opportunity.

Unemployment

The degree of unemployment in the state continues to be a cause of serious concern. According to the Govt. survey only 416 persons are employed Worker Population Ratio (per 1000) for persons of age 15 years and above according to usual principal status approach (Government of Punjab). Amongst the educated 93% was non technical and 23.07% had technical qualifications. Here it can be said that FDI in service can result as boom for the state as by setting up provision of service sector it can provide employment opportunities for the unemployed youth of Punjab.

Challenges in Service Sector in Punjab

Increase in Population

The population of Punjab has been increasing at rapid rate over the last decades and according to some projections by 2025 it will increase to 128 million. The challenge facing the province is to create ample number of jobs every year to absorb the increasingly large number of entrants into the labor force. A continues increase in investment and productivity in the service sector is therefore imperative to create employment and income (International Growth Centre).

Electricity

The lack of electricity is considered the most severe issue by firms in the province. In Punjab, more than 50 percent of total firms facing electricity shortages as the most serious obstacle in environment. But recently the State recognizes that power is one of the most crucial inputs for the industry sector. So accordingly the state makes the provision for better quality and cost-effectiveness power to give a great boost to the Industry.

Corruption and hoarding

Across the seven key industrial hubs in Punjab, more than one third of the firms identified corruption (ICA, 2007). The various method of corruption is through inconsistent interpretation and ad-hoc application of government regulation and policies related to tax, labor, and other licensing issues. An overwhelming majority of Punjab's service sector believe that officials interpret policies and regulations inconsistently. The application of policies by government officials is purposely complicated to extract as much rent as possible by threats or even harassment. The other notable constraints identified by sectors are access to finance, evasion of taxes and crime, theft and other disorder in political manner.

Macroeconomic instability

The overall investment in a country is negatively impact on economic growth due to macroeconomic instability as it also increases uncertainty of future growth and returns. At the Punjab level almost 46 percent of firms declared macroeconomic instability among these constraints. This uncertainty further arise fluctuation and volatility in demand, and relative prices adds to the cost in business. It emerges restraint by all firms in the Punjab. Macroeconomic instability has been identified great hurdles in productivity and output growth (ICA, 2007).

Inadequate workforce

Punjab is endowed with a young and a fast growing labor force. This demographic trend and pattern presents an immense challenge for the economy which is to both educate and technological trained. But the (ICA, 2007) survey has identified that inadequately trained workforce as major impediment to sector performance.

Analyzing the Various Policies of Government of India on FDI in Service Sector

FDI in services sector slumps with 23 percentage and declined to USD 6.7 billion in 2017-18. The services sector includes finance, banking, insurance, outsourcing, R&D, courier, tech testing and analysis. FDI inflows was fall by about 23 percent to USD 6.7 billion in the services sector Department of Industrial Policy and Promotion (DIPP). The services sector had attracted FDI inflows worth USD 8.68 billion (2016-17). The services sector includes finance, banking, insurance, outsourcing, R&D, courier, tech testing and analysis. As FDI inflows are concerned, the growth rate seen a five-year low of 3 percent USD 44.85 billion (2017-18). According to Anis Chakravarty (Lead Economist & Partner, Deloitte India, 2018) the slowdown in FDI inflows because of re-routing of investments to economies like the US which witnessed as continuously increase in interest rates. The slump down of growth rate, FDI inflows are more of an exogenous effect and the policy makers also have continue focus on economic management and stability with growth prospective. In chemicals sector also FDI, was marginal decline in growth rate in (2017-18). Services sector contributes up to 60 percent India's GDP. FDIs are crucial for India as it would require huge investments in the next coming years to revamp the infrastructure sector to boost growth. Continuously decline in foreign inflows not only put pressure on the country's balance of payments but impact the currency too. The DIPP had issued the updated and revised Foreign Direct Investment Policy 2017. The FDI Policy 2017 incorporated various notifications issued by the Government of India over the past year. The most significant amendment to the FDI regime has been the institutional change brought issued by the Department of Economic Affairs confirming the abolition of the FIPB and the introduction of the 'Foreign Investment Facilitation Portal' (FIFP), an administrative body to facilitate FDI applicants. The FDI Policy 2017 defines and lists sector-specific administrative ministry and department as 'Competent Authorities' empowered to grant government approval for FDI which include the DIPP in respect of applications for FDI in the Single Brand, Multi Brand and Food Product retail trading and the Department of Economic Affairs of India for FDI in the financial services sector. The DIPP had also issued the Standard Operating Procedure which sets detailed procedure, timeline for applications and the list of 'competent authorities' for processing government approvals for FDI in India. The FDI Policy 2017 has introduced 'Convertible Notes' by Start-ups to persons resident outside India; and equity or equity linked/ debt instruments by Start-ups to Foreign Venture Capital Investors.

The Sector-Specific Significant Amendments in Previous Years

Manufacturing: The manufacturing sector which allowed 100% FDI under the automatic route under government approval route was allowed for retail trading, e-commerce, food products manufactured and produced in India.

Civil aviation: The threshold for FDI in existing projects under the automatic route was increased from 74% to 100%.

Other financial services: All financial sector activities which is regulated by financial sector regulators and fall under the 100% automatic route of investment with applicability of sector laws.

CONCLUSIONS

The service sector is fastest growing sector in Punjab, it has highest efficiency in agro- productivity, and projected to continue to grow at a fast pace. The share of services in India's total trade is higher than the global average, and India is among the top 10 WTO members in service exports and imports. But India does not have effective policy that can lead to inclusive growth and numerous governing bodies and a lack of coordination among them, corrupted system and management which adversely affect the growth of the sector. In many types of services, the regulations are outdated, and there are FDI restrictions and regulatory barriers. A major proportion of Punjab does not have access to basic services such as healthcare and education. Infrastructure is weak, so the cost of service delivery is high. Although Punjab wants to develop in road connectivity, knowledge hub but there is no uniformity in the quality and standards of education, and formal education does not guarantee employability because of lack of training and macro instability.

The service sector will be able to contribute to inclusive growth by enhancing investment, creating employment and developing infrastructure, and technology enhancement. It is important for Punjab with a huge youth population to generate quality employment and to grow the economy. It can attract FDI and private investment only with a stable, transparent, well planned and competitive policy environment. If the reforms suggested here are implemented definitely Punjab will sooner enhance the efficiency of the service sector which leads to inclusive growth.

REFERENCES

Ansari, M.I. (1995). "Explaining the service sector growth: An empirical study of India, Pakistan and Sri Lanka". *Journal of Asian Economics*, 6(2): 233–246.

Azman-Saini, W.N.W., Law, S.H., & Ahmad, A.H. (2010). "FDI and economic growth: New evidence on the role of financial markets". *Economics Letters*, 107(2): 211–213.

Badade, K., & Katkar, M. (2011). "Foreign direct investment in banking sector: A boon in disguise". *Professional Banker*, 3: 46–49.

Banga, R. (2005). "Critical issues in India's service-led growth". Working paper no. 171 International Economic Relations (ICRIER). New *Delhi: ICRIER*.

Chakravarti, R. (2009). "An Empirical Analysis of Investment Determinants in Indian States: 1998-2006". *The Michigan Journal of Business*, 2(2): 9–53.

Chandrasekhar, C.P., & Ghosh, J. (2012). "India's External Sector". *Business Line*, 9.

Chee, Y.L., & Nair, M. (2010). "The impact of FDI and financial sector development on economic growth: Empirical evidence from Asia and Oceania". *International Journal of Economics and Finance*, 22: 107.

Deloitte (2011). "Inclusive Growth a Challenging Opportunity". *Deloitte and All India Management Association.* Retrieved from: *http://www.deloitte.com/assets/DcomIndia/Local%20Assets/Documents/Inclusive_Growth*

Department of Industrial Policy and Promotion Government of India. Retrieved from: *http://dipp.nic.in/foreign-direct-investment/foreign-direct-investment-policy*

Dollar, D., Iarossi, G., & Mengistae, T. (2002). Investment climate and economic performance: Some firm level evidence from India. Center for Research on Economic Development and Policy Reform, Stanford University, Working Paper, (143).

Gordon, J., & Gupta, P. (2003). "Understanding India's Services Revolution", Paper prepared for IMF-NCAER Conference. *A Tale of Two Giants: India's and China's Experience with Reform.*

Government of Punjab, State Power Corporation. Retrieved from: *www.pspcl.in*

Hussain, S.T., Khan, U., Malik, K.Z., & Faheem, A. (2012). "The constraints to industry in Punjab, Pakistan". *The Lahore Journal of Economics,* 17(SE): 135–189.

International Growth Centre. Retrieved from: *www.theigc.org*

International Monetary Fund. Government Finance Statistics Division

(1986). *Government Finance Statistics Yearbook*. International Monetary Fund.

Jain, S., & Ninan, T.N. (2010). “Servicing India’s GDP growth”. India’s Economy Performance and Challenges, Essays in Honour of Montek Singh Ahluwalia, pp. 328–365.

Lipsey, R.E. (2001). ”Foreign direct investment and the operations of multinational firms: Concepts, history and data”. Working paper no. 8665. National Bureau of Economic Research.

Ministry of Commerce Government of India. Retrieved from: www.ibef.org

Ministry of Social Justice, Government of India. Retrieved from: *http://socialjustice.nic.in*

Punjab: *“The State Profile”- (November 2011) by PHD Research Bureau, PHD Chamber of Commerce and Industry.*

UNCTAD, G. (2006). *World Investment report.*

Veeramani, C., & Goldar, B. (2004). ”Investment climate and total factor productivity in manufacturing: Analysis of Indian states”. Working paper no.127.

Warsi, A.Z., Mubarik, M.S., & Hussain, J. (2013). “Effect of workers’ remittances on balance of trade, inflation and economic growth in Pakistan”. *Pakistan Business Review*, 204.

6

Exploring the Potential of Dark Tourism of India: A Revival of the Past

ADIL AMIN NAZKI[1]* AND ABID SUHAIL NIKA[2]

ABSTRACT

The current study wants to analyze the potential of Dark tourism of India which has emerged as a result of various shocking events. As most of the tourists are leisure, pleasure and religious loving, some of them are interested in Adventure and other activities but it has been seen that Indian youth is very much interested to visit dark sites because of high patriotism. The paper wants to highlight the important dark tourism sites in India so that people visit these sites and also promote them word-of mouth globally to boom tourism. This will definitely give birth to dark tourism in India as it has been a growing trend in other countries also. The objective of the current study is to uplift-the-wale for the great potential of dark tourism and the ways to attract the tourists towards this form of tourism in India. The study is qualitative in nature.

Key words: Dark tourism, Grief tourism, Indian tourism.

INTRODUCTION

Dark tourism, Phoenix tourism, Thanatourism, Black tourism and Grief tourism is a type of tourism which involves traveling to places historically linked with death, suffering, torture and tragedy. This

[1] Department of Tourism Studies, Central University of Kashmir, J&K.
Corresponding author: Email: nazkiadi@gmail.com; abids157@gmail.com

tourism is becoming popular day by day especially among youth all over the globe. Dark tourism has gained more importance through media imagination and academic scholarship. Despite a good account of literature available on the representation and tourist experience of deaths capes, tragedies, horror and sufferings, dark tourism as a field of study is still in its infancy stage and needs to be explored. Phoenix tourism is now a research brand in which scholars can locate a diverse range of death related destinations to enhance tourist experience. Phoenix tourism is not simply a fascination with death or the macabre, but a multi disciplinary academic lens through which to scrutinize fundamental interrelationships of the modern commodification of death with the cultural environment of society.

Within the contemporary visitor economy, deaths, disasters and atrocities in touristic form are becoming an increasingly per-vasive trait. "People who desire to travel and gaze upon real or recreated death, a plethora of sites, attractions and exhibitions is now emerging across the world to cater to the *darker side of travel*" (Shar-pley & Stone, 2009). In fact, morbid practices within tourism vary from tourists who are gazing upon the sites of brutality at former World War One battlefields of northern France, to tourists buying souvenirs of atrocity at Ground Zero, to tourists sightseeing in the ruins of New Orleans (after Hurricane Katrina), touring of excursionists to sites of genocide and tragedy such as Auschwitz-Birkenau or the Killing Fields of Cambodia.

There is no worldwide established framework of dark tourism, and globally accepted definition of dark tourism. Sharpley and Stone (2009) "addressed presentations of tragedy and located dark tourism interpretation within a conceptual framework and the commodification of remembrances". However, there has been a mounting interest among researchers to use dark tourism as a research area. For instance, Lee *et al.* (2011) analyzed dark tourism in context to peace paradigm between South and North Korea. Seaton (2009) suggested how dark tourism sites could be managed properly and concluded that dark tourism sites are unique places whose evolutionary assortment and nature demand various managerial strategies that differ from other tourism destinations.

REVIEW OF RELATED LITERATURE

'Dark tourism' or 'Thanatourism' for the first time was used by Foley and Lennon (1996) in their article published in International Jour-nal of Science of cultural and historical heritage (Stone & Sharpley, 2008) and stated as "tourism involving locations associated with death and great suffering" (Gibson, 2006). Tourists generate heterogeneity in their motivations which comes only through their unique fascination towards the sites linked with pain, death and horror. With the passage of time, human being has always shown tendency towards Dark tourism. In order to promote dark tourism, ethical points arise which asks whether it is morally right to promote the sites of dark tourism and provide them freely available for commercialization. The main issue of ethical dimension pertaining to dark tourism is that it leads publicity of dark sites which are actually meant for mourning. "But death has been a part of tourism longer than any other form of tourism supply, often through religious or pilgrimage purposes". The early examples of dark tourism attractions are the Roman Colosseum where death and suffering took place due to the gladiatorial games. In the first guided tour in England (1838) whereby the hanging of two convicted murderers took place in a railway excursion in Cornwall. From the last century, dark tourism has become more widespread and varied. Various researchers think that the sites or destinations linked with war most likely compose the biggest single category of tourist attractions in the world. Stone (2005) states that "dark tourism involves visits to sites, attractions and exhibitions where the main or one of the main themes have real or animated scenes of death, suffering, or in an appropriate manner displayed massacres". Tarlow (2005) identifies dark tourism as "visitations to places where tragedies or historically noteworthy death has occurred and that continue to impact our lives". "This focused on tourists' motivation which seems to exclude many dimensions of this type of tourism but it does not mean that it excluded disaster and death" (Miles, 2002; Stone, 2006). In Philip R. Stone's article Marcel (2004) investigated whether or nor not "death makes a holiday" and propagated that "dark tourism is the tourism industry's dirty little secret". Stone (2006) also discussed the explanation given by Blom (2000) who writes that "morbid tourism" is centre of attraction for those who shows their interest in real or artificial death. "The tragic incidents which happened on sites of dark tourism affect our lives politically and socially" (Tarlow, 2005). A good number of studies associated to visits to graveyards and cemeteries (Seaton, 1996), Holocaust sites (Beech, 2009) places of atrocity (Ashworth & Hartmann, 2005), prisons (Strange & Kempa, 2003; Wilson, 2008) and slavery-heritage attractions (Dann & Seaton, 2001; Rice, 2009) are also devoted to this specific type of tourism. Cohen (2011) indicated location aspect by taking into account geographically authenticity while Biran *et al.* (2011) discussed the various benefits of dark tourism. Jamal and Lelo (2011) explored dark tourism construct in view of social point. Seaton (2009) in his study stressed upon the management of dark tourism sites.

It is mostly the Anglo-Saxon terminology which lists a number of terms associated with dark tourism *e.g.,* dark tourism, thanatourism, grief tourism and cemetery tourism, which have been described by a number of overseas researchers. The most well-known authors, who had worked on dark tourism and have published papers on it includes Lennon, Stone and Foley (1999, 2005 & 2006) and others who have been describing it for last two decades. As per Lennon, terminology of dark tourism is still in its infancy stage. Lennon and Foley denominated this phenomenon as the dark tourism (1999, 2000). The descriptions and definitions given by various authors on this phenomenon differ while going through the literature. It has been termed, for instance, 'fatal attraction tourism' (Rojec, 1993), 'disaster and conflict tourism', 'holidays in hell', 'morbid tourism' (Blom, 2000) and 'black-spot tourism' (Rojec, 1993). But in the current literature on tourism, it is frequently referred as "dark tourism", (Lennon & Foley, 2000).

Dark tourism is also visiting the memorial sites and memorial cemeteries. The emergence of dark tourism cannot be clearly determined, but from the past literature we make out that first trips to the major sacral and burial sites were already known in prehistoric times, respectively, in ancient times (Menhir fields in Carnac, Stonehenge, Gladiatorial games, etc.). Tourist spots of tragedies may be the area with a large growth potential, but it can't be termed as a new phenomenon. The watching of gladiatorial games by Ancient Romans, travelling of hundreds of pilgrims miles ago to the graves and places of religious martyrdom, watching battles, executions, burning at the stake, etc.

RESEARCH METHODOLOGY

The current study is qualitative in nature and the data has been collected from various reputed journals, national and local newspaper archives. The data has been also encapsulated from online resources like UGC Inflibnet, EBSCOhost and Google Scholar etc. The dark tourism sites mentioned in the study have been identified through review of related literature.

DISCUSSION

It has been seen through literature review, that there is a wider scope of dark tourism all over the world. The trend is changing very fast towards this form of tourism across countries. Dark tourism is flourishing day by day. Many countries have started to promote dark sites as the as one of the important type of tourism at their places other than religious, leisure, pleasure, cultural and adventure. These dark tourism sites include: castles and battlefields such as Culloden in Scotland and Bran Castle and Poenari Castle in Romania; former prisons such as Beaumaris Prison in Anglesey, Wales and the Jack the Ripper exhibition in the London Dungeon; sites of natural disasters or man-made disasters, such as Hiroshima Peace Memorial Park in Japan, Chernobyl in Ukraine and the commercial activity at Ground Zero in New York one year after September 11, 2001. It also includes sites of human atrocities and genocide, such as the Auschwitz concentration camp in Poland, the Nanjing Massacre Memorial Hall in China, the Tuol Sleng Genocide Museum in Cambodia; the sites of the Jeju Uprising in South Korea and the Spirit Lake Internment Camp Centre near La Ferme, Quebec as an example of Canada's internment operations of 1914–1920. In the US, visitors can tour the Holocaust Memorial Museum in Washington D.C. "with an identity card which matches their age and gender with that of a name and photo of a real holocaust victim. Against a backdrop of video interpretation portraying killing squads in action, the pseudo holocaust victim enters a personal ID into monitors as they wander around the attraction to discover how their real-life counterpart is faring".

The researcher is of this thought that the main attraction to dark sites is their historical value rather than their associations with death and suffering only. The main aim of the current study is to identify the important dark tourism sites of India which are having great potential than other countries. The study will focus on some selected dark tourism sites which are lying across India.

Amritsar (Jallianwala Bagh)

This is very important dark tourism site which is having higher potential to attract tourists all over the globe. It reminds one about the harsh attitude of an army general towards innocent people. It was 13th April 1919, General O Dyer (British General) ordered to fire randomly upon unarmed innocent people of Amritsar including infants who even could not have called for help, who had gathered to celebrate the festival of Baisakhi. A good number of the people were uninformed about the martial law imposed outlawing freedom of assembly because of the arrest and deportation of two important national leaders namely Satya Pal and Dr. Saifuddin Kitchlew.

The armed soldiers were standing at the main gate which was acting as a way for both entrance as well as exit. General O Dyer ordered his troops to close the door and ruthlessly start firing upon the people who very fully engaged in the celebrations of the Baisakhi. There was a mass shooting so as to disperse the crowd. More than 1,000 people including women and children were killed and 1,000 injured at the spot. Apart from being wounded by gunshots, many victims died in the stampede. Mostly the sad part of the story is that many tried to protect themselves from this massacre and they jumped inside a well in the garden, only to drown to death. The event which took place has leaded a very bad impression of this act of humanity on an earth. While setting foot inside the Jallianwala Bagh in Amritsar, Punjab (north India), one can see the names of martyrs embossed in gold at the base of the entrance wall and the adjacent bullet marks on the walls, is enough to recount that the place has witnessed something very horrific event which now cannot be overshadowed upto the day of judgement.

There are still the impressions and insertions of bullets on the walls which even today reveal a true picture of this kind of massacre. While entering the Jallianwala Bagh through the 'historical lane'(a narrow passage leading to the park that was blocked by the British troopers), a board saying 'people were fired at from here', really chills down ones spine. One after paying homage to those persecuted inside the 'Martyrs' Gallery', can move to the exhibition that accounts harsh pictures of the incident, other artifacts including a coin which has been damaged by a bullet of trooper which actually belonged to one of the victims of the massacre.

There is huge potential for attracting tourists who love to visit such sites. People love to visit and want to make themselves well versed about the way massacres have taken place which have killed thousands of people in a one go. They want to visually see and practically experience the dark tourism sites like Jallianwala Bagh. They want to recapitulate each and every thing about what they have read in the books in the past. While visiting such spots a person really gets much emotional and himself realizes what kind of harsh moment the people have seen in the past and after visiting many travelers share their experience through writings and lay more focus that such harsh events should not be repeated again in future. This in turn can help us in spreading the message of peace throughout the world.

Bhopal (Gas Tragedy)

This is a kind of disaster which took place due to an industrial accident. On 3 December 1984, in the city of Bhopal, India Union Carbide subsidiary pesticide plant released 42 tons of toxic methyl isocyanides (MIC) gas, which exposed 5 lakh people to toxic gases.

People when woke up in the morning were having a burning sensation in their lungs. Thousands of people died instantly from the effects of the toxic gases. People were trampled in the panic due to the incident. The first official abrupt death toll was 2,259. Another estimate revealed that 8,000 died within two weeks. The research also revealed that further 8,000 people have since died from gas related diseases which affected them. The irony was like that innumerable people ran on the streets, vomiting and dying, the city literally ran out of cremation grounds. There is well-demonstrated museum dedicated to the Bhopal Gas tragedy.

The tragic places in India are increasingly luring gigantic crowds from all over the globe. In the central parts of the country, Bhopal is one such site. It is the only city which has witnessed world's worst industrial disaster ever – the tragedy of Bhopal gas. Ministry of tourism Govt. of India is having a good chance to capitalize the Bhopal (Gas Tragedy) in a sense that they by way of promotion can attract large number of tourists. They should make strategies to portrait the image of this dark tourism site at the global level so that people all over the world could come and see the place which has seen this tragic incident. People from the industrial sector from all over the world can be attracted to visit the place so that they might get firsthand experience about the consequences of leakage of industrial gases so that proper mechanism/shields should be in place at their places of industrial hub in order to stop such leakages and prevent such disasters in near future.

Taj Palace Hotel, (26/11 Mumbai Terror Attacks)

It was 26–29 November 2008, when Mumbai (financial capital) a place of hustle bustle witnessed a series of terrorist attacks by 10 terrorists, which carried out a series of 12 coordinated shooting and bombing attacks which lasted for four days across Mumbai. The attack drew widespread global condemnation. It killed 164 people and 308 were severely wounded. One of the terrorist attacks was on Taj Palace Hotel, Mumbai which created a panic situation all over India. Mumbai was on high alert. Many tourists which were having accommodation in this hotel had to go with the worst day of their life. The attack resulted in the drastic decline of tourist arrivals.

As the attack killed number of people at a time, the place is attached with high strength of grief, sorrow and emotions. Due to this fact, the place which is the financial capital is having high potential for dark tourism as it can attract domestic as well as foreign tourists from all over the globe. Now the outcome of this attack can help India to gain foreign exchange by attracting foreign arrivals to this place through dark tourism. Tourists can feel themselves about the kind of environment which could have been there on the terror attack day. They can visually see the entrances through which the terrorists entered into the hotel. They can easily understand the situation of the people who were on top floors at the time of the attack. Today the tourist guides at this site of the blast have already started to recreate the scenes of the incident–talking to travelers about the Taj Hotel and the footbridge which is opposite to Victoria Terminus, to show where the bullets were once buried in walls. This inside triggers everyone to visit the place but the only need of the hour is to promote it as a dark tourism site.

Kuldhara (Rajasthan)

As dark tourism is the tourism activity, associated with visiting historical places that are related to tragedy, grief and death of the people. The village of Kuldhara known as the Abandoned and Cursed village depicts the mayhem of the villagers before two centuries. The place has tragic and grief story to offer, for dark tourism enthusiast. Kuldhara lies 20 kilometers to the west of Jaisalmer in Rajasthan, a place with ruined houses and scant presence of human existence. It is said that the place was once prosperous village, but now it has remained into the ruins of old site, the place which was abandoned by its own people. It is said about 200 years ago when powerful kings and their ministers were ruling India, Kuldhara was the home to Paliwal Brahmins. And during this time Salim Singh was the Diwan of Jaisalmer, he was well known for his corruption, dishonesty and immoral tax collecting methods. It was said that Salim Singh has set his evil eye on the beautiful daughter of village chief. Salim Singh was hell bent on having the chief's daughter and has threatened villagers he would levy a huge amount of tax on them, if they came in his way. Villagers fear the wrath of Salim Singh (Diwan) on one side, and on the other side their humanity does allow them to sacrifice their daughter in the dirty hands of Diwan Salim Singh. Eventually all the villagers fled away on one dark night, leaving behind their homes and every memory associated with this place. It was said that no one even saw the thousands of members of village leave and where did they resettle. Only one thing that is known is when they fly they cursed the town "No one would ever be able to settle down in Kuldhara again". The curse has stayed true even till date as the whole town is still uninhabited and remained barren till date. The place is just a barren town of ruined homes with scant humans' inhabitants reminding us the grief and sorrow of the village who abandoned their own village as a result of cruel Diwan.

In 2010, government of Rajasthan has decided to develop Kuldhara as tourist spot and has now been maintained by the Archaeological Survey of India as a heritage site. Kuldhara has accrued the reputation as a Haunted Place, and has a huge potential to become the dark tourism site.

Cellular Jail (Andaman and Nicobar)

Cellular Jail is also famous by the name of "Kala Pani", It lies in the splendid archipelago of Andaman and Nicobar Island. The place stands as a dark nostalgia of British colonial rule in the Indian subcontinent. The British used this remote archipelago to exile Indian Political prisoners who revolted against the high handedness of British rule. It is said that around eighty thousand prisoners who revolted against the British rule in India and Burma were admitted to Cellular Jail. And here they were regularly harassed, punished and tortured by oppressive and cruel jail wardens. Prisoners were subjected with oppressive inhumane tortures, and were fed through there nostrils, filing their lungs not there stomach. These cruel tortures results in exhaustion and even brutal death of poor prisoners. The cries of innocent Indian patriots are still roaming in this dreaded and grueling prison.

The Prison constructed by British in the beginning of 20th century was finally closed after India become free and independent in 1947, and this barbaric prison was later converted into the memorial. Anyone who visits the jail, get a picture of the tortures, which these prisoners was facing. The corridors and cells have no proper windows, and they had constructed in such a way that prisoners could never see each other inside these cells. It has said that once, two brothers was admitted in the jail at the same time, and for the period of two years both of them remained unaware of each other's presence in jail. The cellular Jail has huge potential as far as dark tourism is concerned. Today people love to visit these types of sites, so that they feel the pain that people have faced in these places. The cellular jail boost patriotism among the people of India, this places always reminds them the sacrifice and suffering which their national heroes has faced during fight for independence against the colonial British Rule.

CONCLUSIONS

Dark tourism is visiting of tourists to battlefields, terrorist attacks, areas of genocide or zones of disasters. To attract tourists for dark tourism is growing because dark tourism gives unusual experiences. It is a special interest tourism in which tourists unwittingly participate. This paper attempted to deliberate on dark tourism and to see if India has resources for this type of tourism. Unfortunately India has not been in a position to capitalize the dark sites so good until now, though it holds abundant potential for dark tourism. The awareness of dark tourism in India is lower when compared with other countries. The need of the hour is to use this untapped potential so that it contributes towards overall development of tourism in India. The sites being highlighted in the paper are prime dark tourism spots because they satisfy all essential prerequisites which a dark tourist craves for. The main focus should be to develop these sites and adopt proper marketing strategies so as to woo more dark tourists to visit India for the purpose of dark tourism. However, development of these sites and attractions should be sustainable and not at the cost of their damage. Dark tourism has not earned the attention and utmost popularity in India but one can't deny the existence and its mega potential which can help in taking tourism industry of India to climax. There is lack of basic infrastructure at these sites and this should be the foremost priority for the government to look into. Tour operators can play a noteworthy role to use dark tourism potential of India by adding these important sites in their Packages. The tourists should be attracted to these sites by formulating the strategies to promote them so that the congestion (mass flow of tourists) at other places like Red Fort, Taj Mahal, Qutub Minar and Golden Temple could be diverted and the concept of sustainable tourism can be made practically applicable in India.

REFERENCES

Ashworth, G.J., & Hartmann, R. (2005). Horror and human tragedy revisited: *The Management of Sites of Atrocities for Tourism*, New York.

Beech, J. (2009). Genocide tourism. *The Darker Side of Travel: The Theory and Practice of Dark Tourism*, pp. 207–23.

Biran, A., Poria, Y., & Oren, G. (2011). "Sought Experience at Dark Heritage sites". *An-nals of Tourism Research*, 38(3): 820–841.

Blom, T. (2000). "Morbid-Tourism – A postmodern market niche with an example from Althrop". *Norwegian Journal of Geography*, 54(1): 29–36.

Cohen, E. (2011). "Educational dark tourism at an in Populo site: The Holocaust Museum in Jerusalem". *Annals of Tourism Research*, 38(1): 193–209.

Dann, G.M.S., & Seaton, A.V. (*eds.*) (2001). Slavery, contested heritage and thanatourism. *Haworth Hospitality Press*, New York.

Foley, M., & Lennon, J.J. (1996). JKF and dark tourism: A fascination with assassination. *International Journal of Heritage Studies*, 2: 198–211.

Gibson, D.C. (2006). The relationship between serial murder and the American tourism industry. *Journal of Travel & Tourism Marketing*, 20(1): 45–60.

Jamal, T., & Lelo, L. (2011). Exploring the conceptual and analytical framing of dark tourism: From darkness to intentionality. *Tourist Experience: Contemporary perspectives*, pp. 29–42.

Lennon, J., & Foley, M. (2000). *Dark tourism: The Attraction of and Disasters*. London, Thomson Learning.

Miles, W. (2002). "Auschwitz: Museum interpretation and darker tourism". *Annals of Tourism Research,* 29(4): 1175–1178.

Rice, A. (2009). Museums, memorials and plantation houses in the Black Atlantic: Slavery and the development of dark tourism. *The Darker Side of Travel: The Theory and Practice of Dark Tourism*, pp. 224–246.

Rojec, C. (1993). Ways of Seeing-Modern Transformations in Leisure and Travel.

Seaton, A.V. (1996). Guided by the dark: From thanatopsis to thanatourism. *International Journal of Heritage Studies*, 2(4): 234–244.

Seaton, T. (2009). Purposeful otherness: Approaches to the management of thanatourism. *The darker side of travel: The theory and practice of dark tourism*, pp. 75–108.

Sharpley, R., & Stone, P.R. (*eds.*) (2009). *The Darker Side of Travel: The Theory and Practice of Dark Tourism*. Channel View Publications.

Stone, P. (2005). Dark tourism consumption – A call for research. *ERTR, E-Review of Tourism Research*, 3(5): 109–117.

Stone, P.R. (2006). A dark tourism spectrum: Towards a typology of death and macabre related tourist sites, attractions and exhibitions. *Turizam: Međunarodni znanstveno- struèni đasopis*, 54(2): 145–160.

Stone, P., & Sharpley, R. (2008). Consuming dark tourism: A thanatological perspective. *Annals of Tourism Research*, 35(2): 574–595.

Strange, C., & Kempa, M. (2003). Shades of dark tourism: Alcatraz and Robben island. *Annals of Tourism Research*, 30: 386–405.

Tarlow, P. (2005). "Dark tourism: The appealing dark side of tourism and more". *Niche Tourism, Contemporary Issues Trends and Cases*. Oxford, Elsevier, pp. 47–5.

Tarlow, P. (2005). Dark tourism. Novelli, M. (*ed.*), *Niche Tourism: Contemporary Issues, Trends and Cases.*

Wilson, J.Z. (2008). *Prison: Cultural Memory and Dark Tourism*. Peter Lang.

7

The Strategic Role of HR in Minimizing Gender Disparity: A Conceptual Framework

ZAHID H. BHAT[1]*

ABSTRACT

Research on workforce diversity at the organizational level gained momentum in the 1990s, because of the growing trend in HR research to link HR practices with organisational performance. This paper critically reviews the literature on managing diversity through Human Resource Management (HRM) techniques. Our review shows that inequality and discrimination still widely exist and HRM has focused mainly on compliance with equal employment opportunity and affirmative action. Less attention has been paid to valuing, developing and making use of diversity. Our review presents key strategic HRM practices which help in combating gender disparity. Our review reveals limited literature examining how diversity is managed in organizations through effective human resource management. Our review also discusses the implications for practice and further research.

Key words: Gender disparity, HRM, Recruitment and Selection, Training, Performance appraisal, Pay.

INTRODUCTION

Having a diverse workforce is increasingly being recognized as instrumental in improving the organization's performance, and

[1] Department of Higher Education, Govt. of Jammu & Kashmir, Srinagar, J&K.
**Corresponding author:* E-mail: zbhat2000@gmail.com

also an imperative that organizations can no longer choose to ignore. It is well recognized today that diversity adds both tangible and intangible value, even if it requires working through the issues and costs that sometimes accompany it. Emphasis on diversity focuses on the composition of work groups around factors that generally distinguishes one individual from the other, mostly in terms of observable demographic characteristics such as gender, race, ethnicity, or age, or in term of non-observable attributes such as education or socio-economic status. Workforce gender diversity is associated with resources that can provide a firm with a sustained competitive advantage. These resources include market insight, creativity and innovation, and improved problem-solving. Men's and women's different experiences (Nkomo & Cox, 1996) may provide insights into the different needs of male and female customers. Further, men and may have different cognitive abilities, such as men's proficiency in mathematics and women's proficiency in verbal and interpersonal skills (Maccoby & Jacklin, 1974). A mix of cognitive abilities in a gender diverse team may enhance the team's overall creativity and innovation. Moreover, a gender diverse team produces high quality decisions (Rogelberg & Rumery, 1996).

REVIEW OF LITERATURE

The increase in workforce gender diversity has attracted the attention of both researchers and practitioners. In particular, a question arises whether different gender compositions in an organisation's workforce will impact individual, group, or organisational level performance. According to the resource-based view, a firm can gain a sustained competitive advantage if it takes advantage of its valuable and inimitable resources (Barney, 1991). A diverse workforce comprises a multitude of beliefs, understandings, values, ways of viewing the world, and unique information. Rapid internationalization and globalization has enhanced the significance of workforce diversity. A cross-cultural and multicultural workforce is a common thread not only in organizations in western economies but also in corporations globally. As a result, diversity has increasingly become a *hot-button* issue in political, legal, corporate and educational arenas. However, the attitude towards a diverse workforce in corporations and researchers has been very mixed. On the one hand, a large number of corporations are reluctant to hire and promote female employees and ethnic minorities, especially for senior positions. On the other hand, there is a wide recognition of the value of workforce diversity. Empirical evidence shows that firms that have effective diversity management stand to benefit through bottom line returns. Information sharing and constructive task-based conflict management are the keys to the 'value in diversity' argument.

Managing diversity is premised on recognition of diversity and differences as positive attributes of an organization, rather than as problems to be solved (Thompson, 1997). McLeod, Lobel and Cox (1996) and Wilson and Iles (1999) found that a diverse workforce has a better-quality solution to brainstorming tasks, displays more cooperative behavior, relative to homogeneous groups, and can raise organizational efficiency, effectiveness and profitability. In addition to the full utilization of the skills and potential of all employees, managing diversity effectively can contribute to organizational success by enabling access to a changing marketplace by mirroring increasing diverse markets (Cox & Blake, 1991; Iles, 1995; Gardenswartz & Rowe, 1998) and improving corporate image (Kandola, 1995). Therefore, valuing diversity may become a source of competitive advantage, increase the quality of organizational life and ultimately be good for business (Cassell, 1996).

However, scholars suggest that the potential benefits will not come into being simply because of greater workplace diversity. Past research has suggested that managers should actively manage and value diversity. If designed and implemented properly, effective diversity management can support key organizational development initiatives (Agocs & Burr, 1996; Liff & Wajcman, 1996; Storey, 1999).

The key to diversity management hinges on strategic thinking and people-centred policies. While diversity management is an approach that revolves around employees, the HRM function is the custodian of the people management processes. These functions have considerable overlap. First, both HRM and diversity management are mainly concerned with the contribution of the human resource function to business strategy. Second, both HRM (especially soft HRM) and diversity management are concerned with individual differences, the development and well-being of each and every individual (Truss *et al.*, 1997). Past studies concluded that using the HRM toolkits addressing inequality in recruitment, appraisal, advancement and reward can enhance equal employment opportunity, improve inclusiveness and enhance creativity in a diverse workforce (Konrad & Linnehan, 1995; Goodman, Fields & Blum, 2003). Research by Goodman *et al.* (2003) revealed a positive relationship between emphasizing employee development and promotion, and the representation of women. Other studies have confirmed the association between identity-conscious or formalized HRM practices which address demographic representation in human resource decision making and greater representation of women and minorities in managerial positions (Kalleberg *et al.,* 1994; Konrad & Linnehan, 1995). It is, therefore, widely recognized by researchers that effective diversity management can be achieved through using appropriate HRM strategies (Litvin, 1997). HRM strategies are critical in overcoming individual and group process problems while improving the triple bottom line. Effective HR strategies focus on increasing organizational learning, flexibility, knowledge creation and the development of a work environment which is conducive to diversity management. Diversity management has a place in HRM and should be at the heart of human resource practices and policies.

Many authors have suggested a range of techniques for improving diversity management through HRM. Strong emphasis has been put on management philosophy that is committed to EEO, AA and appreciating and making use of diversity at the strategic level. As Truss (1999) argued, leadership and administrative heritage influence the nature and form of careers offered to both men and women. Effective diversity management requires a culture of inclusion that creates a work environment nurturing teamwork, participation and cohesiveness (Carnevale & Stone, 1994; Dwyer, Richard & Chadwick, 2001). Diversity culture should be emphasized in organizational vision, mission and business strategy and the HRM strategy. The formation of a diversity culture requires a significant commitment of resources and leadership. Formalization of HR diversity policies is also necessary as Reskin and McBrier (2000) argued that organizations with written documents for hiring and firing had higher percentages of women in management.

Key HRM Practices

HRM is a set of distinctive activities, functions and processes that are aimed attracting, directing and maintaining an organization's human resources (Lado & Wilson, 1994). The HR function has grown substantially over the past few decades and now covers the whole gamut of people management processes. There are different views about the nature of HRM and there exists an enormous variety of HR practices adopted by various organizations (Boselie *et al.*, 2005). Nevertheless, it is widely recognized that the key practices of HRM include recruitment and selection, training and development, performance management and pay.

Recruitment and selection

Empirical evidence suggests that many employees and managers regard diversity management as being equal to having an equal opportunity for any person to enter the organization. Many world class organizations have been effective in hiring women and minorities to mirror the increasingly diverse markets and win over new customers (Perlman, 1992). Managerial attention to increased work force diversity has been mandated in IBM, Xerox and J.C. Penney (Ted, 2005).

However, despite several decades of equality legislation and declared commitment to equal opportunities, there still exists a systematic discrimination in the recruitment and selection process. Worldwide, only 54% of working-age women are in the workforce compared to 80% of men (Kossek *et al.*, 2005). Morrison (1992) conducted a survey of managers in 16 'model' US organizations. He found that most organizations introduced just one approach to equality, instead of an array of measures intended to make the organizational climate more supportive. Organizations need to ensure that employment policies and practices provide developmental opportunities, career planning, reduction of work–family conflict, and mentoring for disadvantaged groups. Morrison

(1992) proposed that managing diversity can complement affirmative action strategies and new employment policies and practices to address the failure of organizations to promote women and racial and ethnic minorities into higher levels of management.

Training and development

There is anecdotal evidence showing diversity training and management development are receiving considerable attention from organizational management. According to Maxwell *et al.* (2001) public sector normally regards diversity management as giving a fair chance to get ahead for everyone. However, many leading corporations have not been successful in training, retaining and promoting women and minorities (Goodman *et al.*, 2003). Managers in organizations where there is a lack of effective HR diversity polices are likely to promote or rate highly subordinates who have similar cultural backgrounds and experience.

There is evidence that training programmes present lower rates of female participation, becoming an obstacle to women's career advancement and access to managerial positions worldwide (Powell & Butterfield, 1994). Women are also widely excluded from informal networks and experience difficulties in the establishment of mentoring relationships. These factors prevent them from reaching top positions, a phenomenon known as 'the glass ceiling effect' (Ragins & Scandura, 1994). Moreover, most diversity training programmes reinforce norms, values and perspectives of the dominant organizational culture (Tung, 1993). Also, ethnic minority employees are not allowed to express their culture and religions in the bank openly (Subeliani & Tsogas, 2005). Furthermore, the context of some diversity training may be different enough from the on-going work context so as to make it difficult for trainees to exhibit behaviours similar to those learned in training (Ford & Fisher, 1996).

Performance appraisal

Many organizations take account of AA (Affirmative Action) and EEO (Equal Employment Opportunity) in their performance appraisal systems (Kramar, 1998). However, appraisal and performance-related pay practices and techniques are often inherently gendered and against women (Rubery, 1995). Tsui and Gutek (1999) reported that there is consistent evidence showing that higher demographic similarity between supervisors and subordinates on age, race or gender correlates with HR outcomes, such as higher ratings on performance, organizational citizenship, and lower role ambiguity and conflict. Other mechanisms of discrimination are pointed out in the performance appraisal processes, in which women seem prone to get lower ratings (Ohlott, Ruderman & McCauley, 1994).

Pay

Pay inequality is a main cause of job dissatisfaction and demotivation, and therefore a major HR diversity issue (McLoughlin & Carr, 1997; Van den *et al.,* 1997). EEO and AA have been integrated with compensation practices by many organizations, again, like Digital, Esso and Westpac (Kramar, 1998). Kramar has been supported by Dagher *et al.* (1998) who also reported that diversity practices in remuneration are widely used by Australian organizations. However, Dagher *et al.* (1998) attributed positive remuneration practices to a 'union effect'. These authors state that a relatively strong trade union movement in Australia has prevented the occurrence of wage discrimination among unionized employees.

While the implementation of equal pay has significantly reduced earnings differences between men and women, gender income inequality still remains a global problem (Blau & Kahn, 1994; Katz & Autor, 1999; Brainerd, 2000). Globally, women earn 20% to 30% less than men (Kossek *et al.,* 2005).

HR Diversity Management

Measuring diversity and diversity management practices is strongly regarded as the initial step of HR diversity management practice (Kossek *et al.,* 2005). Diversity capabilities in organizations could be undermined by the lack of attention to the documented policies and practices and proper record keeping. Therefore, many scholars have suggested organizations measure the identity profile or demographics of defined work groups (Cox, 1993) the dominant organizational culture, and the perceptions of various employee groups in order to identify cultural barriers that may hinder the full and effective participation of all employees (Kossek *et al.,* 2005). A critical analysis of the current HR diversity practices, such as recruitment and selection procedures, criteria for entry into jobs, selection tools, and diversity training programmes, performance appraisal and compensation is also important. Such an analysis helps to overcome unfairness, remove the glass ceilings and eradicate tokenism and resistance (Human, 1993). Periodic audits of diversity are necessary to identify the areas that require improvement to manage diversity effectively. Organizations can compare this data with benchmarking in an industry or a region in order to rate and increase the representation of women and minorities in the workforce or management.

Managing growth in workforce diversity and increasing the representation of women and minorities is a critical HRM strategy of recruitment and selection for most organizations (Thomas & Ely, 1996). Human resource managers usually tend to bring people into the organization and promote employees who fit or have values similar to the decision makers or gatekeepers. Therefore, recruitment and selection should avoid what Schneider (1987) called 'The A-S-A (Attraction-Selection-Attrition) cycle' in order to develop multiple cultures in the organization. Human resource professionals and line managers who recruit and interview job seekers in a multicultural workforce need to be aware of the ways in which the interviewers' beliefs, attitudes, and stereotypes influence interview behaviour.

High quality diversity awareness training is one HR function that enhances the effective integration of diverse group members. Awareness training builds a common understanding of the value of diversity, assisting in building social cohesion so that it improves individual and organizational outcomes. Participants should know whether the training programme seeks to raise diversity awareness or develop multicultural skills. A top down training strategy may be valuable – providing awareness training to senior managers first and team-building training last. Education and training should be tailored to the specific needs of the organization, division, level, team or individuals. Critical to the success of education and training is the important step of linking training to the strategic objectives of the organization. Kossek *et al.* (2005) suggested that external facilitators involved in diversity training may help to achieve higher levels of productivity in a shorter time given work group diversity can lead to increased conflict among members in the short-term. Professional development and career planning is another area where discrimination is visible and needs careful attention while designing diversity management policies. If the HR practices concerning career progression do not effectively reflect diversity issues, diverse employees would have negative perceptions of the whole process (Richard & Kirby, 1999). Organizations should ensure providing equal opportunities for promotion and personal development to all employees. Minorities should be regularly included on panels that evaluate, select and promote managers.

Effective performance appraisal practices in the area of diversity management should be objective not subjective, relevant to the job and the company, and fair to all employees and offer no special treatment (Schuler, Dowling & De Cieri, 1993). When conducting appraisals, the language of appraisal should focus on the individual's performance and not on the personality or race. Hence, the aim should be to make the appraisal as culturally neutral as possible (Fulkerson & Schuler, 1992). Also, some scholars suggest that when assessing each manager's performance, actions taken by the manager to hire and promote minorities and women can be used as performance criteria in order to promote diversity (Morrison, 1992).

Pay equality contributes to effective diversity management and organizational performance. Diversity management in remuneration requires complete application of the principle of equal pay and a performance-based pay system. Empirical evidence suggests that the compensation structure, the wage determinants and the benefit schemes should be designed not only on common principles but also considering individuals in terms of their ability, knowledge and skill.

To implement HR diversity practices, scholars also placed strong emphasis on educating employees to understand diversity principles and accept their responsibilities, developing identity-based networking groups and targeting communications to different affinity group members (Kramar, 1998; Friedman & Holtom, 2002).

Reflecting the discussions above, at the strategic level, what is required is a management philosophy that recognizes diversity is critical for organizational success. Top management commitment to diversity should be reflected in the organizational vision, mission and business strategy in order to remove psychological and operational barriers to managing diversity. At the tactical level, a range of HRM diversity policies can be formulated in order to support this management philosophy. Measuring the employees' perception of the existing HRM diversity practices and their expectations may be conducted to facilitate policy development. HRM diversity policies at the operational level are implemented at the workplace, involving mainly educating employees, identity-based networking groups, targeting communications to different affinity group members, flexible employment and support for generating a work–life balance. At all levels, line managers should play a more important role in diversity management. Decentralization of responsibility for people management is a central theme of HRM (Storey, 1992) and of diversity management as well (Kandola & Fullerton, 1994).

DISCUSSION AND CONCLUSIONS

HR diversity management has gained momentum because of the pressures on business that become internationally competitive, the changing labour force composition, growing awareness of the importance of human resources management and a backlash created by perceptions of special treatment for women and ethnic minorities.

The findings of this study have significant practical implications. The review indicates that there is a continuing need for effective diversity management and for HRM to play an irreplaceable role in this regard. Effective diversity management through good HR practices and procedures leads to positive outcomes. Therefore, diversity management must become a priority agenda in HRM practices for all organizations. Due to the fact that most organizations consider diversity mainly as an issue of compliance with legal requirements and recruiting ethnic minorities, there is a great need for improved HR diversity strategies focusing on appreciating and making use of diversity.

This study has identified several avenues for further research. Despite wide recognition of its significance, diversity management in HR has to date received surprisingly little attention in the diversity management literature. There are some HRM studies concerning diversity issues. However, the fact that these studies are normally regarded only as part of the HR literature makes it difficult to draw complete conclusions on HR diversity management by analysing only the diversity management literature. As mentioned earlier there are different diversity issues in different national contexts. Research in non-western contexts would develop a better understanding of the effects of different socio-cultural environments on diversity management. Also, due to the fact that managers, employees and different groups within an organization may have different perceptions of diversity management, such perceptions can often be the result of poor implementation of HR diversity policies. Future research should examine diversity management from multiple perspectives. Moreover, past studies are usually prescriptive in exploring the relationship between HR diversity practices and organizational performance. As a result, there is, so far, no study statistically examining the contribution of diversity management in HR to organizational performance from financial and non-financial perspectives. Further empirical research on this aspect would advance our understanding of the contributions of HR diversity management.

REFERENCES

Agocs, C., & Burr, C. (1996). Employment equity, affirmative actions and managing diversity: Assessing the differences. *International Journal of Manpower*, 17 (4/5): 30–45.

Allen, R.S., Dawson, G.A., Wheatley, K.K., & White, C.S. (2004). Diversity practices: Learning responses for modern organizations. *Development and Learning in Organizations*, 18(6): 13–15.

Barney, J. (1991). Firm resources and sustained competitive advantage. *Journal of Management*, 17(1): 99–120.

Bennington, L., & Wein, R. (2000). Anti-discrimination legislation in Australia – Fair, effective, efficient or irrelevant? *International Journal of Manpower*, 21(1): 21–33.

Blau, F.D., & Kahn, L.M. (1994). Rising wage inequality and the U.S. gender gap. *American Economic Review*, 84(1): 23–28.

Blum, T.C., Fields, D.L., & Goodman, J.S. (1994). Organizational-level determinates of women in management. *Academy of Management Journal*, 37(2): 241–266.

Boselie, P., Dietz, G., & Boon, C. (2005). Commonalities and contradictions in research on human resource management and performance. *Human Resource Management Journal*, 15(3): 67–94.

Brainerd, E. (2000). Women in transition: Changes in gender wage differentials in Eastern Europe and Former Soviet Union. *Industrial and Labor Relations Review*, 54(1): 138–162.

Carnevale, A.P., & Stone, S.C. (1994). Diversity beyond the golden rule. *Training and Development*, 48(10): 22–39.

Cassell, C. (1996). A fatal attraction? Strategic HRM and the business case for women's progression. *Personnel Review*, 25(5): 51–66.

Cox, T., & Blake, S. (1991). Managing cultural diversity: Implications for organizational competitiveness. *Academy of Management Executive*, 5(3): 45–56.

Dagher, J., D'Netto, B., & Sohal, A.S. (1998). 'Managing Workforce Diversity in the Australian Manufacturing Industry'. *Journal of Human Factors and Ergonomics in Manufacturing*, 8(2): 1–15.

Dwyer, S., Richard, O., & Chadwick, K. (2001). Gender diversity in management and firm performance: The influence of growth orientation and organizational culture. *Journal of Business Research*, 55: 1–11.

Eagan, M., & Bendick, M. (2001). Workforce diversity initiatives of U.S. multinationals in Europe. *Research Report*. Washington, DC: Bendick and Egan Economic Consultants.

Ford, J., & Fisher, S. (1996). The role of training in a changing workplace and workforce: New perspectives and approaches. *In: Managing Diversity: Human Resource Strategies for Transforming the Workplace*. Kossek E., & Lobel S., (*eds.*), Oxford: Blackwell, pp. 164–193.

Friedman, R., & Holtom, B. (2002). The effects of network groups on minority employee retention. *Human Resource Management*, 41(4): 405–421.

Fulkerson, J.R., & Schuler, R.S. (1992). Managing worldwide diversity at Pepsi-Cola international. *In*: *Diversity in the Workplace: Human Resources Initiatives*. Jackson, S.E. (*ed.*), New York: Guilford Press.

Gardenswartz, L., & Rowe, A. (1998). Why diversity matters. *HR Focus*, 75(7): s1–s3.

Goodman, J., Fields, D., & Blum, T. (2003). Cracks in the glass ceiling: *In*: What kind of organizations do women make it to the top? *Group and Organization Management*, 28(4): 475–501.

Gordon, J. (1995). Different from what? Diversity as a performance issue. *Training*, 32(5): 25–33.

Gustaffsson, B., & Li, S. (2000). Economic transformation and the gender earnings gap in urban China. *Journal of Population Economics*, 13(2): 305–329.

Horwitz, F.M., Bowmaker-Falconer, A., & Searll, P. (1996). Human Resource Development and Managing Diversity in South Africa. *International Journal of Manpower*, 17(4/5): 134–151.

Hughes, J., & Maurer-Fazio, M. (2002). Effects of marriage, education, and occupation on the female/male wage gap in China. *Pacific Economic Review*, 7(1): 137–156.

Iles, P. (1995). Learning to work with difference. *Personal Review*, 24(6): 44–60.

Joplin, J.R.W., & Daus, C.S. (1997). Challenges of leading a diverse workforce. *The Academy of Management Executive*, 11(3): 32–48.

Kalleberg, A., Knoke, D., Marsden, P., & Spaeth, J. (1994). The national organizations study: An introduction and overview. *American Behavioral Scientist*, 37: 860–871.

Kandola, R. (1995). Managing diversity: New broom or old hat? *In: International Review of Industrial and Organizational Psychology*(vol. 10), Cooper C.L., & Robertson, I.T., (*eds.*), Chichester: Wiley.

Katz, L., & Autor, D. (1999). Changes in the wage structure and earnings inequality. *In*: *Handbook of Labour Economics* (vol. 3). Ashenfelter, O., & Card, D., (*eds.*), North Holland: Elsevier Science, pp. 1463–1555.

Konrad, A., & Linnehan, F. (1995). Formalized Human Resource Management Structures: Coordinating equal opportunity or concealing organizational practices. *Academy of Management Journal*, 38: 787–820.

Kossek, E.E., Lobel, S.A., & Brown, A.J. (2005). Human Resource Strategies to Manage Workforce Diversity. *In: Handbook of Workplace Diversity*, Konrad, A.M., Prasad, P., & Pringle, J.M. (*eds.*), Thousand Oaks, CA: Sage, pp. 54–74.

Kramar, R. (1998). Flexibility in Australia: Implications for employees and managers. *Employee Relations*, 20(5): 453–460.

Lado, A.A., & Wilson, M.C. (1994). Human resource systems and sustained competitive advantage: A competency-based perspective. *Academy of Management Review*, 19(4): 699–727.

Lawler, J. (1996). Managing diversity at work. *In: Human Resources at Work*, Molander, C. (*ed.*), Lund: Studentlitteratur, pp. 159–185.

Liff, S., & Wajcman, J. (1996). "Sameness" and "Difference" Revisited: Which way forward for equal opportunity initiatives? *Journal of Management Studies*, 33(1): 79–94.

Litvin, D. (1997). The discourse of diversity: From biology to management. *Organizations*, 4(2): 187–209.

Maccoby, E.E., & Jacklin, C.N. (1974). Myth, reality and shades of gray-what we know and don't know about sex differences. *Psychology Today*, 8(7): 109–112.

Maxwell, G.A., Blair, S., & McDougall, M. (2001). Edging towards managing diversity in practice. *Employee Relations*, 23(5): 468–482.

McLeod, P.L., Lobel, S.A., & Cox, T.H. (1996). Ethnic diversity and creativity in small group. *Small Group Research*, 27(2): 248–264.

McLoughlin, D., & Carr, S.C. (1997). Equality sensitivity and double De-motivation. *Journal of Social Psychology*, 137(55): 668–670.

Morrison, A. (1992). *The New Leaders: Guidelines on Leadership Diversity in America*. San Francisco, CA: Jossey-Bass.

Nkomo, S.M., & Cox, T., Jr. (1996). Diverse identities in organization. *In: Handbook of Organization Studies*, Clegg, S.R., Hardy, C., & Nord, W.R. (*eds.*), London: Sage, pp. 338–356.

Ohlott, P., Ruderman, M., & McCauley, C. (1994). 'Gender Differences in Managers' development job experiences. *Academy of Management Journal*, 37(1): 46–67.

Perlman, L. (1992). *Turning Diversity into Opportunity. Conference Board Report 75th Anniversary Symposia Series, In: Diversity's Strength: Capitalizing on the New Workforce, New York: Conference Board*, pp. 15–16.

Powell, G.N., & Butterfield, D.A. (1994). Investigating the 'Glass Ceiling' phenomenon: An empirical study of actual promotions to top management. *Academy of Management Journal*, 37(1): 68–86.

Ragins, B.R. (2002). Understanding diversified mentoring relationships: Definitions, challenges and strategies. *In*: *Mentoring and Diversity: An International Perspective*, Clutterbuck, D., & Ragins, B. (*eds.*), Oxford: Butterworth-Heinemann, pp. 23–53.

Ragins, B.R., & Scandura, T. (1994). Gender differences in expected outcomes of mentoring relationships. *Academy of Management Journal*, 37(4): 957–971.

Reskin, B., & McBrier, D. (2000). Why not ascription? Organizations' employment of male and female managers. *American Sociological Review*, 65(2): 210–233.

Richard, O.C. (2000). Racial diversity, business strategy, and firm performance: A resource-based view. *Academy of Management Journal*, 43(2): 164–177.

Richard, O.C., & Kirby, S. (1999). Organizational Justice and the justification of work force diversity programs. *Journal of Business and Psychology*, 14(1): 109–118.

Roberson, L., Kulik, C., & Pepper, M. (2003). Using needs assessment to resolve controversies in diversity training design. *Group and Organization Management*, 28(1): 148–174.

Rogelberg, S.G., & Rumery, S.M. (1996). Gender diversity, team decision quality, time on task, and interpersonal cohesion. *Small Group Research*, 27(1): 79–90.

Rubery, J. (1995). Performance related pay and the prospects for gender pay equality. *Journal of Management Studies*, 33(2): 209–236.

Rynes, S., & Rosen, B. (1995). A field survey of factors affecting the adoption and perceived success of diversity training. *Personnel Psychology*, 48(2): 247–270.

Sanchez, J.I., & Brock, P. (1996). Outcomes of perceived discrimination among Hispanic employees: Is diversity management a luxury or a Necessity? *Academy of Management Journal*, 39(3): 704–719.

Sanglin-Grant, S., & Schneider, R. (2000). *Moving on up?* Racial Equality and the Corporate Agenda, London: Runnymede Trust.

Schneider, B. (1987). The people make the place. *Personnel Psychology*, 40(3): 437–456.

Schuler, R.S., Dowling, P.J., & DeCieri, H. (1993). An integrative framework of strategic international human resource management. *International Journal of Human Resource Management*, 5(3): 717–764.

Shen, J., Chanda, A., D'Netto, B., & Monga, M. (2009). Managing diversity through human resource management: An international perspective and conceptual framework. *International Journal of Human Resource Management*, 20(2): 235–251.

Snape, E., & Redman, T. (2003). Too old or too young? The impact of perceived age discrimination. *Human Resource Management Journal*, 13(1): 780–789.

Storey, J. (1992). *Developments in the Management of Human Resources*, Oxford: Blackwell Business.

Storey, J. (1995). Human Resource Management: Still marching on, or marching out? *In*: *Human Resource Management: A Critical Text*. Storey, J. (*ed.*), London: International Thomson Business Press, pp. 3–32.

Storey, J. (1999). Equal opportunities in retrospect and prospect. *Human Resource Management Journal*, 9(1): 5–8.

Subeliani, D., & Tsogas, G. (2005). Managing diversity in the Netherlands: A case study of Rabobank. *International Journal of Human Resource Management*, 16(5): 831–851.

Ted, J.T. (2005). Diversity at IBM, global workforce diversity. *Human Resource Management*, 44(1): 73–77.

Thomas, D.A., & Ely, R.J. (1996). Making differences matter: A new paradigm for managing diversity. *Harvard Business Review*, pp. 79–90.

Thomas, R. Jr. (1990). From affirmative action to affirmative diversity. *Harvard Business Review*, 68(2): 107–117.

Thompson, N. (1997). *Anti Discriminatory Practice*, Basingstoke: Macmillan.

Truss, C. (1999). Human Resource Management: Gendered terrain? *The International Journal of Human Resource Management*, 10(2): 180–200.

Truss, C., Gratton, L., Hope-Hailey, V., McGovern, P., & Stiles, P. (1997). Soft and hard models of human resource management: A reappraisal. *Journal of Management Studies*, 34(1): 53–73.

Tsui, A., & Gutek, B. (1999). *Demographic Differences in Organizations*, Lanham, MD: Lexington Books.

Tung, R. (1993). Managing cross-national and intra-national diversity. *Human Resource Management*, 32: 461–477.

Van den Bos, K., Lind, E.A., Vermunt, R., & Wilke, H.A.M. (1997). How do I judge my outcome when I do not know the outcome of others? The psychology of the fair process effect. *Journal of Personality and Social Psychology*, 72(5): 1034–1046.

Walsh, K. (1995). *Public Services and Market Mechanisms Competition, Contracting and the New Public Management*, Basingstoke: Macmillan.

Webb, J. (1997). The politics of equal opportunity. *Gender, Work and Organization*, 4(3): 159–169.

Wilson, E.M., & Iles, P.A. (1999). Managing diversity – An employment and service delivery challenge. *The International Journal of Public Sector Management*, 12(1): 27–49.

8

Effect of Antecedents of E-Retailing on Customer Satisfaction: The Role of Perceived Usefulness, Perceived Ease of Use and Trust

DANISH MEHRAJ[1]* AND ISHTIAQ H. QURESHI[2]

ABSTRACT

This study examines the effect of different factors that influence customer's satisfaction using three factors of Technological Acceptance Model (TAM) perceived usefulness, perceived ease of use and Trust. The main intention of this paper is not only to investigate the effectiveness of e-services provided by the online retailers but also considers how customers can get benefited by these services in India. To examine the data of a conceptual model, author used multiple regression analysis technique. Result of 265 respondents' reveals that, perceived usefulness, perceived ease of use, and trust positively influence customer satisfaction. Future scope of research and recommendations for marketing manager's and practitioners are conferred in the end.

Key words: Customer satisfaction, Perceived usefulness, Perceived ease of use, Trust.

INTRODUCTION

Buying through internet is one of the most rapidly growing forms of shopping, with over almost 4.2 billion people were internet users and 3.4 billion were social media users worldwide in year 2017.

[1, 2] Department of Management Studies, University of Kashmir, Srinagar, J&K.
**Corresponding author:* E-mail: khandanish11@gmail.com; ishtiaqiq@yahoo.co.in

China, India and the United States rank ahead all other countries in terms of internet users (Internet World Statistic, 2017). The internet has created tremendous opportunities for both businesses and customers. Distribution channel members can extend their reach and visibility to partners beyond geographical boundaries. In this regard, the internet is a widely used medium that acquires and delivers information and services to customers and business. It is incessantly transforming the way people and businesses interact with each other (Khatibi, Haque & Karim, 2006). With such transformation, impressions of expressed ethical conduct by both parties are now at the forefront. E-retailing has witnessed extensive growth. Dozens of Internet-only companies have surfaced in many industries and numerous conventionally-operated companies have adopted the internet (Kim, J.H., Kim & Kandampully, 2007). Accordingly, competition among online companies has become rigorous. Most online companies publish price information and feature price in their advertising campaigns. Therefore, customers can become informed of the optimal prices for sought products/services (Khatibi *et al.,* 2006).

Since the advent of internet in India and its use by different business enterprises, many of the challenges triggering competitors to satisfy customers relatively better than others do. The key challenge is how well they offer and perform services to the customers while holding the significant importance of customer satisfaction in Customer's behavioral loyalties are now changing mind (Yang, Jun & Peterson, 2004). Website usability factors are the key factors that allow e-businesses to gain customers trust online. In other words, website usability means, how well website visitor interact with their website. More specifically apparent website usability increase user's website experience and in result in future it moves website behavior towards visitor (Casaló, Flavián & Guinalíu, 2008). Different Studies reveal that quality website had the largest impact on customers' beliefs. Good website usability is to develop it according to the site visitor needs and wants (Kim, E.K.E. & Tadisina, 2005). Website "which focuses on the visitor's expectations have a better chance for success". Therefore, service quality delivery through website has gradually become one of the most important aspects influencing Business Customer success (Dai, Huang & Yi, 2005). The old rules of interaction among the retailers and customers are now changed; advancement of information technology revolutionizes the conventional way of doing businesses. Customers are now more knowledgeable and informed about their needs and wants. It is now need of the day for businesses to assess what their customers need and how they can do and fulfill these needs in such a way to successful in the current era of revolution and change.

Customer's behavioral loyalties are now changing and varying with different services and products offered by businesses, there is no guarantee of success for e-businesses by just only to show up. Therefore, this study considers (interaction of retailers with the customer, considering the effect of different e-service factors that a retailer's website include) to understand more easily the implications of these important categories between online retailer and customer interaction.

Based on Technology Acceptance Model (TAM) (Davis, 1989) current study proposes to investigate the relationship and effects of different variables on customer satisfaction in India, as such findings and results are beneficial to marketing professionals, managers, researchers and those who have an interest in customer relationship marketing business.

REVIEW OF LITERATURE

Perceived ease of use and perceived usefulness are key constructs in the TAM (Davis, 1989) and have been researched in a number of contexts and among different users. Ndubisi, Gupta and Ndubisi (2005) examined the role of the two constructs in inrormation systems (ISs) adoption by entrepreneurs and found to be instrumental. Perceived ease of use in the context of this research refers to the extent to which a consumer believes that online shopping will be free of effort (Chiu, Chang, Cheng & Fang, 2009). The WWW is a medium that allows users arbitrary connections in an open environment; within this environment, users have computer skills ranging from novice to expert (Pearson, Pearson & Green, 2007). With all the available websites and the diverse set of user skills, what motivates users to choose one site over another may lie in their ease of use perceptions. If a user finds a site difficult to use, cannot find the desired product on a business-to-consumer (B2C) website, or is not clear on what a site offers, the user will typically leave that site (Pearson *et al.,* 2007). Website design quality is crucial for online stores (Lee & Lin, 2005) and has strong impact on user perception of ease of use. Website design describes the appeal that user interface design presents to customers (Lee & Lin, 2005). A recent empirical study found that website design factors are strong predictors of customer quality judgments, satisfaction and loyalty for internet retailers (Lee & Lin, 2005). According to J.H. Kim *et al.* (2007) online features that are customer centered have an impact on online shoppers' positive attitude toward the internet. J.H. Kim *et al.* (2007) found that retail websites with more customer-centered web attributes had higher annual web sales and higher market shares than those retail websites with fewer customer-centered web attributes. In addition, J.H. Kim *et al.* (2007) indicate that the buying environment characteristics of retail websites impact the financial performance of e-retailers, and many e-retailers under-perform in offering web service attributes that can accommodate individual customers' needs and facilitate online shopping. Thus, when consumers perceive website to be ease to use, it would affect their intentions to repurchase in future.

Perceived usefulness is defined as the extent to which a consumer believes that online shopping will enhance his or her transaction performance (Chiu *et al.,* 2009). An individual is more likely to undertake continued usage when such usage is perceived to be useful. Customers who have accomplished the shopping task of product acquisition in an efficient manner will be more likely to exhibit stronger online customer satisfaction. Prior research shows that perceived usefulness has a significant effect on customer loyalty (Chiu *et al.,* 2009). Perceived usefulness has also shown to be an important determinant of ISs adoption in general (Davis, 1989; Ndubisi *et al.,* 2005).

On other hand Customer's trust plays a fundamental role in maintaining long-term relationships with the retailer. Trust is viewed as a set of specific beliefs dealing primarily with the benevolence, competence and integrity of another party. Benevolence is the belief that the trustee will not act opportunistically against the trust or, even given the opportunity (Chiu *et al.,* 2009; Ndubisi *et al.,* 2005). Competence is the belief in the trustee's ability to fulfill its obligations as expected by the trust or. Integrity is the belief that the trustee will be honest and will honor its commitments (Chiu *et al.,* 2009; Ndubisi *et al.,* 2005). Customer's trust implies that the good intentions of the firm are not questioned by the consumer, that the promises made do not generate uncertainties in the purchaser, and that the communication between the parties is honest. Customer's uncertainty can imply the potential for service failure and negative outcomes therefore, trust becomes vital to long-lasting relationships (Eisingerich & Bell, 2007). Lack of trust reduces the chances of buyers to engage in online shopping because they are unwilling to deal with a vendor whom they do not trust. Indeed, prior research indicates that trust plays a pivotal role in driving customer satisfaction (Chiu *et al.,* 2009). While customer satisfaction means how a company provides supply, or deliver products or services to meet the customer needs and wants (Ha & Janda, 2008). In e-business context, company should pay special concentration on the policies and applications in marketing services and products online because well-designed and well-practiced policies will make sure customer service experience and buy intentions positively with their Website (Zhou, Dai & Zhang, 2007). While, another study reveals that customer satisfaction with the website and its impact on customer, repurchase intent plays an important role in enhancing customer likeliness in shopping online (George, 2002). However, In e-business context to understand user's preferences, plays an important role in developing and creating satisfactory technological, strategic and marketing decisions, because it increase their level of satisfaction and improves business performance and returns in future (Chen & Corkindale, 2008). Websites having consumer awareness and usability factors positively influence trust and satisfaction of customer in B2C environment (Dholakia & Zhao, 2009).

Conceptual Framework and Hypothesis Development

Fig. 1 shows the research framework for this paper and illustrates three independent variables namely perceived ease of use, perceived usefulness and trust. We generated three hypotheses based on this framework to test the influence of each independent variable on online customer satisfaction. The TAM developed by

(Davis, 1989) underpins the development of this framework. The extended TAM model which integrates eight constructs was adopted in this study to help understand the role of user process, customer confidence, as well as customer trust in e-retailing.

Hence, the following hypotheses were formulated:

H_1: Perceived ease of use will have a positive influence on customer online satisfaction.

H_2: Perceived usefulness will have a positive influence on customer online satisfaction.

H_3: Trust will have a positive influence on customer online satisfaction.

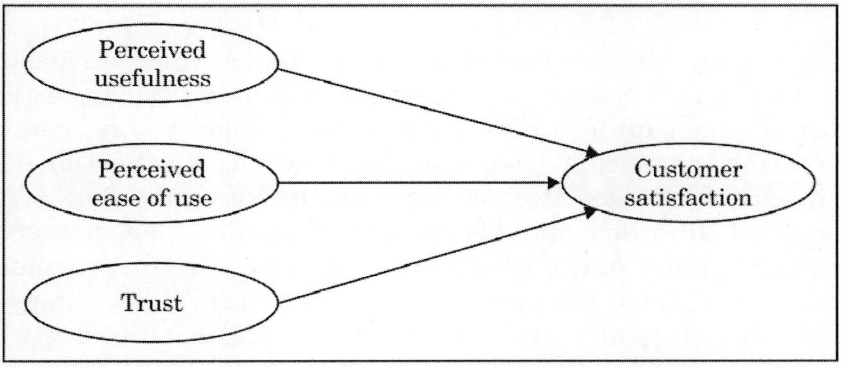

Fig. 1: Showing hypothetical framework

METHODOLOGY

The information and data for this research paper were gathered from primary. The primary data was derived from survey questionnaire. Survey questionnaires were used to obtain responses from participants from north India. We employed snowballing sampling method to select the participants for this research. This was to ensure that the participants have used the internet to purchase a product or service. Since, we were interested in participants' willingness and ability to purchase products/services online, it was considered reasonable to collect data from those who have prior experience in buying products or services online in line with the key informant technique (Ndubisi *et al.,* 2005). The key informant method was used and only customers with online shopping experience were requested to respond to the questions. Key informants are viewed as appropriate respondents if appropriate selection procedures are used (John & Reve, 1982). Thus, using guidelines on selecting key respondents from previous research (Campbell, 1955) key informants were screened and chosen on the basis of their knowledge of the research issues, their experience with online shopping, and willingness to respond. The snowball approach used in this study enabled us to achieve this objective and the wider research objective and is a sampling method widely used in internet-based research.

QUESTIONNAIRE DESIGN

The questionnaire for this research is divided into two parts – Sections A and B. Section A of the questionnaire contains questions on the demographic profile such as respondents' age, gender, occupation, education level and monthly income. Section B of the questionnaire solicits responses on the key constructs of the research framework namely perceived ease of use, perceived usefulness, trust and customer satisfaction. The measurement items were adapted from previous studies and revalidated for this study. Measures of perceived usefulness and ease of use were adapted from (Chiu *et al.,* 2009) and (Davis, 1989). Trust was measured with items adapted from (Pavlou & Fygenson, 2006) and online customer satisfaction was measured items adapted from (Khalifa & Liu, 2007). The data was collected on five-point scale.

DATA ANALYSIS

We used inferential statistics to make deductions based on the results and the significance. Descriptive analytical tools such as mean and standard deviation were used to summarize the respondents' feedback. For reliability of the variables, reliability tests were conducted before subjecting the data to inferential analysis. The three variables were tested for their relationship with customer satisfaction using correlations and regression analysis. SPSS was used for the analysis.

RESULTS AND FINDINGS

A total of 295 completed questionnaires were returned out of 350 distributed questionnaires and 30 questionnaires out of this were found invalid due to incomplete responses, and outliers which results to 265 usable responses. Table 1 illustrates the demographic profile of the 265 respondents who participated in this research.

Table 1: Showing demographic profile of the respondents.

Item	*Categories*	*Frequency*	*Percentage*
Gender	Male	140	52.8
	Female	125	47.1
Age	>25	94	35.5
	25 – 50	106	40.0
	<50	65	24.5
Income(Per month)	>10000 INR	66	24.9
	10000-20000 INR	105	39.6
	<20000 INR	94	35.4

Source: Authors' own

Table 2 presents the mean values, standard deviations and the number of items for each variable. For the independent variables, trust yielded the highest mean (3.92), followed by perceived ease of use (3.89) and lastly perceived usefulness (3.77). Since all variables yielded mean value more than 3, one can conclude that the respondent's perceptions on these variables are mostly favorable. Table 2 also shows the Cronbach's alpha values for the independent and dependent variables in this research. The result indicates that Cronbach's alpha value range from 0.711 to 0.873. Accordingly, the value for Cronbach's alpha of 0.7 or higher is considered acceptable (Nunnally, 1978). Thus, the data on these variables are reliable and consistent with research standards.

Table 3 reveals the correlation matrix of the conceptual variables. A two-tail test at significance level 0.01 indicates that there are positive relationships among dependent variable and the independent variables.

Table 2: Showing descriptive statistics of variables.

ID	*Variable name*	*Mean*	*S.D*	*No. of items*	*Cronbach's alpha*
PE	Perceived ease of use	3.89	0.879	7	0.711
PU	Perceived usefulness	3.77	0.983	7	0.742
TR	Trust	3.92	0.932	7	0.873
CS	Customer satisfaction	3.67	0.876	3	0.823

Source: Authors' own

Table 3: Reveals Pearson correlation coefficient matrix.

ID	*PE*	*PU*	*TR*	*CS*
PE	1			
PU	.800**	1		
TR	.765**	.789**	1	
CS	.728**	.743**	.753**	1

***Source*:** Authors' own *Note:* Correlation is significant at the **0.01 level

From Table 4, R = 0.802 and R^2-value =.644. This means that 64 percent of the variation in Y can be explained by all three predictors (or accounted for by) the variation in X. The results in Table 5 shows the three independent variables predict 64 percent of the variation in online customer satisfaction. This is a considerable amount of variance. The result shows that all three variables are significant at 0.01 significance level (0.01). This indicates that there is linear relationship between the dependent variable (customer satisfaction) and the predictor variables (perceived ease of use, perceived usefulness, and trust). *Hence all hypotheses (H_1, H_2 and H_3) stand accepted.*

Table 4: Showing multiple regression analysis (R and R^2).

Model	*R*	*R square*	*Adjusted R square*	*Std. error of the estimate*
1	.802[a]	.644	.641	.59348

Source: Authors' own *Notes:* Predictors: (constant), PE, PU, TR; Dependent variable – CS; let Y – Customer satisfaction (CS); X – Perceived ease of use (PE), Perceived usefulness (PU), and Trust (TR).

Table 5: Showing regression coefficients.

Model		Unstandardized coefficients		Standardized coefficients	t	Sig.
		B	Std. error	Beta		
1	(Constant)	.542	.102		5.324	.000
	PE	.234	.046	.237	5.050	.000
	PU	.276	.050	.272	5.538	.000
	TR	.353	.045	.357	7.788	.000

Dependent variable: CS

Source: Authors' own

DISCUSSION AND CONCLUSIONS

Existing research has dealt extensively with the factors affecting customers' offline satisfaction. Relatively, the amount of research that have considered online customer satisfaction is small, as such this paper adds value by contributing to the relatively sparse literature in the area by integrating different models from past studies. The results from this study indicate that all the factors identified in the study influence the customer satisfaction. The outcome of this research not only corroborates some of the findings of prior studies, but is also an advance over many as the integrated model explains a greater amount of variance in customer satisfaction than any former model. As such, the integrated model is more helpful in understanding customer's satisfaction. Practitioners can avail the knowledge and information unveiled in this study, especially in strategy decision. Clearly, as the coefficients suggest, some factors emerged with stronger impact compared to others, online retailers are therefore able to make informed decision on which factors to pay greater emphasis. Online businesses could use the findings to boost their service by deploying more information and knowledge management systems with stronger capabilities.

Online retailers should strive to build good reputation and trust which will enable customers to endure to buy from them. Businesses should continue to focus on improving their goodwill by maintaining good business ethics, which will help in building trust and confidence among customers. Besides, ensuring privacy of information provided by customers, building trust and good reputation, added value and usefulness of this mode should be enhanced and communicated to customers. The greater the value and/or usefulness perceptions of customers, the greater their likelihood of returning, therefore, online retailers should clearly demonstrate these benefits in their benefits proposal to the public. Outcomes are not the only important elements. While outcome orientation of the respondents is clearly demonstrated in this study, the respondents are also process oriented. It is crucial for the respective online firms in India to recognize the importance of managing consumer expectations and be able to provide functional, reliable and easy-to-use systems that enable enjoyable online purchase experiences. As the study shows, customers will be happy to purchase products and services from an online store that offers an excellent functional store front that is free of hiccups and other constraints that could frustrate potential customers. Online businesses must understand what a great online shopping experience is for its customers. To achieve business success in the marketplace, online businesses would need to invest resources and time to understand their customers and their buying motives. Based on this research, the online firms should capitalize on the ethical, outcome, and process orientations of customers, and through that develop applicable marketing strategies to retain their customers, which would enhance repurchase activities in the future. A good customer relationship management will enable a firm to provide excellent service quality to satisfy customers' needs. This can enhance customer satisfaction, and help to reduce customers switching behaviors. It is therefore possible for online firms to improve their competitiveness by effectively managing and delivering services to customers that guarantee highest level of ethical standards, efficient processes and beneficial outcomes. Relevant government agencies could find the outcomes of this paper useful, particularly with respect to developing internet infrastructure in India. There is the need to enhance competition among internet service providers. With greater competition, customers would have greater options and better services at competitive prices. It is necessary at this point to mention some of the weaknesses of this paper and to draw some future research directions. First, we consider the number of usable responses in this research small. Whereas, the research objectives were fully met, future research should strive for higher response rate. This will increase the representativeness of the sample and consequently the generalizability of the findings. In addition, future research may also consider the responses from businesses. This will enable a stronger and a more balanced perspective on the research issues.

REFERENCES

Casaló, L., Flavián, C., & Guinalíu, M. (2008). The role of perceived usability, reputation, satisfaction and consumer familiarity on the website loyalty formation process. *Computers in Human Behavior*, 24(2): 325–345. *https://doi.org/10.1016/j.chb.2007.01.017*

Chen, Y.H.H., & Corkindale, D. (2008). Towards an understanding of the behavioral intention to use online news services: An exploratory study. *Internet Research*, 18(3): 286–312. *https://doi.org/10.1108/10662240810883326*

Chiu, C., Chang, C., Cheng, H., & Fang, Y. (2009). Determinants of customer repurchase intention in online shopping. *Online Information Review*, 33(4): 761–784. *https://doi.org/10.1108/14684520910985710*

Dai, L., Huang, L., & Yi, Y. (2005). How B2C Service Quality Influences Website Continuance. *Pacific Asia Conference on Information Systems 2005 Sections 18 and Poster Sessions,* 16: 1375–1381.

Davis, F.D. (1989). Perceived usefulness, perceived ease of use and user acceptance of information technology. *MIS Quarterly*, 13(3): 319. *https://doi.org/10.2307/249008*

Dholakia, R.R., & Zhao, M. (2009). Retail website interactivity: How does it influence customer satisfaction and behavioral intentions? *International Journal of Retail & Distribution Management*, 37(10): 821–838. *https://doi.org/10.1108/09590550910988011*

Eisingerich, A.B., & Bell, S.J. (2007). Maintaining customer relationships in high credence services. *Journal of Services Marketing*, 21(4): 253–262. *https://doi.org/10.1108/08876040710758559*

George, J.F. (2002). Influences on the intent to make Internet purchases. *Internet Research*, 12(2): 165–180. *https://doi.org/10.1108/10662240210422521*

Ha, H., & Janda, S. (2008). An empirical test of a proposed customer satisfaction model in e services. *Journal of Services Marketing*, 22(5): 399–408. *https://doi.org/10.1108/08876040810889166*

Internet World Statistic (2017). World Internet Users Statistics and 2017 World Population Stats. *https://doi.org/10.1016/S0009-739X(07)71253-8*

John, G., & Reve, T. (1982). The reliability and validity of key informant data from dyadic relationships in marketing channels. *Journal of Marketing Research*, 19(4): 517–524. *https://doi.org/10.2307/3151724*

Khalifa, M., & Liu, V. (2007). Online consumer retention: Contingent effects of online shopping habit and online shopping experience. *European Journal of Information Systems*, 16(6): 780–792. *https://doi.org/10.1057/palgrave.ejis.3000711*

Khatibi, A., Haque, A., & Karim, K. (2006). E-commerce: A study on internet shopping in Malaysia. *Journal of Applied Sciences*, 6(3): 696–705. *https://doi.org/10.3923/jas.2006.696.705*

Kim, E.K.E., & Tadisina, S. (2005). Factors impacting customers' initial trust in e-businesses: An empirical study. *In: Proceedings of the 38th Annual Hawaii International Conference on System Sciences,* Vol. 00, pp. 1–10. *https://doi.org/10.1109/HICSS.2005.272*

Kim, J.H., Kim, M., & Kandampully, J. (2007). The impact of buying environment characteristics of retail websites. *Service Industries Journal*, 27(7): 865–880. *https://doi.org/10.1080/02642060701570529*

Lee, G., & Lin, H. (2005). Customer perceptions of e service quality in online shopping. *International Journal of Retail & Distribution Management*, 33(2):161–176. *https://doi.org/10.1108/09590550510581485*

Ndubisi, N.O., Gupta, O.K., & Ndubisi, C. (2005). The Moguls' model of computing: Integrating the moderating impact of users' persona into the technology acceptance model. *Journal of Global Information Technology Management,* 8(1): 27–47. *https://doi.org/10.1080/1097198X.2005.10856389*

Nunnally, J. (1978). *Psychometric Theory. New York: McGraw-Hill. https://doi.org/10.1037/018882*

Pavlou, P.A., & Fygenson, M. (2006). Understanding and Predicting Electronic Commerce Adoption: An Extension of the Theory of Planned Behavior. *Mis Quarterly*, 30(1): 115–143. *https://doi.org/10.2307/25148720*

Pearson, J.M., Pearson, A., & Green, D. (2007). Determining the importance of key criteria in web usability. *Management Research News*, 30(11): 816–828. *https://doi.org/10.1108/01409170710832250*

Yang, Z., Jun, M., & Peterson, R.T. (2004). Measuring customer perceived online service quality. *International Journal of Operations & Production Management*, 24(11): 1149–1174. *https://doi.org/10.1108/01443570410563278*

Zhou, L., Dai, L., & Zhang, D. (2007). Online shopping acceptance model: Critical survey of consumer factors in online shopping. *Journal of Electronic Commerce Research*, 8(1): 41–62. *https://doi.org/10.1086/209376,*

9

Workforce Diversity and Discrimination - A Study of Indian Telecom Organizations

URSIL MAJID MAKHDOOMI[1*], FAYAZ AHMAD NIKKA[2] AND MUBASHIR MAJID BABA[3]

ABSTRACT

With the increase in globalization, there has been a rise in the economic development of different countries and this increase has led to a number of changes in workplaces with respect to the characteristics of people. The organisations which do not embrace the diversity of the workforce are not able to eliminate discrimination due to which it affects the organisation adversely both in terms employees as well as customers. This paper analyzes whether discrimination on the basis of diversity exists in the telecom organizations on a sample of 382 employees. The findings revealed that discrimination has been found to be almost non-existent in terms of gender, age, marital status, language, religion, ethnicity, socioeconomic status and qualifications in both the organisations. Discrimination was found significant in terms of tenure in the present organisations in both public and private organisations. Also discrimination was found to be significant in terms of experience in private organisations but not in public organisation.

Key words: Workforce diversity, Discrimination, Telecom.

[1,2] Department of Management Studies, Central University of Kashmir, J&K.
[3] National Institute of Technology (NIT), Srinagar, J&K.
**Corresponding author:* E-mail: ursilmakhdoomi@gmail.com

INTRODUCTION

With the increase in globalization, there has been a rise in the economic development of different countries and this increase has led to a number of changes in workplaces with respect to the characteristics of people. These changes have acquired all the areas of life whether social, political, cultural or economic. There has been an increase in migration, which has intensified the diversity of the workforce. It is the cause of increase in contact among people of different backgrounds, cultures and societies. Nowadays people work in an environment where there are people from multiple backgrounds coming from different parts of the world, and working together in such an environment requires understanding of their behavior towards work, their style of communicating and their values. In order to work successfully in such environment it is necessary to develop good relationships with different people in the workplace. Diversity exists not only inside the organisations but as well as outside organisations, whether it is the employees or the consumers both are diverse with a large variety of distinct skills and characteristics. Diversity is growing at such a pace that organisations have no choice but to accept it and take measures to put it to good use.

Researchers have suggested that a diverse workforce enhances the performance of the employees thus increasing the productivity of the organisation. It also has many other positive impacts on the environment of an organisation. There are many studies which show that diversity and organisational performance are positively correlated. However there have been studies which reveal that workforce diversity make lead to poor performance. A diverse workforce can also result in some negative implications like prejudices and cultural insensitivity. In order to understand what impacts a diverse workforce may have, the effects of distribution of resources, *inter se* relationships among employees and teams, and the compositional effects of job, occupation, firm or society must be considered (Skaggs & DiTomaso, 2004). Thus workforce diversity can have positive as well as negative effects on the organisation and in order to enhance its positive impacts it is important to maintain a positive workplace climate within the organisation by learning and profiting from the proper management of workforce diversity. Diversity at workplace helps the employees in improving their personal growth and development. Interacting with people from different cultures and backgrounds helps to have a global understanding of the environment. The more these diverse employees communicate with each other, they become comfortable and understand each other and it helps to remove discrimination, racism and ethnocentrism etc.

LITERATURE REVIEW

Discrimination means making distinctions among people (Gomez-Mejia *et al.*, 2007). An organization that shows discrimination directly or indirectly towards its employees restricts their potential is not able to utilize them properly and also cannot retain them. In Indian workplaces, gender discrimination is a major problem (Saxena, 2014). Not only gender but also age, language and having a different mindset also results in contradictions among the workforce. Unfair work practices influence the organisations in many ways, thus organisations need to create a bias-free workplace for better productivity. Bias can occur in organisations in the processes of recruitment, retention, recognition, promotion etc. The social identity theory suggests that managers will use social categories as a similarity indicator and will prefer and recruit individuals similar to them (Tajfel & Turner, 1979). In diverse firms, informal groups are created on the basis of race, ethnicity etc. due to which the important information bypasses the formal groups and goes in favour of the informal groups (Schneider & Northcraft, 1999) and the employees left out of these informal groups face problems in succeeding and growing in such firms (Ibarra, 1993). Minorities are considered to be facing discrimination and prejudice from a long period of time and removing any such acts of discrimination should be one of the major concerns of the top management in the organisations (Brief *et al.*, 1997). In organisations where people of diverse backgrounds exist, there are very fewer chances of discrimination to occur (Cox, 1991). Moderate levels of diversity in organisations are a cause of favoritism in groups and discrimination outside groups (Richard *et al.*, 2004).

The Thorat Committee Report, 2007 suggests that even though public sector organisations have to hire employees considering a fixed representation of employees from backward class and tribe's etc. discrimination or unfair treatment still exists in the organisations. In India, there are many laws protecting against exploitation and discrimination at workplaces for women and minorities but the implementation of these laws is found to be very poor. Discrimination related to gender and race (category) is prevalent in the Indian organisations, male employees think women are less qualified, less productive and less competent, also employees from general category think that socially disadvantaged employees are less productive and less competent (Kundu, 2003).

Some studies show that gender stereotypes still favour male candidates (Callan, 1993) while hiring. Female candidates are given lower interview ratings than male applicants with similar qualifications and skills (Arvey, 1979). It is also found that there was discrimination also in the positions that were traditionally occupied by men (Rich, 1995) and for such positions qualified women are less likely to be hired (Heilman, 1997) but in case they are hired they are paid less as compared to men. The work done by women is valued less compared to the same work done by men due to which there are differences in pay but no differences in the job title (Truman & Baroudi, 1994). Not only in terms of wages but minorities have also been discriminated in terms of performance ratings (Martell, 1991). In case of accountability and capability, men are considered more often for the managerial positions. A small percentage of women have been CEO's of Fortune 500 companies, in 2004 only 1.6% of women were CEO's of these companies (Acker, 2006). A study conducted by Hass and Huwang (2007) to calculate the number of women in top management that two-thirds of the companies had no women in the senior management.

Studies show that discrimination also exists in hiring and firing decisions in the organisations towards mature aged workers (Billett *et al.,* 2011). A study by Heywood *et al.* (1999) found that there were reductions in the hiring of older employees, a preference was shown towards hiring young workers. Literature has shown that organisations are biased against hiring older employees due to their concerns about the ability to change and adapt to changes, and their ability to acquire and learn new skills (Encel & Studencki, 2004).

Religion also plays an important role and the differences in religions and religious practices can also be a cause of discrimination. There is a global rise in conflicts within and among different religions (Grim, 2014). Employees who have similarities in certain characteristics and attitudes regard each other as similar (Byrne, 1971) which creates an interpersonal attraction which in turn result in positively biased decisions and evaluations. Another group of employees which are a part of the workforce is the people with disabilities. Discrimination against them has also been going on because of their disabilities. Generally such employees are being considered as noncapable employees (Henderson, 1994).

Research also shows that lesbians and gay men also fear discrimination. In a study conducted by Levine and Leonard (1984) on 203 lesbians, it was found that 60% expected job discrimination, harassment, termination, ostracism, taunts or even violence against them if their sexual orientation was known. Studies related to gay men's perceptions of job discrimination towards their sexual orientation were found to give similar results (Levine, 1979).

The organisations which do not embrace the diversity of the workforce are not able to eliminate discrimination due to which it affects the organisation adversely both in terms employees as well as customers.

OBJECTIVES

- To analyze whether discrimination on the basis of diversity exists in the Indian organizations.

RESEARCH METHODOLOGY

This paper aimed at evaluating the workforce diversity of private and public telecom sector *i.e.*, Bharti Airtel and MTNL in Delhi NCR from the perspective of lower and middle level employees. Cluster sampling followed by simple random sampling was used for the selection of telecom companies from the five regions of Delhi NCR (Delhi, Gurgaon, Faridabad, Noida and Ghaziabad).

Field survey method was adopted for the collection of data, for which a comprehensive structured questionnaire was used. The sample size for the study was chosen according to the items (itemized sampling) in the study. The final sample was taken as 382 from both the organisations.

DATA ANALYSIS

H_{01}: Employee diversity does not cause any discrimination.

In order to study whether there has been discrimination on the basis of diversity of the employees, Independent samples test and One Way ANOVA were applied on different dimensions of diversity. For gender and marital status with discrimination independent test was applied and for age, ethnicity, religion, education, experience, position, language and tenure with discrimination one way ANOVAs was used to test the relationship.

Table 1: Independent samples test-discrimination.

			Levene's test for equality of variances		***t-test for equality of means***				
			F	***Sig.***	***T***	***Df***	***Sig. (2-tailed)***	***Mean Difference***	***Std. error Difference***
Gender	Public	Equal variances assumed	.426	.515	–1.539	189	.125	–.10917	.07092
	Private	Equal variances assumed	.260	.611	3.445	189	.001	.19740	.05731
Marital Status	Public	Equal variances assumed	.093	.761	–.595	189	.552	–.04390	.07373
	Private	Equal variances assumed	.014	.905	–.429	189	.669	-.02401	.05603

Source: Authors' own

After the application of independent sample test on discrimination and gender and discrimination and marital status for both the public and private organisations (Table 1) assuming equal variances the significance value for both public and private organisations was found to be higher than the p value of 0.05 due to which null hypothesis is to be accepted implying that there is no discrimination based on gender and marital status in both public and private telecom organisations.

One way ANOVA (Table 2) on discrimination and the various dimensions of diversity which are age, ethnicity, religion, education, experience, position in the organisation and tenure for both the public and private organisations.

In case of public organisation it was found that there was no discrimination due to the diversity of age, ethnicity, education, religion, language, experience, and position as the p value for all the dimensions was higher than 0.05 (Table 2). The organisations where people from diverse backgrounds exist, there is lesser discrimination (Cox, 1991). But the p value was less than 0.05 for tenure in the present organisation and discrimination implying that there is discrimination in the organisation on the basis of tenure in the present organisation.

Table 2: ANOVA – discrimination

			Sum of squares	*Df*	*Mean square*	*F*	*Sig.*
Age	Public	Between groups	1.036	4	.259	1.188	.318
		Within groups	40.541	186	.218		
		Total	41.577	190			
	Private	Between groups	.264	3	.088	.624	.600
		Within groups	26.379	187	.141		
		Total	26.643	190			
Ethnicity	Public	Between groups	.347	2	.173	.790	.455
		Within groups	41.230	188	.219		
		Total	41.577	190			
	Private	Between groups	.218	2	.109	.776	.462

Table 2: (*Contd...*)

Table 2: (*Contd...*)

			Sum of squares	*Df*	*Mean square*	*F*	*Sig.*
		Within groups	26.425	188	.141		
		Total	26.643	190			
Religion	Public	Between groups	.211	4	.053	.237	.917
		Within groups	41.366	186	.222		
		Total	41.577	190			
	Private	Between groups	.634	4	.158	1.133	.342
		Within groups	26.009	186	.140		
		Total	26.643	190			
Education	Public	Between groups	.022	2	.011	.051	.950
		Within groups	41.554	188	.221		
		Total	41.577	190			
	Private	Between groups	.154	2	.077	.547	.579
		Within groups	26.489	188	.141		
		Total	26.643	190			
Position	Public	Between groups	.331	3	.110	.501	.682
		Within groups	41.245	187	.221		
		Total	41.577	190			
	Private	Between groups	.835	3	.278	2.018	.113
		Within groups	25.808	187	.138		
		Total	26.643	190			
Language	Public	Between Groups	1.142	3	.381	1.760	.156
		Within groups	40.435	187	.216		
		Total	41.577	190			
	Private	Between groups	.184	3	.061	.432	.730

Table 2: (*Contd...*)

Table 2: (*Contd...*)

			Sum of squares	***Df***	***Mean square***	***F***	***Sig.***
		Within groups	26.459	187	.141		
		Total	26.643	190			
Tenure	Public	Between groups	3.517	6	.586	2.834	.012
		Within groups	38.060	184	.207		
		Total	41.577	190			
	Private	Between groups	.886	2	.443	3.233	.042
		Within groups	25.757	188	.137		
		Total	26.643	190			
Exper-ience	Public	Between groups	1.727	6	.288	1.329	.246
		Within groups	39.850	184	.217		
		Total	41.577	190			
	Private	Between groups	1.236	3	.412	3.033	.031
		Within groups	25.407	187	.136		
		Total	26.643	190			

Source: Authors' own

For private organisation discrimination and various dimensions of diversity which are age, ethnicity, religion, language, position and education reveal a higher p value ($p>0.05$) implying that there is no discrimination on the basis of age, ethnicity, religion, language, position and education. But tenure in the present organisation and experience reveal p value lesser than 0.05 implying that there is a presence of discrimination on the basis of tenure and experience in the private organisations. The final hypotheses testing results are presented in Table 3.

The basis of various dimensions of diversity was also supplemented through percentage results, it was found that 7% respondents were discriminated on the basis of experience in private organisation while as 6% in the public organization (Figs.

1 & 2). And a very small percentage of 2%, 3%, 2% and 1% were discriminated in public organisation on the basis of language, religion, qualifications and disability respectively while as 2%, 1%, 1% were discriminated in private organisation on the basis of language, socioeconomic status and qualifications respectively, as properly shown in the graphs below.

Table 3: Hypotheses results-discrimination and workforce diversity.

Hypotheses		***Public***	***Private***
H_{01}:	Employee diversity does not cause any discrimination.		
$H_{01.1}$:	*There is no discrimination on the basisc of gender.*	Supported	Supported
$H_{01.2}$:	*There is no discrimination on the basis of marital status.*	Supported	Supported
$H_{01.3}$:	*There is no discrimination on the basis of age.*	Supported	Supported
$H_{01.4}$:	*There is no discrimination on the basis of ethnicity.*	Supported	Supported
$H_{01.5}$:	*There is no discrimination on the basis of religion.*	Supported	Supported
$H_{01.6}$:	*There is no discrimination on the basis of education.*	Supported	Supported
$H_{01.7}$:	*There is no discrimination on the basis of position in the organisation.*	Supported	Supported
$H_{01.8}$:	*There is no discrimination on the basis of language.*	Supported	Supported
$H_{01.9}$:	*There is no discrimination on the basis of tenure in the present organisation.*	Not supported	Not supported
$H_{01.10}$:	*There is no discrimination on the basis of Experience.*	Supported	Not supported

FINDINGS

Discrimination has been found to be almost non-existent in terms of gender, age, marital status, language, religion, ethnicity, socioeconomic status and qualifications in both the organisations. Discrimination was found significant in terms of tenure in the present organisations in both public and private organisations.Also discrimination was found to be significant in terms of experience in private organisations but not in public organisation.

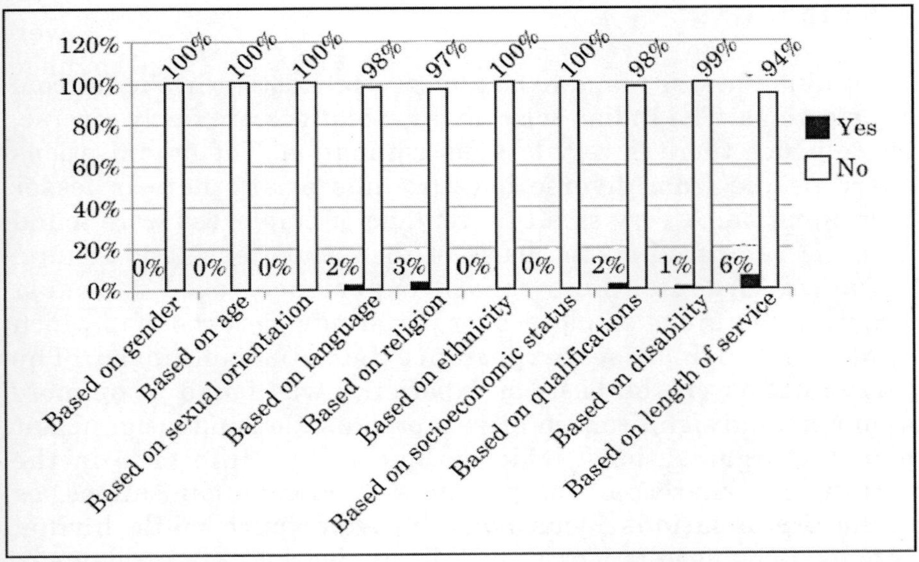

Fig. 1: Discrimination-MTNL (Public organisation)

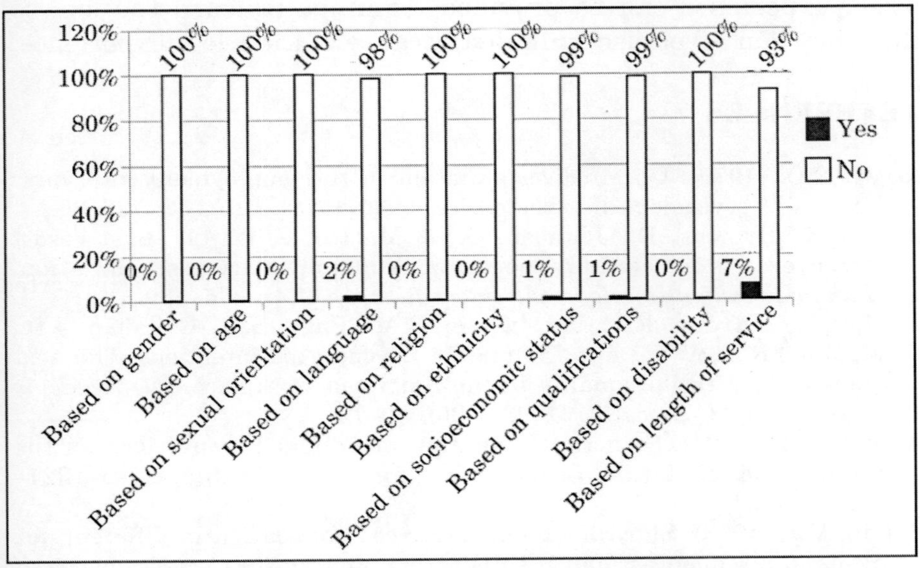

Fig. 2: Discrimination-Airtel (Private organisation)

CONCLUSIONS

Discrimination was found to be almost non-existent in the telecom organisations. The Indian telecom organisations are fairly diverse, due to which there is very less discrimination. The organisations where people from diverse backgrounds exist, there is lesser discrimination. A very small percentage of employees were found to be discriminated on the basis of their experience and tenure. Nowadays organisations regard experience to be the most important feature of employees for performing better due to which employees with lesser experience feel discriminated. The discrimination on the basis of experience was found to be more prominent and significant in private organisation and insignificant in public organisations, which is due to the difference in the recruitment criteria's of the private and public organisations, as public organisations focus more on experience while hiring. Organisations need to look into skills and various other talents of employees who have lesser experience so that they also get opportunities get hired and also perform better. Employees with lesser experience can be provided trainings to learn the job, so that they don't feel discriminated because of their less experience.

REFERENCES

Arvey, R.D. (1979). Unfair discrimination in the employment interview: Legal and psychological aspects. *Psychological Bulletin*, 86: 736–65.

Billett, S., Dymock, D., Johnson, G., & Martin, G. (2011). Last resort employees: Older workers' perceptions of workplace discrimination. *Human Resource Development International,* 14(4): 375–389.

Brief, A.P., Buttram, R.T., Reizenstein, R.M., Pugh, S.D., Callahan, J.D., McCline, R.L., & Vaslow, J.B. (1997). Beyond good intentions: The next steps toward racial equality in the American workplace. *The Academy of Management Executive* (1993-2005), 59–72.

Byrne, B.M. (2001). Structural equation modeling: Perspectives on the present and the future. *International Journal of Testing*, 1(3–4): 327–334.

Callan, V.J. (1993). Subordinate–manager communication in different sex dyads: Consequences for job satisfaction. *Journal of Occupational and Organizational Psychology*, 66(1): 13–27.

Cox Jr, T. (1991). The multicultural organisation. *Academy of Management Executive*, 5(2): 34–37. *Pennsylvania, Wharton School, Universidad de Pennsylvania.*

Encel, S., & Studencki, H. (2004). Older workers: Can they succeed in the job market? *Australasian Journal on Ageing*, 23(1): 33–37.

Gomez-Mejia, L.R., Balkin, D.B., & Cardy, R.L., (2007). *Managing Human Resources* (5th ed.). Upper Saddle River: NJ. Pearson Prentice Hall.

Grim, B.J. *ed.* (2014). Religious hostilities reach six year high. Pew research center.

Haas, L., & Hwang, C.P. (2007). Gender and organisational culture: Correlates of companies' responsiveness to fathers in Sweden. *Gender & Society*, 21(1): 52–79.

Heilman, M.E. (1997). Sex discrimination and the affirmative action remedy. The role of sex stereotypes. *Journal of Business Ethics*, 16: 877–89.

Henderson, G. (1994). *Cultural Diversity in the Workplace: Issues and Strategies.* Westport, CT: Quorum Books.

Heywood, J.S., Ho, L.S., & Wei, X. (1999). The determinants of hiring older workers: Evidence from Hong Kong. *Industrial and Labor Relations Review*, 52: 444–59.

Ibarra, H. (1993). Personal networks of women and minorities in management: A conceptual framework. *Academy of Management Review*, 18(1): 56–87.

Kundu, S.C. (2003). Workforce diversity status: A study of employees' reactions. *Industrial Management & Data Systems*, 103(4): 215–226.

Levine, M.P. (1979). Employment discrimination against gay men. *International Review of Modern Sociology*, pp. 151–163.

Levine, M.P., & Leonard, R. (1984). Discrimination against lesbians in the work force. *Signs*, 9(4): 700–710

Martell, R.F. (1991). Sex Bias at Work: The effects of attentional and memory demands on performance ratings of men and women[1]. *Journal of Applied Social Psychology*, 21(23), 1939–1960.

Richard, O.C., Barnett, T., Dwyer, S., & Chadwick, K. (2004). Cultural diversity in management, firm performance, and the moderating role of entrepreneurial orientation dimensions. *Academy of Management Journal*, 47(2): 255–266.

Saxena, A. (2014). Workforce diversity: A key to improve productivity. *Procedia Economics and Finance*, 11: 76–85.

Schneider, S.K., & Northcraft, G.B. (1999). Three social dilemmas of workforce diversity in organisations: A social identity perspective. *Human Relations*, 52(11): 1445–1467.

Skaggs, S., & Di Tomaso, N. (2004). Understanding the effects of workforce diversity on employmen outcomes: A multidisciplinary and comprehensive framework. *In*: Diversity in the Work Force Emerald Group Publishing Limited, pp. 279–306.

Tajfel, H., & Turner, J.C. (1979). An integrative theory of intergroup conflict. *The Social Psychology of Intergroup Relations*, 33(47): 74.

Truman, G.E., & Baroudi, J.J. (1994). Gender differences in the information systems managerial ranks: An assessment of potential discriminatory practices. *MIS Quarterly*, pp. 129–142.

10

Understanding Self-Service Technologies

Shahid Amin[1*], Aditya Tripathi[2], Keshav Kansana[3] and Jahangir Malik[4]

ABSTRACT

Self-service technologies enable companies to reduce their costs and help them provide a better quality service. By deploying self-service technology companies can apply the productivity benefits of information and technology to their business. The successful businesses in the future will be those that are able to leverage most from the information and communication technology revolution. Increasingly consumers are demanding more and more efficient services. The winners will be those businesses that are able to harness on the capability of information and communication technology in making strategic decisions in terms of enhancing value offerings, its organizational capacity and capability, risk management and building better customer relationships. Life is never so easy, but the science and technology is gifting humans the comfort, luxury and feel easy. But a new technology brings with it not only the potential for success but also a never-ending series of questions regarding its design, its value to its users, ultimate use and acceptability. The current chapter is an attempt to understand the self-service technologies from a research perspective. The aim is to help researchers get insights into the concept and undertake more good research in this direction. In India, the concept of self-service technology is relatively new but the potential is massive. There is a greater need of research in this direction.

***Key words*:** Service, Self-service, SST, Research, Satisfaction, Opportunity.

[1, 2, 3] SOM, ITM University Gwalior, Gwalior, Madhya Pradesh.
[4] Higher Education Department, Jammu and Kashmir.
**Corresponding author:* Email: dr.shahidamin15@gmail.com

INTRODUCTION TO SERVICES

Services are essentially intangible benefits and provide value to the consumers. Being dissimilar from a physical good, service has its unique characteristics, including intangibility, heterogeneity as well as inseparability. It is quiet challenging to imagine a life without the services. The most economies around the globe are increasingly becoming service economies. Services are widely used by people today in practically all aspects of life. Services nowadays are increasingly being used by the corporate as well as the house hold sector. Services or the "tertiary sector" of the economy covers a wide range of activities in the areas like Banking, Insurance, Trade, Hotels and Restaurants, Dwellings, Real Estate, Railways, Other Transport and Storage, Communication (Post, Telecom), Business Services, Public Administration, Defense, Personal Services, Community Services, and other Services.

Huge Growth of Services

In alignment with the global trends, Indian services sector has witnessed a major boom and has led to the enormous rise in employment and contributing heavily to the Indian national income. The sector is not only the dominant sector in India's GDP, but has also attracted significant foreign investment flows, contributed significantly to exports. The sector is offering a large-scale employment to the Indian population. The services sector is the key driver of India's economic growth. The sector has contributed 55.65 percent of India's Gross Value Added at current price in Q1 2018-19 and employed 28.6 percent of the total population. Net service exports stood at US$ 18.7 billion in Q1 2018-19 (P). Services sector has received the most FDI inflows between April 2000 and June 2018 totalling US $ 68.62 billion. The Government of India also recognises the significance of promoting growth in services sectors and offers many incentives in wide variety of sectors such as engineering, communications, transportation, health care, tourism, education, banking and finance, information technology, management, among others.

Self-Service -A New Revolution in Services

Self -Service is an old concept that has proved significant with the time. A consumer on visiting a restaurant or attending a marriage now serves himself rather than depending on others are better examples of a self-service. But the world grooming with the advent of technology has transformed the life of complexities into the life of simplicities. The concept of self service has now been transformed into a new delightful function of Self-Service Technology (SST). Originally Dabholkar (1994) gave the concept of 'TBSS' (Technology Based Self Service). Dabholkar (1996), Ladik (1999), Dabholkar *et al.* (2003) and Anselmsson (2001), among others later developed the concept of Self-Service Technologies (SST's).

Since the satisfaction from services is increasing and resulting its high demand it has often meant increasing the number of employees. But the capital-labor substitution and customer-labor substitution because of the rapid advancement in service technologies has made it possible for service providers to become the biggest consumers of new information technologies and leading many services to become technology based. Service firms can use technology in three basic ways: (1) Employees who do not interact with customers use technology in the back office to increase the overall efficiency of the service production, (2) Employees who interact with customers use technology to provide faster and more comprehensive service to customers, and (3) Customers use technology to perform services for themselves, which may diminish the need for labor input in the service company (Ojasalo, 1999).

Meaning of Self-Service Technologies

Self-Service Technology is an innovative channel of marketplace transactions in which no interpersonal contact is required between customer and service provider (Meuter *et al.,* 2000) while self-service activities are necessarily completed by customers themselves (Globerson & Maggard, 1991). SST (Self-Service Technology) or TBSS (Technology Based Self-Service) is termed as an activity or benefit based on hard technologies that service providers offer so that customers can perform the service or parts of service by themselves (Anselmsson, 2001). SSTs (Self-Service

Technologies) are the technological interfaces that enable customers to take advantage of a service without any service employee involvement (Meuter *et al.,* 2000). Conducting bank transactions through Automated Teller Machines (ATM), self-service gas stations, self-health diagnosis, shopping through the Internet, making reservations and purchasing tickets through kiosks, checking out of hotel rooms through interactive television,using self-scanning systems at retail stores, vending machines, internet banking, phone banking, kiosks, self-scanning check out, are some of the examples of Self-service technologies.

Self Service Technologies and Customer Satisfaction: Research Perspective

The satisfaction of customers drive customer loyalty and customer loyalty drives revenue growth and profitability (Anderson *et al.,* 1994). But on the other side extremely unsatisfied customers which is most dangerous for a firm always speaks out against a poorly delivered service and stop buying. The customers will spread a strong word of mouth when satisfied and loyal with the service firms. Self-service technologies improve the quality of services that firms provide to their customers. The services are made easier and manageable by virtue of technology. Self-service technologies add up to the customers' convenience and enable their time as well. Self-service technologies may lead to improved customer service, empowered customers and employees and increased efficiency.

The rapid advancement in technology enables service firms to increasingly incorporate technology and their operations. These new technologies are revolutionizing the services environment; however many consumers do not necessarily see the incorporation of technology as an improvement (Meuter *et al.,* 2003). Today consumers often have the choice of using self-service technology; at a bank a customer may choose between using an ATM and using a teller; at a hotel a traveler may choose between using a vending machine and using room service and at a gas station, a customer can choose between pumping his own gas and having an attendant to do it. Consumers choose self-service technologies for a good number of reasons including monetary savings, convenience, faster service and ease of use etc. Businesses are often available 24 hours a day, seven days a week, to customers rather than traditional working hours by virtue of self-service technologies. Self-service technologies empower the consumers and using the technology the customer controls the service and not feels rushed or pressured (Castro *et al.,* 2010).

Self-service technologies may lead both the success as well as failure. The customers generally may recall the failures rather than the successes of self-service technologies. Nakata *et al.* (2003) suggests that in nearly all cases (96%), customers blame companies and their technologies, not themselves, for these dissatisfying experiences. Customers are always in need of better purchasing opportunities. But very often firms fail to visualize the customers 'vision'. What the customers expects and what he perceives he gets has a great impact on their satisfaction or dissatisfaction and their propensity to return to service, or to seek alternatives from competitors. Firms pursue SST's for many reasons. Some of these are; customer demand, cost reduction, to improve service levels, to improve customer satisfaction, the firms need for new delivery channels (for both new and old customers) and to gain competitive advantage.

Anselmsson (2001) and Dabholkar (1996) are among the researchers who have noteworthy contributions on service quality and customer satisfaction from the consumer perspective. Anselmsson, 2001 found the customers need for independence, self-esteem, social escapism, risk aversion, commitment, socially integration and attitude towards using technology in general as the customer characteristic determinants of service quality. The speed of delivery, enjoyment, reliability, ease of use, physical appearance, personnel based support and decision control were found to be technology/system specific determinants of service quality. Time was found to be a salient and only factor that is easily observable by the service provider.

Self-service technologies are highly viable for banks and other financial intermediaries because information processing is essential to their services. Self-service banking which is to make use of SST's in banking has uplifted the banking and resulted in the increased demand and satisfaction for consumers. Self-service banking includes banking by telephone and internet, EFTPOS (Electronic Funds Transfer Point of Sale) terminals, ATM's and other interactive kiosks and are highly facilitating the needs and convenience of consumers (Sannes, 2001). The current consolidation in banking (Davis, 2000) together with an expected technology driven globalization of banking infrastructure, threaten to marginalize the parties who choose not to participate in the game. The costs of processing and transmitting information can be highly reduced through self-service and information technology use.

The ATM's, telephone banking, PC banking and internet banking are examples of such a revolution in banking industry. Developing alternative distribution channels not only increases effectiveness and efficiency but also strengths the financial institutions to retain the existing customer base. The new customers may also get attracted towards a bank offering benefits through alternative distribution channels. Generally the customers are better informed about the alternative options in banking and thus are highly conscious of the expenses associated with banking.

Competition is now happening on price, packaging and promotion but for the future consumers will be more focused on the operational excellence, good product quality and a strong customer service (The Times of India, 21 Dec., 2010). The concept of quality is very important to marketers because quality drives the development of all marketing strategies (Ravi Shanker, 2008). This means that operational excellence, quality, and a strong customer service must be a major focus of all service providers making use of self-service technologies.

Matic and Prskalo (2016) explored customer readiness towards new self-service technologies in retail. The research findings indicated that consumers show a high level of readiness toward new self-service technologies and moderate high level of perceived trust toward smart self-service carts in retail stores. Additionally, it indicated that customers show positive attitudes toward new self-service technology trends such as smart self-service carts and most of them intend to use that technology in their future purchases.

Marler *et al.* (2016) suggested that implementation of Employee Self-Service (ESS) technology presents a variety of challenges for organizations as they strive to maximize return on investment and change management. The study examined factors that enhance user acceptance of ESS technology both before and after implementation. The results suggested that employees are more likely to intend to use ESS technology when they have positive attitudes toward using it and when subjective norms in the organization support use of the technology. Perceived Organizational Support (POS) enhanced the effect of managerial pressure on perceptions of normative beliefs supporting use of the technology post-implementation.

Scherer *et al.* (2015) suggested that advancements in information technology have changed the way customers experience a service encounter and their relationship with service providers. Especially technology-based self-service channels have found their way into the 21st century service economy. The paper concluded that firms should not shift customers toward self-service channels completely, especially not at the beginning of a relationship. The study underlined the importance of understanding when and how self-service technologies create valuable customer experiences and stresses the notion of actively managing customers' co-creation of value.

CONCLUSIONS

Self-service technologies enable companies to reduce their costs and help them provide a better quality service. By deploying self-service technology companies can apply the productivity benefits of information and technology to their business. The successful businesses in the future will be those that are able to leverage most from the information and communication technology revolution. Increasingly consumers are demanding more and more efficient services. The winners will be those businesses that are able to harness on the capability of information and communication technology in making strategic decisions in terms of enhancing value offerings, its organizational capacity and capability, risk management and building better customer relationships. The growing competition coupled with higher customer expectations and greater use of technology is bound to give totally new opportunities to businesses in India. Undoubtedly Indian companies are trying their best but still there is a vast significant opportunity to enable customers to use technology to make the delivery of a good or service more efficient. Science and technology is shaping the nature of the human life. Life is never so easy, but the science and technology is gifting humans the comfort, luxury and feel easy. But a new technology brings with it not only the potential for success but also a never-ending series of questions regarding its design, its value to its users, ultimate use and acceptability. In India, the concept of self service technology is relatively new but the potential is massive. There is a greater need of research in this direction.

REFERENCES

Anderson, E.W., Fornell, C., & Lehmann, D.R. (1994). "Customer satisfaction, market share and profitability: Findings from Sweden". *Journal of Marketing,* 58: 53–66.

Anselmsson, J. (2001). *"Customer-perceived service quality and technology-based self-service",* Unpublished doctoral dissertation, Lund University, Lund.

Castro, D., Atkinson, R., & Ezell, S. (2010). "Embracing the self-service Economy". *The Information Technology and Innovation Foundation.,* Washington, DC.

Dabholkar, P.A. (1994). Incorporating choice into an attitudinal framework: Analyzing models of mental comparison processes. *Journal of Consumer Research*, 21: 100–118.

Dabholkar, P.A. (1996). "Consumer evaluations of new technology-based self-services.

Dabholkar, P.A., Michelle Bobbitt, L., & Lee, E.J. (2003). Understanding consumer motivation and behavior related to self-scanning in retailing: Implications for strategy and research on technology-based self-service. *International Journal of Service Industry Management*, 14(1): 59–95.

Davis, S.I. (2000). "*Bank Mergers: Lessons for the Future*", London: MacMillan.

Globerson, S., & Maggard, M.J. (1991). "A conceptual model of self-service". *International Journal of Operations & Production Management*, 11(4): 33–43. *https://www.ibef.org/industry/services.aspx, Accessed on Nov. 11, 2018*

Ladik, D.M. (1999). "A technology-based self-service delivery system: An exploration adoption model in a supermarket delicatessen". *Proceedings of Annual Meeting of the Society Marketing Advance,* Atlanta, GA.

Marler, J.H., Fisher, S.L., & Ke, W. (2016). "Employee self-service technology acceptance: A comparison of pre-implementation and post-implementation relationships. *Personnel Psychology,* 62: 327–35

Matic, M., & Prskalo, D. (2016). "*The Analysis of Customer Readiness towards New Self Service Technologies in Retail*". *Oeconomica Jadertina*, pp. 32–41

Meuter, M.L., Ostrom, A.L., Roundtree, R.I., & Bitner, M.J. (2000). "Self-service technologies: Understanding customer satisfaction with technology-based service encounters". *Journal of Marketing,* 64(3): 50–64.

Meuter, M.L., Ostrom, A.L., Bitner, M.J., & Roundtree, R.I. (2003). "The influence of technology anxiety on consumer use and experiences with self-service technologies". *Journal of Business Research*, 56(11): 899–906.

Nakata Cheryl & Zhen Zhu (2003). "Self-Service Technology Failure: Understanding the Customer Perspective", Power-point Presentation. As retrieved from *http://www.uic.edu/cba/crim/CrimNewsFiles/Colloquia/*

Ojasalo, K. (1999). "Conceptualizing productivity in services", Hanken Swedish School of Economics Finland, Helsinki/Helsingfors. options: An investigation of alternative models of service quality". *International Journal of Research in Marketing,* 13(1): 29–51.

Sannes, R. (2001). "Self-service banking: Value creation models and information exchange". *Informing Science*, 4(3): 139–148.

Scherer, A., Wünderlich, N.V., & Wangenheim, F.V. (2015). "The value of self-service: Long-term effects of technology-based self-service usage on customer Retention". *MIS Quarterly*, 39(1): 177–200.

Shanker, R. (2008). Services Marketing-the Indian Perspective, Excel Books New Delhi.

11

Health Micro Insurance as a Healthcare Financing Mechanism and Its Impact

SHEIKH AFTAAB-UL-MAROOF[1]*

ABSTRACT

While setting the goal of ensuring healthy lives and promoting well-being for all, the United Nations in 2015 has placed an objective of achieving universal health coverage, including financial risk protection, access to quality essential healthcare services. Universal Health Coverage Programs have been found to be quite useful in restricting the poor households to use the inefficient strategies to cope up with the adverse financial consequences of health shocks, and at the same time improve the healthcare utilization by reducing the affordability constraints of access to healthcare. Universal Health Coverage programs have been found playing significant part towards contributing the earlier Millennium Development Goals (MGDs). The current study is an effort to assess the impact of health coverage program focusing the poor in India (Rashtriya Swasthya Bima Yojana) in terms of its impact on financial protection to a household. The program covers the inpatient treatment expenditure up to rupees thirty thousand for a household. The study besides looking at the inpatient treatment aspect, has also thrown light on the out-patient treatment variables to track out the spill-over effects of the program. The study following a quasi-experimental research design has two groups of respondents i.e., treatment and control group and the data have been collected from three North-Indian states (Haryana, Punjab and Himachal Pradesh). The study has applied Propensity Score Matching technique to assess the impact. The results reveal that RSBY has been quite successful in providing the financial protection by reducing the health expenditure of the policy

[1] AAA Memorial Degree College, Bemina, Cluster University, Srinagar, J&K.
**Corresponding author:* E-mail: sheikhaftaabulmaroof@gmail.com

holders and their need to raise finance through costlier means together with smoothing the essential household consumption. Therefore health micro insurance by way of universal health coverage programs is a way forward for achieving sustainability development in healthcare together with playing a part in poverty eradication.

Key words: Sustainability development, Financial protection, Healthcare utilization, Millennium development goals, Quasi-experiment, Propensity score matching.

INTRODUCTION

Micro insurance is the insurance for low income people, who generally because of poverty, unawareness and lower affordability do not have an access to insurance facilities. Micro insurance is having the potential to assist the poor people to cope up with shocks, such as health shocks, death, crop loss and natural hazards (Dror & Jacquier, 1999). Risks which are uninsured have a welfare implication which go beyond consequences for short term consumptions and is a cause of persistent poverty (Dercon, 2004; Townsend, 1994). Micro insurance as having a protective mechanism has the potential to reduce these welfare costs. By offering a payout on happening of some unfavorable outcome, it reduces their need to adopt costlier strategies thus protecting their income earning opportunities.

Of all the risks facing poor households, health risks probably pose the greatest threat to their lives and livelihoods. Health shocks have a direct impact on human capital formation. It thrusts health expenditure on a poor household precisely at a time when they can ill-afford it due to income shortfall resulting from the shock. Moreover, the uncertainty of the timings of illness and unpredictability of its costs make financial provision for illness difficult for households receiving low and irregular income (Tenkorang, 2001).

Health Micro Insurance (HMI) offers a promising way to mitigate risks of disease and ill health, which are disproportionately borne by the world's poorest citizens. In developing countries, illness is mentioned more frequently then job loss as the main cause of poverty (Dodd & Munck, 2002; Asfaw,

2003) and many low-income individuals cannot afford medical treatment. Health risks pose dangerous threats to the lives and livelihoods of the poor, and health security remains integral to accomplishing many of the Millennium Development Goals. HMI is one many potential healthcare financing options for the poor. Research indicates that 26 percent of households in low- and middle-income countries resort to selling assets and borrowing to cover healthcare expenses (Kruk *et al.,* 2009) suggesting that there is a huge gap in healthcare financing. Although health care is increasingly perceived as a human right and public good, in reality resource constraints slow the deployment and scale-up of national health care financing. In these cases, HMI can be a possible alternative; hybrid strategies that combine private-sector-led HMI with the strengths of the public sector also promise to push the frontier in healthcare financing for the poor. The present study is an attempt to evaluate a health coverage program started by the Government of India in the year 2008 (Rashtriya Swasthya Bima Yojana) in terms of providing financial protection to the poor households and improving their healthcare utilization.

REVIEW OF LITERATURE

Impact encompasses the changes that micro insurance makes to the economic or social circumstances of insured people or their households, enterprises or communities. Since micro insurance is a relatively new intervention. Few impact assessment studies have been performed, which is exacerbated by a lack of standard indicators and research protocols for evaluating programs. Many of the existing studies also faced methodological problems that make it difficult to determine whether the reported effects were caused by the policies under consideration.

Health-Micro Insurance and Financial Protection

Financial protection occurs when micro insurance safeguards low-income households form using inefficient coping mechanisms in response to shocks and stress these mechanisms can include depleting savings and additional supplies of goods like food land livestock, selling valuable and sometimes income-generating possessions, borrowing at typically high interest rates, adjusting labour supply, altering purchasing and consumption patterns, engaging in reciprocal mutual support practices, capitalizing on self-help group memberships and withdrawing children from school to generate the resources necessary to handle the shocks involved (Radermacher *et al.,* 2014). Besides reducing reactive measures taken by households in crisis, the financial protection provided by micro insurance theoretically allows individuals to proactively make decisions that improve their incomes and standards of living. These include choices related to asset accumulation; individuals are believed to be more likely to purchase productive goods, such as ovens or tractors, when the financial repercussions of losing or breaking them are mitigated. Similarly, micro insurance is believed to encourage "households to allocate resources to more profitable ends (which were previously precluded for being too risky)" (Morduch, 1995). Therefore financial protection is a wider concept and in order to evaluate the impact of Health Micro insurance on financial protection, the due care should be taken to include all the above mentioned areas.

Financial Protection Indicators

After reviewing the current literature on HMI, the major indicators of financial protection has been identified as:

- Health expenditure (which includes out-of-pocket expenditure and catastrophic expenditure).
- Fund mobilisation.
- Income and consumption smoothing.

(Wagstaff and Yu, 2007; Wagstaff and Lindelow, 2008; Wagstaff *et al.*, 2009; Galarraga *et al.*, 2010; Thornton *et al.*, 2010; Jowert *et al.*, 2004; Wagstaff and Pradhan, 2005; Aggarwall, 2010; Diop *et al.*, 2006; Franco *et al.*, 2008; Jutting, 2004).

Health expenditure

The most important and direct impact of health insurance is on Out-of-Pocket (OOP) health expenditure. Studies from Vietnam like Jowertt *et al.* (2003) have observed that health insurance reduces average OOP expenditure by approximately 200%. In the same line Healthcare Fund for Poor (HCFP), not only reduces sharply the OOP expenditure, but was also successful in reducing the catastrophic payment following the health shock. A very popular health insurance scheme in Mexico known as Seguro Popular (SP) has been successful in reducing the OOP and catastrophic health expenditure (Galarraga *et al.,* 2010). Another study conducted by Wirtz (2012) has found that households covered under SP had a lower probability of incurring OOP expenditures for medicines than their comparison group. The same observation is true of a couple of studies from China where a positive impact of health insurance on OOP and catastrophic expenditures has been found (Wagstaff & Lindelow, 2008; Wagstaff *et al.,* 2009). Evidence from Ghana (Naguyen *et al.,* 2011) also indicate that the National Health Insurance Program running in the country has been able to achieve a reduction in OOP expenditure that ranges from 0.5 percentage points to 1 percentage point (which amounts to a reduction of 36% to 67% of the sample mean).

Reviewing the literature, the researcher has come across the number of studies which have shown a negative impact of health insurance on OOP expenditure *i.e.,* the HMI has not been able to reduce the OOP health expenditures of insured persons (Jowert *et al.,* 2003; Wagstaff *et al.,* 2008; Wagstaff *et al.,* 2009; Galarraga *et al.,* 2010; Wirtz, 2012). There have been lots of reasons found to be responsible for negative impact of MHI on OOP expenditure. HMI is believed to make people more likely to use health care providers (Wagstaff *et al.,* 2008; Wagstaff *et al.,* 2009; Galarraga *et al.,* 2010). The reason can be that low income individuals have worse health status at the time of purchasing the policy and use health insurance to access otherwise unaffordable services (Jowert *et al.,* 2003). Theoretically health insurance should prevent excessive OOP, but supply driven demand may restrict this object of HMI, as people who otherwise would not have availed the service to use several treatments and procedures, which may not be insured. The researchers also observed that insurance makes people more likely to move up the provider 'ladder' *i.e.,* preferring Township Health Centers (THC) to village clinics, and hospital to THCs (Wagstaff *et al.,* 2008). So we can say that HMI does not always reduce OOP health expenditures. HMI should reduce the incidence of catastrophic health expenditure. Some studies have observed this dimension within health expenditure.

The lack of impact on OOP expenditure does not necessarily mean failure of a program, given that this result might be explained -at least partly- by a desirable effect (increased utilization). The same outcome (lack of impact on OOPE) might suggest a need for totally different approach (Giedion *et al.*, 2013). Studies should be conducted to study the health expenditure while considering both direct and indirect costs associated with it. For example OOP or catastrophic expenditure variables, as constructed by most of the researchers usually do not include health-seeking related costs (such as transportation costs) not paid at the point of delivery. Ekman (2007) has observed this by evaluating the impact of different health insurance schemes in Zambia not only on OOP payment at the point of service, but on a wider concept of health related OOP expenditures. He finds that being exempted from paying for care and having access to private or employment-based health insurance significantly reduces the risk increasing a catastrophic OOP expenditures. However, when other costs related to health-care seeking were included-such as transportation, food, and other costs, the study finds that the probability of suffering from catastrophic health care related expenditures actually increases. Thus when examining only the OOP expenditures at the point of services, the effect of reduction in price dominates, and these seems to be greater financial protection. However, when the other costs related to health seeking are included, the conclusions are reversed (Giedion *et al.*, 2013).

Fund mobilization

There are number of strategies available to a household to support OOP health expenditure like using cash and existing savings, sale of assets, loans, income diversification, wage labour, etc. There are other time-coping strategies like intra-house labour substitution, changing the capital labour mix of production, hiring labour, free community labour etc (Sauerborn *et al.,* 1996). Out of the above mentioned strategies depleting savings, selling productive assets (livestock etc.) and taking loan at higher cost affects the household in longer run. Parmar *et al.* (2012) in their study mentioned that in the absence of adequate savings household resort to selling productive assets like live stock, which could have asserted the household in agricultural production (*e.g.*, Ox or Donkeys). Moreover, loss of livestock leads to loss of their produce, *e.g.*, milk that could have been used for self-consumption or sold in the market (*e.g.*, cow, goat etc.) or people with inadequate amount of income face very hardships while repaying the borrowed amount, which result in reduction of essential consumption, which in turn have adverse impact on health.

There are hardly a couple of studies which have evaluated the impact of health insurance on Assets, borrowing etc. Parmar *et al.* (2012) in their study attempted to find out whether community based health insurance protect household assets in rural Burkina Faso, Africa. Within the Assets, durable goods and livestock were considered for evaluation. Finally impact has been evaluated by finding out the effect of insuring an additional member in the household on per capita household assets. All the models used in the study (OLS, 2OLS & FE) provide evidence that the community based health insurance scheme in the Nauna district protected household assets. Specifically the models predicted that Community Based Health Insurance (CBHI) significantly increased household assets. This is not surprising, given that the scheme is highly subsidized. Benefits of being insured outweigh the cost of purchasing the insurance. The researchers themselves have realized the lack of other studies and stated that there is no other study that has analyzed the impact of CBHI on household assets, therefore becomes difficult for the researcher to bench mark these results with other studies. Aggarwal (2010) in her impact study also studied financial protection of insured and used borrowings/sale of assets resulting from medical payments as an indicator of financial protection. Results of the study revealed that health payments caused significantly less indebtness/sale of assets which have the most pronounced impoverishing effects. The results are more positive in case of surgical procedures. However result is not so significant for hospitalization a maternal case. In fact, inpatient treatments other then surgery resulted in increase of borrowing for the Yeshweni health group. Taking into account the availability of a few studies in this area, there is a need of further research as also realized by Parmar *et al.* (2012) and Radermacher *et al.* (2012).

Income and consumption smoothing

Severe adverse health event imposes the twin challenges of both coping with the expenses of the events in question and continuing to meet on-going household needs (Radernacher *et al.*, 2012). Under such pressing circumstances, low-income people may pursue an undesirable action like eating less or less nutritious food. By reducing the financial burden of shocks, micro insurance aims to enable policy holders to maintain their incomes and standards of living in times of crises (Radermacher *et al.*, 2012).

OBJECTIVES

1. To study the impact of health micro insurance on inpatient healthcare expenditure.
2. To assess the incidence of catastrophic expenditure among the policy holders as compared to non-policy holders.
3. To critically evaluate the source of finances availed by the households for supporting healthcare expenditure.
4. To study the spillover effects of the program (RSBY) on out-patients treatment side variables.

RESEARCH METHODOLOGY

Data Collection

Data collection was done using a pre-tested and structured interview schedule beneficiaries of RSBY which is Government of India sponsored health coverage scheme which was launched on 1st April 2008 by Ministry of Labour and Employment to provide health insurance cover to BPL and other unorganized sector workers. A total of 450 respondents have been involved in the survey, consisting of 150 RSBY enrolled and 300 not-covered under RSBY.

Sampling Design

The impact of micro insurance is assessed by using a quasi-experimental survey design, which required comparison of a 'treatment' group, consisting of programme participants, to a 'control' group of non-participants. Participant group of respondents were selected after receiving list of insured households, where at least one hospitalization was occurred and where the household has received the treatment, from the state nodal agencies. Each non participant household for comparison was selected from the same locality where a participant household was located after taking the due care that the characteristics of participant and non-participant should be similar.

Participant group of respondents were selected through a multi-stage sampling method. In the first stage, three North-Indian states namely Himachal Pradesh, Punjab and Haryana were selected as being at the extreme of North-India. Jammu and Kashmir State was not selected as RSBY is not functional in the state.

In the second stage, one district from each state was selected after giving due consideration to performance of RSBY in all districts of a particular state. Kangra was selected from Himachal Pradesh. In Punjab Amritsar was selected, and Rohtak was selected from Haryana. The sample composition is given in Table 1.

Table 1: Sample composition.

Sl. no.	*State (District)*	*No. of insured HH*	*No. of uninsured HH*	*Total*
1	Himachal Pradesh (Kangra)	50	100	150
2	Punjab (Amritsar)	50	100	150
3	Haryana (Rohtak)	50	100	150
	Total Households			450

In the third stage of sampling 4 blocks showing more enrolment were selected from each district. After considering rural urban differences, out of 4 blocks two are rural and two from urban blocks.

In the fourth stage, data was collected from the treatment and control group respondents from each block, representing a district and ultimately a state.

Period of the Study

The present study has collected the data from the respondents pertaining to the year 2013-14.

Implementation of propensity score matching

Propensity score matching method is used for the impact evaluation of a programme. The basic idea is to find in a group of non-participants those individuals who are similar to the participants in all relevant observable characteristics X. That being done, differences in outcomes of the control (untreated) group and of participants (treated) can be attributed to the programme. This essentially means that the outcomes of members are compared with the potential outcomes of untreated households had they been members of the programme. More specifically, if P=1 for treated group and =0 for untreated group, then the average treatment effect on treated (ATT) on an outcome variable Y is

$$ATT= E\,(Y1-Y0\,|\,P=1),$$

which means,

$$ATT= E\,(Y1\,|\,P=1)-E(Y0\,|\,P=1)$$

While data on E (Y1 | P=1) are available from the programme participants, estimation of the counter factual $E\ (Y0\,|\,P=1)$ is based on the assumption that after adjusting for observable differences, the mean of the potential outcome is the same for P = 1 and P = 0.

Application of PSM technique involves number of steps and these have been explained below.

Estimating the propensity score

When estimating the propensity score, two choices have to be made. The first one concerns the model to be used for the estimation, and the second one the variables to be included in this model. Little advice is available regarding which functional form to use. For the binary treatment case, where we estimate the probability of participation *vs.* non-participation, logit and probit models usually yield similar results. Hence is not too critical, even though the logit distribution has more density mass in the bounds (Caliendo & Kopeinig, 2008). The present study has used logistic regression to calculate propensity score for matching. After reviewing the literature on the factors determining the demand for micro insurance and particularly health micro insurance, number of factors has been identified to be included in the model. Most studies focus on individual/household specific factors such as income, nature of their economic activity, demographic patterns, age structure, health patterns, social status, education, and personal preferences. However socio economic contexts within which households live cannot be ignored. The study therefore has explicitly taken into account area specific characteristics. They include health infrastructure, distance from the nearest health facility and transport facilities. The 'statistical significance approach' was adopted in the final selection of model. The study has started with few important variables and then added new variables to test their performance. Variables were kept if they were statistically significant and increased the prediction rates notably.

Balancing test

It is believed that imposing the common support restriction in the estimation of propensity scores improves the quality of the estimates. But there are also arguments against imposing this restriction. Lechner (2001) for instance, argues that besides reducing the sample considerably, imposing the restriction may lose high quality matches at the boundary of the common support region. However, following the standard practice to limit comparisons to a subset of cases lying on the common support of propensity scores, we also dropped households off the common support. We thus restricted our balancing test in the common support region with a trim value of 5%.

Assessing the quality of matching

For assessing the quality of matching, the situation before and after matching needs to be compared to check if there remain any differences after conditioning on the propensity score. Various indicators of assessing the quality of matching are available in the literature (Caliendo & Kopeinig, 2008). The present study has used the mean absolute standardized bias (Rosenbaum & Rubin, 1985; Lechner, 1999; Sianesi, 2004) and pseudo R^2 (Sianesi, 2004) (Table 2).

Table 2: Result of the mean absolute standardized bias and Pseudo R^2 tests.

Measure		
Standardized bias	Pre matching mean bias	22.4
	Post matching mean bias	17.8
	Absolute change in bias	4.6
	Change (%)	20.53
Pseudo R^2	Pre matching Pseudo R^2	0.338
	Pre matching likelihood Ch^2	193.46
	Chi sq	0.00
	Post matching Pseudo R^2	0.081
	Post matching likelihood Ch^2	32.84
	Chi sq	0.00
	Change (%)	76.03

The results here reveal that matching for the present study has been able to reduce the mean bias to the extent of 20.53% and pseudo-R^2 also shows a considerable fall, setting a sound base for using propensity score matching.

Assessing common support region

ATT (Average Treatment Effect on Treated) and ATE (Average Treatment Effect) are defined only in the region of common support hence; an important step is to check the overlap and the region of common support between treatment and comparison group. The simple way is to visually analyze the density distribution of the propensity scores in both groups (Lechner, 2001). The present study has imposed common support restriction (Table 3) with a trim of 5%. The Fig. 1 shows the propensity score density distribution.

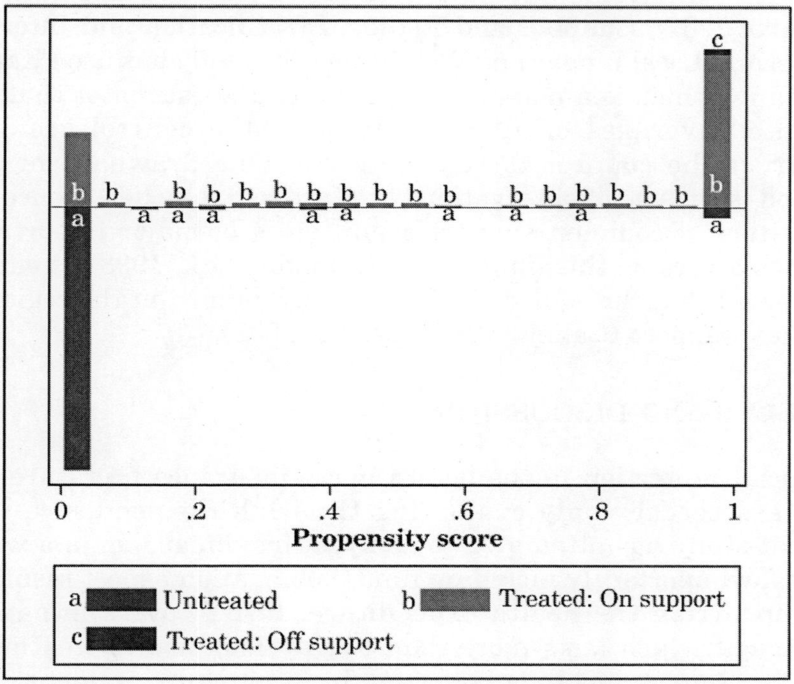

Fig. 1. Propensity score histogram.

Table 3: Showing households under common support.

Psmatch2: Treatment assignment	*Psmatch2 common support*		*Total*
	Off support	*On support*	
Untreated	0	300	300
Treated	3	147	150
Total	3	447	450

From the propensity score graph and table showing common support restriction results, it is clear that most of the households fall within the common support region, thus provides the sufficient reason for using ATT.

Choosing a matching algorithm

There are different matching estimators in PSM like Nearest Neighbor (NN), Calipher and Radius, Stratification and Interval, Kernel and Local Linear and Weighting. The study has used Kernel matching, which is a non-parametric matching estimator that use weighted averages of all individuals in the control group to construct the counter factual outcome. One drawback of this method is the use of observations that are bad matches. Hence the imposition of common support condition is of major importance and has overcome this limitation (Heckman *et al.,* 1998) as earlier mentioned that the ATT and ATE are only defined in the region of common support (Caliendo & Kopeinig, 2008).

RESULTS AND DISCUSSION

Financial protection in the health micro insurance literature has been assessed by only evaluating the health expenditure. The present study has attempted to analyze this dimension in a wider angle, by importantly including fund mobilization aspect resulting from incurring the health expenditure. RSBY covers in-patient (treatment which lasts more than twenty four hours) treatment; therefore impact has to be assessed for in-patient treatment only. An attempt has been made to additionally present the data related to the out-patient treatment variables as well to assess the spillover effects on the out-patient treatment indicators.

Health Expenditure

Out of pocket expenditure

Health expenditure being a crucial aspect of financial protection has always remained a focus of assessment for the researchers. The present study has attempted to through a light on two important issues within health expenditure and these are *Out-of-pocket expenditure* (OOPE) and *Incidence of Catastrophic Expenditure.* Table 4 clearly shows that Households (HHs) with RSBY have incurred an average of Rs. 1418.17 OOPE per hospitalization, where as it is Rs 8005.75 for the HHs without RSBY and therefore shows a huge difference.

Out-patient (where patients are treated without being admitted in a hospital) OOPE as expected does not differ too much for the treatment and control HHs, but still HHs with RSBY show a lower out-patient OOPE per visit, which is because the people with RSBY have developed a habit of visiting government hospitals for treatment, which might be the reason for lower outpatient OOPE.

Table 4: Showing out-of-pocket expenditure per hospitalization / healthcare visit.

Variable	***Control***		***Treatment***	
	Mean	***St. dev.***	***Mean***	***St. dev.***
In-patient OOPE per hospitalization	8005.75	10183.7	1418.17	3331.07
Out-patient OOPE per healthcare visit	243.00	247.6383	217.65	225.62

Incidence of catastrophic expenditure

Out-of-Pocket Expenditure (OOPE) becomes catastrophic when it absorbs a considerable amount of annual household income (often defined as 10 percent) (Radermacher *et al.,* 2012). Table 5 shows the incidence of catastrophic expenditure. Among the sampled RSBY households, 4.67% have incurred catastrophic healthcare expenditure where-as it is 53.67% in case of households not covered under RSBY, which clearly highlights a protective shield.

Table 5: Showing the incidence of catastrophic expenditure (In-patient treatment).

Incidence of in-patient CE	***Status of sampled household***		***Total***
	Control	***Treated***	
Not incurred CE	139 (46.33%)	143 (95.33%)	282 (62.67%)
Incurred CE	161 (53.67%)	7 (4.67%)	168 (37.33%)
Total	300 (100%)	150 (100%)	450 (100%)

Incidence of catastrophic expenditure related to the out-patient treatment does not show a larger difference between treatment and control group (Table 6). The marginal difference here is because of the larger OOPE per visit for the control group.

Table 6: Shows the incidence of catastrophic expenditure (Out-patient treatment)

Incidence of out-patient CE	*Status of sampled household*		*Total*
	Control	*Treated*	
Not incurred CE	135 (45%)	85 (56.67%)	220 (48.89%)
Incurred CE	165 (55%)	65 (43.33%)	230 (51.11%)
Total	300 (100%)	150 (100%)	450 (100%)

Fund Mobilization

Poor households generally have three sources of finance to support healthcare expenditure and these are HH savings or HH income, borrowings, and in worst condition, sale of HH Assets. Table 7 shows that HHs have majorly used HH savings and HH savings plus borrowings as the source of finance to support in-patient healthcare expenditure. While comparing treatment and control group, it is revealed that 96% of the HHs with RSBY have used HH savings to support in-patient healthcare expenditure, whereas in case of HHs not-covered under RSBY, only 42.67% have used the HH savings for treatment. 54.67% of HHs among control group have raised borrowings which is only 3.34% in case of treatment group. Further 0.67% of the control group HHs have sold HH assets, whereas HHs under RSBY have not sold assets to support healthcare expenditure. For out-patient treatment, people mostly have relied upon their HH savings (Table 8).

After critical analysis, it has been understood that because of the coverage of health expenditure by RSBY, treatment group HHs were not compelled to use the costlier sources of finance, as they have not incurred the large healthcare expenditure like the HHs without RSBY.

Households raise money through borrowings which in most of the cases are interest based, hence further imposes financial burden on them. Table 9 shows that 59.17% of the HHs out of 169 HHs have paid interest on borrowings.

Table 7: Source of finance (In-patient treatment).

Source of finance to support in-patient treatment	***Status of sampled household***		***Total***
	Control	***Treated***	
HH savings (A)	128 (42.67%)	145 (96.67%)	273 (60.67%)
Raised borrowings (B)	26 (8.67%)	1 (0.67%)	27 (6%)
Sold household assets (C)	2 (0.67%)	0 (0%)	2 (0.44%)
D=A+B	138 (46%)	4 (2.67%)	142 (31.55%)
E=A+C	4 (1.33%)	0 (0%)	4 (0.88)
F=A+B+C	2 (0.67%)	0 (0%)	2 (0.44%)
Total	300 (100%)	150 (100%)	450 (100%)

Table 8: Source of finance (Out-patient treatment).

Source of finance to support out-patient treatment	***Status of sampled household***		***Total***
	Control	***Treated***	
HH savings (A)	280	139	419
Raised borrowings (B)	6	3	9
Sold household assets (C)	2	0	2
A+B	12	8	20
Total	300	150	450

Table 9: Type of borrowings (In-patient treatment).

Type of borrowing (in-patient)	***Status of sampled household***		***Total***
	Control	***Treated***	
Not incurred CE	135 (45%)	85 (56.67%)	220 (48.89%)
Interest based	98 (59.76%)	2 (40%)	100 (59.17%)
Non-interest based	66 (40.24%)	3 (60%)	69 (40.83%)
Total	164 (100%)	5 (100%)	169 (100%)

The percentage of interest-based borrowings for treatment and control group are 40% and 59% respectively. The reason for lesser percentage for the treatment group is that most of them were not required to raise huge amount of money because of RSBY coverage, hence have mostly managed the borrowings from friends, relatives and neighbors (Table 10).

Table 10: Type of borrowings (Out-patient treatment).

Type of borrowing (out-patient)	*Status of sampled household*		*Total*
	Control	*Treated*	
Interest based	10 (83.33%)	8 (80%)	18 (81.82%)
Non-interest based	2 (16.67%)	2 (20%)	4 (18.18%)
Total	12 (100%)	10 (100%)	22 (100%)

It has been found that most of the HHs in rural areas raise borrowings and pay interest on monthly basis, which is also a matter of concern. At average HHs paid interest at average 2% per month. HHs from control group at average have paid interest at 2.5% per month and HH from the treatment group have paid interest at 2% per month (Table 11).

The present study has further elaborated the sale of HH assets as a source of finance. It has been found that generally HHs are not compelled to sell their HH assets, still 8 are the HHs from the control group where sale of assets has happened. Further because of urgency people are compelled to sell their assets less than their market value. Table 12 shows that out of 8 HHs, 6 HH (75%) have reported incidence of loss from the sale of assets.

Table 11: Average rate of interest (monthly) at which borrowed.

Rate of interest	*Status of sampled household*	
	Control	*Treated*
	2.51%	2%

Table 12: Shows occurrence of loss on the sale of asset (In-patient treatment).

Occurrence of loss (in-patient)	*Status of sampled household*		*Total*
	Control	*Treated*	
0 (No loss)	2 (25%)	0 (0%)	2 (25%)
1 (loss)	6 (75%)	0 (0%)	6 (75%)
Total	8 (100%)	0 (0%)	8 (100%)

Additionally to mention 2 HHs from control group have sold HH assets for out-patient treatment, whereas such incidence has not been observed from the treatment group (Table 13).

Table 13: Shows occurrence of loss on the sale of asset (Out-patient treatment).

Occurrence of loss (out-patient)	*Status of sampled household*		*Total*
	Control	*Treated*	
0 (No loss)	2	0	2
1 (loss)	0	0	0
Total	2	0	2

The study has attempted to find out the type of HH assets being sold by the poor. Positively, it has been found that all the assets being sold were non-income generating. Thus HHs have not lost any asset as a source of income (Tables 14 & 15).

Table 14: Shows kind of asset sold (In-patient treatment).

Type of asset sold (in-patient)	*Status of sampled household*		*Total*
	Control	*Treated*	
Income generating	0 (0%)	0 (0%)	0 (0%)
Non-income generating	8 (100%)	0 (0%)	8 (100%)
Total	8 (100%)	0(0%)	8(100%)

Table 15: Shows kind of asset sold (Out-patient treatment).

Type of asset sold (out-patient)	*Status of sampled household*		*Total*
	Control	*Treated*	
Income generating	0 (0%)	0 (0%)	0 (0%)
Non-income generating	2 (100%)	0 (0%)	2 (100%)
Total	2 (100%)	0 (0%)	2 (100%)

Increased healthcare expenditure often disturbs essential non-medical consumption in a poor household. People are forced to reduce essential HH expenditure, like, expenditure on food, children education, clothing etc. Table 16 shows that 40.67% of the HHs reported reduction of essential consumption due to increased healthcare expenditure, but it is only 15.34% in case of HHs under treatment group, which highlights consumption smoothing effect of health micro insurance.

Table 16: Shows impact of illness on essential household consumption.

Household consumption	*Status of sampled household*		*Total*
	Control	*Treated*	
Reduced	122 (40.67%)	23 (15.34%)	145 (32.23%)
Remained same	178 (59.34%)	127 (84.67%)	305 (67.78%)
Total	300 (100%)	150 (100%)	450 (100%)

Results Based on Propensity Score Matching

Health micro insurance basically aims at reducing health expenses for the poor, thereby protecting them from adverse financial implication. In-patient Out-of-Pocket Expenditure (OOPE) per hospitalization shows an average treatment effect (ATT) of Rs 6566.33 on treated (RSBY households) and this difference is significant at 5% α level, hence rejecting the null hypothesis that there is no significant difference between households covered under RSBY and not-covered under RSBY in terms of in-patient OOPE per hospitalization.

At average treatment group households have 2.78% of monthly household income as in-patient health expenditure, whereas it is 17.14% for the control group households. ATT value is 14.855 which mean RSBY has been able to reduce at average 14.855% of in-patient monthly expenditure out of average monthly income of the households under RSBY. Here in this case also the null hypothesis is rejected that there is no significant difference between treatment and control group households in terms of incidence of catastrophic expenditure as the p value is < 0.05.

As mentioned earlier RSBY by indirectly improving the standard of availing out-patient healthcare treatment as by developing a habit of visiting the public hospitals and avoiding the informal sources of treatment reduces the outpatient treatment expenditure as well. But the results (Table 17) here do not show a statistically significant difference and therefore does not allow the researcher to conclude that RSBY has been able to reduce the outpatient expenditure for policy holders.

Table 17: Differences in financial protection indicators based on propensity score matching (Kernel method).

Variable	*Treated*	*Control*	*Bootstrapped ATT*	*S.E*	*T -stat*	*P value*
In-patient OOPE per hospitalization.	1459.61	7959.19	–6566.332	1152.209	–5.70	0.000
In-patient catastrophic health expenditure (Percentage of monthly HH income).	2.78	17.14	–14.855	3.324	–4.47	0.000
Out-patient OOPE per visit.	221.66	225.69	-6.352	34.908	-0.18	0.856
Out-patient catastrophic health expenditure (Percentage of monthly HH income).	13.93	14.07	-0.295	3.038	-0.10	0.923

CONCLUSIONS

Health micro insurance provides a promising protective mechanism against adverse health shocks which often have pressing financial implications. Rashtriya Swasthya Bima Yojana (RSBY) being a government of India sponsored health coverage scheme has been successful in providing the financial protection by reducing health expenditures of policyholders significantly. It has restricted the poor households to use costlier sources of finances by providing the financial support. Poor households are less compelled to sell their household assets. It has helped in smoothing the essential household consumption in times of health shock. Although the out-patient treatment expenditure has shown a marginal difference between treatment and control group households, but the results are not statistically significant. As focusing inpatient treatment, RSBY seems to have been able to provide financial protection to the households under poverty.

REFERENCES

Aggarwal, A. (2010). "Impact evaluation of India's Yeshasvini' community - Based health insurance programme". *In: Health Economics*, 19(Supplement 1): 5–35.

Ahmed, S., Mbaisi, J., Moko, D., & Ngonzi, A. (2005). "Health is wealth: How low-income people finance health care". *In: Journal of International Development*, 17(3): 383–396.

Arhin-Tenkorang, D. (2001). Mobilizing resources for health: The case for user fees revisited (No. 81). Center for International Development at Harvard University.

Asfaw, A. (2003). "Cost of illness, demand for medical care, and the prospect of community health insurance programs in the rural areas of Ethiopia (Frankfurt).

Bane, Mary Jo & Ellwood David T. (1983). "Slipping Into and Out of Poverty: The Dynamics of Spells". *National Bureau of Economic Research Working Paper* No. 1199 (November).

Banerjee Abhijit, Duflo Esther, Glennerster Rachel & Cynthia Kinnan (2013). The Miracle of Microfinance? Evidence from a randomized evaluation. NBER Working Paper 18950.

Bauhoff Sebastian, Hotchkiss David & Smith Owen (2010). "The impact of medical insurance for the poor in Georgia: A regression discontinuity approach". *Health Economics.*

Bonnevay, S., Dror, D., Duru, G., & Lamure, M. (2002). "A model of microinsurance and reinsurance", *In:* Dror, D., & Preker, A. (*eds.*), A new approach to sustainable community health financing (Washington, D.C. & Geneva, World Bank & ILO), pp. 153–186.

Brown, W., & Churchill, C.F. (1999). Providing insurance to low income households — part I: A Primer on insurance principles and products, microenterprise best practices. Bethesda: Development Alternatives Inc.

Brown, W., Green, C., & Lindquist, G. (2000). A cautionary note for microfinance institutions and donors considering developing microinsurance products, microenterprise best practices. Bethesda: Development Alternatives Inc.

Caliendo, M., & Kopeinig, S. (2008). Some practical guidance for the implementation of propensity score matching. *Journal of Economic Surveys*, 22(1): 31–72.

Chankova, S., Sulzbach, S., & Diop, S. (2008). "Impact of mutual health organizations: Evidence from West Africa". *In*: *Health Policy and Planning*, 23(4): 264–276.

Churchill, C. (2006). "What is insurance for the poor", *In*: Churchill, C. (*ed.*), Protecting the poor a microinsurance compendium, International Labour Organisation, pp. 12–24.

Churchill, C. (2006). What is insurance for the poor? *In*: Churchill, C. (*ed.*), Protecting the poor. A microinsurance compendium. Munich: ILO, Geneva and Munich Re Foundation.

Churchill, C. (2007). "Insuring the low-income market: Challenges and solutions for commercial insurers". *In:* Geneva Papers on Risk and Insurance. *Issues and Practice*, 32(3): 401–412.

Churchill, C., Liber, D., McCord, M.J., & Roth, J. (2003). Making insurance work for microfinance institutions — A technical guide to developing and delivering microinsurance. Geneva: ILO.

Cuevas Facundo & Parker, Susan W. (2011). "The Impact of Health Insurance on Use, Spending, and Health in Indonesia". *In*: The impact of health insurance on low-and middle-income countries. Escobar Maria-Luisa, Griffin, Charles C., & Paul Shaw, R. (*eds.*) Washington, DC: The Brookings Institution Press.

Dekker, M., & Wilma, A. (2009). "Can health insurance be the magic bullet? The case of Microcare in Uganda (Netherlands, African Studies Center Info Sheet).

Dercon, S. (2004). Growth and shocks: Evidence from rural Ethiopia. *Journal of Development Economics*, 74(2): 309–329.

Derriennic, Y., Wolf, K., & Kiwanuka-Mukiibi, P. (2005). "An assessment of community-based health financing activities in Uganda, The Partners for Health Reformplus Project (Bethesda, MD, Abt Associates).

Develtere, P., & Fonteneau, B. (2001). "Member-Based Organizations for Social Protection in Health in Developing Countries", Katholieke Universiteit Leuven, Mimeo.

Diop, F.P., Sulzbach, S., & Chankova, S. (2006). "The impact of mutual health organizations on social inclusion, address to health care and household income protection: Evidence from Ghana, Senegal and Mali, Partners for Health Reformplus project (Bethesda, MD, Abt Associates).

Dodd, R., & Munck, L. (2002). "Dying for change: Poor people's experience of health and ill health (Geneva, World Health Organization, World Bank, Voices of the Poor).

Dror (2007). "Why 'one size fits all' health insurance products are unsuitable for low-income persons in the informal economy in India". *In*: *Asian Economic Review*, 49(1): 1–11.

Dror (2008). "Community-based micro health insurance as an enabler of solidarity and self-help amongst poor communities". *In*: *Microfinance Focus*, 2(8).

Dror, D. (2001). "Reinsurance of health insurance for the informal sector". *In*: *Bulletin of the World Health Organization*, 79(7): 672–678.

Dror, D., & Jacquier, C. (1999). "Micro-insurance: Extending health insurance to the excluded". *International 'Social Security Review*, 52(1): 71.

Ekman, P. (2007). *Emotions revealed: Recognizing faces and feelings to improve communication and emotional life.* Macmillan.

Fields, Gary S. (1993). "Poverty and income distribution: Data for measuring poverty and inequality changes in the developing countries". *Journal of Development Economics,* 44.

Fischer, K., & Qureschi, Z. (2006). Cooperatives and insurance: The mutual advantage. *In:* Churchill, C. (*ed.*), protecting the poor. A microinsurance compendium. Munich: ILO, Geneva and Munich Refoundation.

Fonteneau, B., & Galland, B. (2006). The community-based model: Mutual health organizations in Africa. *In:* Churchill, C. (*ed.*), protecting the poor. A microinsurance compendium. Munich: ILO, Geneva and Munich Re Foundation.

Franco, L.M., Diop, F.P., Burgert, C., Kelly, A.G., Makinen, M., & Siampara, C.H.T. (2008). "Effects of mutual health organizations on use of priority health care services in urban and rural Mali: A case-control study". *Bulletin of the World Health Organization,* 86(11): 830–838.

Galarraga, O., Sosa-Rubi, S.G., Salinas-Rodriguez, A., & Sesma-Vazquez, S. (2010). "Health insurance for the poor: Impact on catastrophic and out-of-pocket health expenditures in Mexico." *Eur. J. Health Econ.,* 11(5): 437–447.

Gertler, P., & Gruber, J. (2002). "Insuring Consumption against illness". *American Economic Review*, 92(1): 51–70.

Gertler, P., Levine, D.I., & Moretti, E. (2009). "Do Microfinance Programs Help Families Insure Consumption against illness". *Health Economics,* 18: 257–273.

Gertler, Paul J., Sebastian Martinez & Celhay Pablo (2011). "Impact Evaluation of Maternal Child Provincial Health Investment Project in Argentina – Plan Nacer".

Giedion Ursula, Beatriz Yadira Díaz & Eduardo Andrés Alfonso (2007). "The Impact of Subsidized Health Insurance on Access, Utilization and Health Status: The Case of Colombia." World Bank, Washington, DC.

Giedion, U., Alfonso, E.A., & Díaz, Y. (2013). "The Impact of Universal Coverage Schemes in the Developing World: A Review of the Existing Evidence", Universal Health Coverage Studies Series (UNICO), The World Bank, UNICO Studies Series No. 25.

Hamid Syed Abdul, Roberts Jennifer & Paul Mosley (2011). "Evaluating the Health Effects of Micro Health Insurance Placement: Evidence from Bangladesh". *World Development,* 39(3): 399–411.

Harris, J.E., & Sosa-Rubi, S.G. (2009). "Impact of 'Seguro Popular' on Prenatal Visits in Mexico, 2002–2005: Latent Class Model of Count Data with a Discrete Endogenous Variable".

Heckman, J.J., Ichimura, H., & Todd, P. (1998). Matching as an econometric evaluation estimator. *The Review of Economic Studies,* 65(2): 261–294.

Jalan Jyotsna & Ravallion Martin (1999). "Are the poor less well insured? Evidence on Vulnerability to Income Risk in Rural China". *Journal of Development Economics,* 58: 61–81.

Jowert, M., Contoyannis, P., & Vinh, N.D. (2003). "The impact of Public Voluntary Health Insurance on Private Health Expenditures in Vietnam". *Social Science & Medicine*, 56: 333–342.

Jowert, M., Deolalikar, A., & Martinsson, P. (2004). "Health insurance and treatment seeking behaviour: Evidence from a low-income country". *Health Economics*, 13: 845–857.

Jutting, J. (2004). "Do community-based health insurance schemes improve poor people's access to health care? Evidence from Rural Senegal". *In: World Development*, 32(2): 273–288.

Khan, Abdullah A., & Bhardwaj, Surinder M. (1994). "Access to Health Care". *Evaluation and the Health Professions,* 17(1): 60–76.

King Gary, Emmanuela Gakidou, Kosuke Imai, Jason Lakin, Moore, Ryan T., Clayton Nall *et al.* (2009). "Public Policy for the Poor? A Randomised Assessment of the Mexican Universal Health Insurance Programme". *The Lancet*, 373(9673): 1447–1454.

Kiwara, A. (2007). "Group premiums in micro health insurance experiences from Tanzania". *In*: *East African Journal of Public Health*, 4(I): 28–32.

Kruk, M.E., Goldmann, E., & Galea, S. (2009). Borrowing and selling to pay for health care in low-and middle-income countries. *Health Affairs*, 28(4): 1056–1066.

Leatherman, S., Christensen, L.J., & Holtz, J. (2012). Innovations and barriers in health microinsurance, *In*: Churchill, C., & Matul, M. (*eds.*), Protecting the poor. A microinsurance compendium, Vol 2. Munich: ILO, Geneva and Munich Re Foundation.

Lechner, M. (1999). Earnings and employment effects of continuous off-the-job training in East Germany after unification. *Journal of Business & Economic Statistics*, 17(1): 74–90.

Lechner, M. (2001). Identification and estimation of causal effects of multiple treatments under the conditional independence assumption. *In:* Econometric evaluation of labour market policies, Physica, Heidelberg, pp. 43–58.

Lei Xiaoyan & Lin Wanchuan (2009). "The New Cooperative Medical Scheme in Rural China: Does more Coverage mean more Service and Better Health?" *Health Economics*, 18(S2): S25–S46.

Marek, T., O'Farrell, C., Yamamoto, C., & Zable, I. (2005). "Trends and opportunities in public-private partnerships to improve health service delivery in Africa, Africa Region Human Development Working Paper 33646 (Washington, D.C., World Bank).

Marek, T., Yamamoto, C., & Ruster, J. (2003). "Private health: Policy and Regulatory Options for Private Participation, Public Policy for the Private Sector Note Number 265 (Washington, D.C., World Bank).

McCord, M.J. (2006). The partner-agent model: Challenges and opportunities. *In:* Churchill, C. (*ed.*), Protecting the poor. A microinsurance compendium. Munich: ILO, Geneva and Munich Re Foundation.

McCord, M.J. (2007b). "Supplying Health Microinsurance: Lessons from East Africa". *In: International Journal of Public Administration*, 30(8): 737–764.

McCord, M.J., & Osinde, S. (2005). "Reducing Vulnerability: The Supply of Health Microinsurance in East Africa". *In*: *Journal of International Development*, 17(3): 327–381.

McLaughlin, Catherine G., & Leon Wyszewianski (2002). "Access to Care: Remembering Old Lessons". *Health Services Research,* 37(6): 1441–1443.

Morduch Jonathan (1995). "Poverty and Vulnerability". *American Economic Review,* 84(2): 221–25.

Morduch Jonathan (1999). Between the State and the Market: Can Informal Insurance Patch the Safety Net? *World Bank Research Observer,* 14(2): 187–207.

Nguyen, N.T., Nguyen, X.M.T., Lane, J., & Wang, P. (2011). Relationship between obesity and diabetes in a US adult population: Findings from the National Health and Nutrition Examination Survey, 1999–2006. *Obesity Surgery*, 21(3): 351–355.

Parmar, D., Reinhold, S., Souares, A., Savadogo, G., & Sauerborn, R. (2012). Does Community-Based Health Insurance Protect Household Assets? Evidence from Rural Africa. *Health Services Research*, 47(2): 819–839.

Radermacher, R., McGowan, H., & Dercon, S. (2012). What is the impact of microinsurance? *In: Protecting the poor: A microinsurance compendium.* Volume II, Churchill, C., & Matul, M. (*eds.*). Geneva: International Labour Organization, pp. 59–82.

Rosenbaum, P.R., & Rubin, D.B. (1985). Constructing a control group using multivariate matched sampling methods that incorporate the propensity score. *The American Statistician*, 39(1): 33–38.

Roth, K., McCord, M.J., & Liber, D. (2007). "The Landscape of microinsurance in the world's 100 poorest countries (Micro-insurance Centre).

Roth, K., Radermacher, R., & Panda Pradeep (2014). "Core outcomes, impacts, and indicators for microinsurance", *In*: Radermacher, R., & Roth, K. (*eds.*), Practical Guide to Impact Assessments in Microinsurance, Microinsurance Network.

Sabri, B. (2003). "Healthcare financing in the African countries of the Eastern Mediterranean. Telephone interview, May 2011.

Sauerborn, R., Adams, A., & Hien, M. (1996). Household strategies to cope with the economic costs of illness. *Social Science & Medicine*, 43(3): 291–301.

Schneider, P., & Diop, F. (2001). "Synopsis of results on the impact of community-based health insurance on financial accessibility to health care in Rwanda", Health, Nutrition and Population Discussion Paper No. 28903 (Washington, D.C., World Bank).

Sepehri, A., Sarma, S., & Simpson, W. (2006). "Does non-profit health insurance reduce financial burden? Evidence from the Vietnam Living Standards survey panel". *In*: *Health Economics*, 15(6): 603–616.

Sianesi, B. (2004). An evaluation of the Swedish system of active labor market programs in the 1990s. *Review of Economics and Statistics*, 86(1): 133–155.

Simith, K., & Sulzbach, S. (2008). "Community-based health insurance and access to maternal health services: Evidence from three West African countries". *In*: *Social Science and Medicine,* 66: 2460–2473.

Sohail Agha (2011). "Impact of a maternal health voucher scheme on institutional delivery among low income women in Pakistan". *Reproductive Health,* 8(1): 10.

Suryahadi Asep & Sudarno Sumarto (2001). "The Chronic Poor, the Transient Poor, and the Vulnerable in Indonesia before and after the Crisis". *SMERU Working Paper*, May.

Thornton, Rebecca L., Hatt, Laurel E., Field, Erica M., Islam Mursaleena, Freddy Solís Diaz & González Martha Azucena (2010). "Social Security Health Insurance for the Informal Sector in Nicaragua: A Randomized Evaluation". *Health Economics,* 19(S1): 181–206

Townsend, Robert M. (1994). Risk and insurance in village India. *Econometrica*, 62(3): 539–91.

Wagstaff Adam & Magnus Lindelow (2008). "Can Insurance Increase Financial Risk? The Curious Case of Health Insurance in China". *Journal of Health Economics,* 27(4): 990–1005.

Wagstaff Adam & Menno Pradhan (2005). "Health Insurance Impacts on Health and Nonmedical Consumption in a Developing Country", Working Paper Series.

Wagstaff Adam & Shengchao Yu (2007). "Do Health Sector Reforms have their Intended Impacts? The World Bank's Health VIII Project in Gansu Province, China". *Journal of Health Economics*, 26(3): 505–535.

Wagstaff Adam, Magnus Lindelow, Gao Jun, Ling Xu & Juncheng Qian (2009). "Extending Health Insurance to the Rural Population: An Impact Evaluation of China's New Cooperative Medical Scheme". *Journal of Health Economics,* 28(1): 1–19.

Wang Hong, Yip Winnie, Zhang Licheng & Hsiao, William C. 2009. "The impact of rural mutual health care on health status: Evaluation of a social experiment in rural China". *Health Economics*, 18(S2): S65–S82.

Wirtz, V.J. (2012). "Heterogeneous Effects of Health Insurance on Out-of-Pocket Expenditure on Medicines in Mexico". *Value in Health*, 15: 593–603. Available online at *www.sciencedirect.com*

World Bank (2001). *World Development Report 2000/2001: Attacking Poverty.* Washington, D.C.

Yip Winnie, Wang Hong & Hsiao William (2008). "The Impact of Rural Mutual Health Care on Access to Care: Evaluation of a Social Experiment in Rural China".

12

Influence of Demographics on the Perceptual Factors of E-Commerce: A Study of TASK Members

SALSABEEL NAZIR[1]*

ABSTRACT

Regardless of the norm that E-commerce is adopted in developed countries, in developing countries it's still an emerging trend. Brick and Mortar companies are finding ways to be visible virtually especially travel and tourism business. E-commerce act as a meditating channel for the Tour and Travel Operators as such it's crucial for survival of their business. Demographical perspective for the adoption of E-commerce is necessary as such this study takes into accounts few demographics and thus studying their impact on the E-commerce adoption factors. Respondents for the study are sourced from J&K states which are the members of TASK association. The study found that tourism related knowledge / training do have a significant impact on E-commerce's perceptual factors, while as qualification doesn't hold the bearing on the said factors. Finally the limitations of the study are put forth creating a scope for further research.

***Key words*:** E-commerce, Perceptual factors, Demographics, J&K, TASK.

INTRODUCTION

E-commerce also known as Electronic-Commerce is the mode of doing business online using a network of computers and internet.

[1] Department of Management Studies, Central University of Kashmir, J&K.
**Corresponding author:* E-mail: salsabeel187@gmail.com

It is the new trend in business since last decade. Companies in the developed world have already shifted their business to E-commerce and now this wave has touched various business sectors progressively in the developing world as well. It operates in various market segments in the form of B2B, B2C, B2G, C2C etc. as it offers tremendous advantages to the business and other stakeholders in the form of low cost and manpower, global reach, efficient utilization of space, etc. Travel and Tourism sector is no different as it is also influenced by E-commerce technology. Earlier a huge involvement of manpower was required for conducting business in this sector but since the invasion of internet and websites, many avenues are available for both customers as well as business holders. Customers can now on their own book their tickets and plan trips by contacting online travel portals and visit different hotel websites. It saves the psychological and monetary cost to them. On the other hand, Tour Operators and Travel Agents expanded their business channels using the internet and owning virtual websites.

E-commerce in Tour and Travel acts as a transactional channel. It has created re-intermediation in this sector. From the supplier's point of view, it provides them with an opportunity to offer their products and services across the globe 24*7 by updating the pricing policies, product, tour and ticket offers, holiday packages etc. The role of Tour and Travel Operators as middlemen has been eliminated by the involvement of internet causing disintermediation. The basic root causing the disintermediation can be the Internet (Inkpen, 1998). As per Barnett and Standing (2001) the introduction of websites enables the travellers to avoid the tour operators and other suppliers' altogether. However, they also postulated in their paper that simple trips can be planned online; complex tours require traditional Tour and Travel Operators as they become cumbersome when dealt *via* web system. For maintaining a competitive place in the high-tech world, it's necessary for them to provide round the clock updated product information services, value-added services, integrate with other large travel agencies in order to penetrate the market (Law, Leung & Wong, 2004) and make most of the internet services.

LITERATURE REVIEW

In India, travel sector was the first in adopting technology which later snowballed in other sectors. Remarkable studies have been conducted in the past to understand the drivers, benefits, and challenges for E-commerce adoption in diversified sectors. For an organization to adopt the technology, challenges from various contexts are to be scrutinized like technological, environmental and organizational. Same is the case with Tour and Travel Agent‘s business. As for them, they face competition from various sources in the form of globalization and deregulation policies, increasing customer needs and also from customers side as now they have become more knowledgeable and accustomed to the upcoming dynamic technologies (Lam & Cheung, 2009). They are the one in danger due to the technological innovations and decommissioning. The internet and other information technology has diminished their role by creating online travel portals where customers bypass the traditional travel agents and book their tours and holidays themselves. The most basic channel in the travel distribution system consists of principals, intermediaries, and customers. Airlines, hoteliers, car rentals etc. are the principals which supply travel products to the customers. Travel Agents and Tour Operators on the other hand act as intermediaries which deliver the suppliers‘ travel product information to the customers and encourage them to purchase these products. They are also involved in handling queries and any kind of paper-works. Basically, travel agencies act as intermediaries between suppliers of travel services and customers (Dolnicar & Laesser, 2007).

Principals (airlines) → CRS or GDS → Travel agents → Customers

E-commerce technology has re-intermediated the role of Tour and Travel Operators. As per Mamaghani (2009) it has enhanced the economic growth of the country and provided various opportunities to the travel and tourism sector. The use of Information Technology enables them to provide customer information on real time basis. In the current scenario, the success of traditional Tour and Travel business depends upon how well they explore and make use of the available technology. For Tour and Travel Operators to recreate their place in the market they can provide value-added services to their customers, a trust which is difficult to create in online portals, customized products and packages and selecting, targeting and positioning the niche market.

However tremendous challenges are faced in E-commerce adoption as discussed by group of authors like insufficient knowledge and resources in its use (Rotchanakitumnuai & Speece, 2003) culture, expertise, resistance to change and resources (Bègin & Boisvert, 2002) fear of unknown, resistance to change, lack of knowledge in ICT and E-commerce, lack of management support and insecurity (Warden & Tunzelana, 2004) and complexity (Roger, 1995). Apart from this, various drivers for E-commerce adoption were mentioned in previous studies like Government involvement (Gibbs, Kraemer & Dedrick, 2003) pool of technologies available and in fit with the firm, relative advantage (increased sales, ease of communication with stakeholders etc.) (Bagale, 2014), (Baldwin, Lymer & Johnson, 2001) and competitive pressure (Zhu, Xu & Dedrick, 2003). All these drivers are considered as motivating factors for E-commerce adoption.

The acceptance of any technology is governed by few factors which various researchers have explained *via* TAM (Technology Acceptance Model). It explains the user's acceptance of technology in the form of perceived usefulness and perceived ease of use (Davis, 1989; Davis, Bagozzi & Warshaw, 1989). For a new technology to be adopted, the user should consider both ease of usefulness and ease of use. But as far as the role of demographics is concerned it‘s not much explored in this study, also the factors that influence the perceived usefulness and ease of use were not discussed, hence it is a relevant contribution to the existing literature to understand its influence on E-commerce technology.

Demographics play a crucial role in the adoption of an innovative technology as they are the main cause for digital divide. Factors like age, gender, qualification and income compose to this divide. Eminent studies have been conducted on the different demographic factors that influence the technology adoption. The education level of any person plays an important role in adopting any innovative technology. As per Baker, Al-Gahtani and Hubona (2007) education is a salient factor influencing employee‘s behaviour and attitude when it comes to technology adoption. It implies that employees know when and how to use that technology when they possess such qualification. Therefore people having less education qualification will be having minimal access to the technology adoption. As per Lee (2010) education not only influences the use of internet but adoption of E-commerce as well. Apart from this gender of the person also affects the adoption of technology as male and female perceive differently even within themselves as well. Age is also considered as an important influencing factor for IT adoption, however many studies has put forth that age is not considered as much important and is closing over time.

This study focuses on the influence of demographic factors on the E-commerce adoption by Tour and Travel Operators of J&K state. Minimal research is conducted in this study as the major focus was shifted to the E-commerce's pros and cons, the rate of adoption and also its influence in different sectors. The Travel and Tourism sector was not much highlighted and worked upon especially in J&K state. So in order to overcome the research gap efforts were made to explore the influence of demographics on the perceptual factors of E-commerce, taking state's registered Tour and Travel Operators into consideration. Seeing the critical impact of demographics on E-commerce adoption, the study takes qualification, tourism knowhow and income level of Tour and Travel Operators into consideration to get more insight of their attitude on demographic grounds.

RESEARCH OBJECTIVES

- To identify the perceptual factors of E-commerce.
- To study the relationship between perceptual factors of E-commerce and select demographic factors.

RESEARCH METHODOLOGY

The study involves a mixed approach of exploratory, descriptive and empirical research. Data was collected from both primary and secondary sources in order to fulfill objectives under study. The questionnaire was constructed for determining the perception of Tour and Travel Operators towards E-commerce in light of select demographic factors. Travel agents which belong to TASK (Travel Agents Society of Kashmir) formed the part of the study's sample. In total 69 responses were received for inclusion in the study and further analysis.

Data Analysis and Interpretation

For the analysis and interpretation of the data, Spss v-20 software was used. Initially the descriptive analysis of the demographics was done in order to know the high means and percentage of the dominating variable, thus Fig.1 shows the graphical representation of the qualification of Travel and Tour Operators. It enables us to give the background of the agents showing that most of them are graduates followed by post graduates and under graduates.

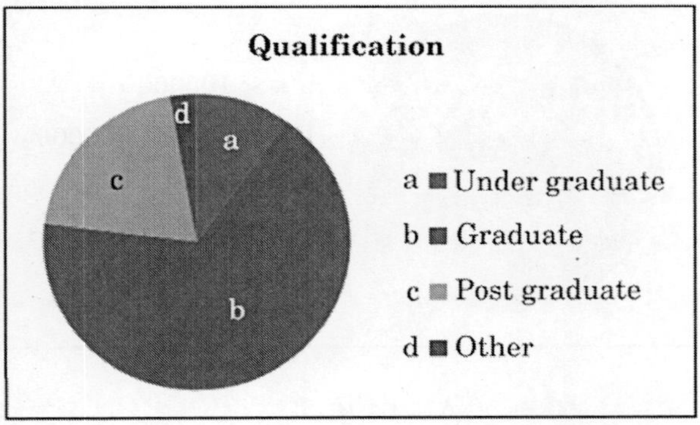

Fig. 1

Another variable was tourism knowhow, which gives an essence of knowledge in their respective profession. Fig. 2 represent that the respondents have multiple degrees but mostly hold advanced degree in the tourism followed by diploma, certified program and degree related tourism.

Last demographic variable was income factor which was depicted on the annual basis. Fig. 3 showed half of the sample population earn more that 1000000 annually while as rest earns within different range.

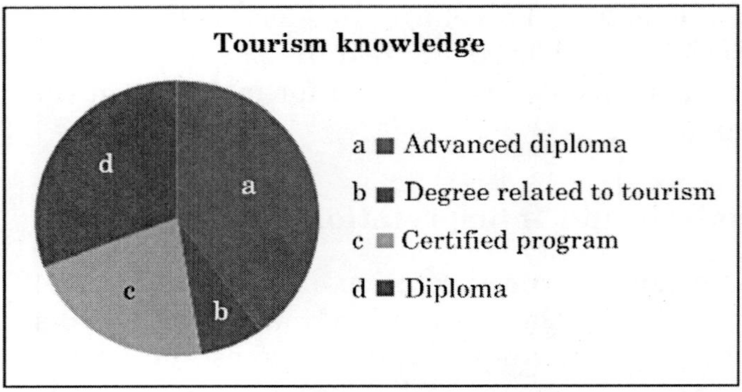

Fig. 2

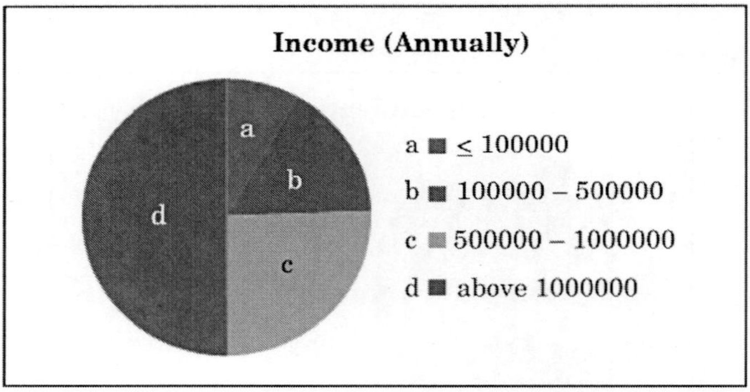

Fig. 3

The overall crux of the descriptive analysis was that majority of Tour and Travel Agents are graduates which do have knowledge of their profession and earn more than 10 lakhs annually.

Initially Cronbach's alpha was conducted for reliability of the scale, resulting 0.85 value which was above the acceptable range of 0.6. KMO and Bartlett's test for sphericity has been used to understand if the factor analysis could be performed, resulting 0.69 as such EFA (Exploratory Factor Analysis) was conducted which lead to the extraction of three factors judged on the basis of perception of Tour and Travel Operators (Perceptual factors), namely Relative Advantage, Governmnet Incentives and Security.

One way ANOVA was performed on demographics of the study to understand the influence on Perceptual factors of E-commerce, which is used to compare several population means.

Ho_1: Perceptual factors and tourism knowledge are independent of each other

Table 1: One-way ANOVA descriptives.

Factors		*N*	*F value*	*P-value (sig.)*
Relative advantage	Advanced diploma	28	4.467	.021
	Degree related tourism	5		
	Certified program	15		
	Diploma	21		
Security	Advanced diploma	28	2.643	.033
	Degree related tourism	5		
	Certified program	15		
	Diploma	21		
Govt. incentives	Advanced diploma	28	.342	.041
	Degree related tourism	5		
	Certified program	15		
	Diploma	21		

Source: Authors' own

From Table 1, its prominent that all the perceptual factors are showing significant relation with the tourism related knowledge (at <0.5 significance level). As such we reject our null hypothesis that perceptual factors and tourism related knowledge are independent of each other.

Another objective was to see the relationship between qualification and perceptual factors.

$Ho_{2:}$ The qualification of Tour and Travel Operators and perceptual factors are independent of each other

One way ANOVA was performed to prove the null hypothesis. Table 2 represents the result of the test. Its predicted that all the values shown by the test are insignificant (at sig< 0.5) as the p value is greater than the threshold value, hence we failed to reject the null hypothesis that is perceptual factors and qualification of Tour and Travel Operators are independent of each other.

Table 2: One-way ANOVA descriptives.

Factors		***N***	***F value***	***P-value (sig.)***
Relative advantage	Under graduate	7	.546	.598
	Graduate	46		
	Post graduate	14		
	others	2		
Security	Under graduate	7	.428	.515
	Graduate	46		
	Post graduate	14		
	others	2		
Government incentive	Under graduate	7	.388	.761
	Graduate	46		
	Post graduate	14		
	others	2		

Source: Authors' own

FINDINGS AND CONCLUSIONS

The study is among the scarce one where the impact is to be seen on the Tour and Travel Operators‘ perceptual factors of E-commerce adoption and that too in J&K state. From the study and relevant tests its evident internet and E-commerce play a central role in the business of Tour and Travel Operators as such they are wholly and solely dependent on it. Three factors namely relative advantage, Security and Government Incentives were extracted as such they are called perceptual factors.

Relative advantage includes the benefits related to E-commerce adoption in the form of ease of communication, collaboration with their business partners, customers etc. This factor was given due importance by other researchers in their study as well (Nazir & Haq, 2017), (Poon & Swatman, 1997) and Lawrence (2002) which emphasizes that relative advantage is important for E-commerce adoption.

Security was another outcome factor which was considered important for E-commerce adoption. Hassle and bug free transactions are important for their business as such it's seen as important factor. This was in queue with other studies as well (Nazir, 2017).

Government incentives is the final factor which highlight the support that the government should provide related to the E-commerce diffusion in travel business. As per Girish, William and Yates (2014) the Government policies and support has shown as having direct relation and hence faster diffusion of technology. The Govt. regulation influences the E-commerce adoption in a positive way as such legal support is necessary on their part which was in line with the study of Al- Alawi (2015). The study has also that Government support is very crucial both legally and financial for the upliftment of the travel business.

Qualification, Income and Tourism knowledge formed the part of demographic variables. Since the main study revolves around E-commerce factors and demographics, it can be put forth that tourism knowledge was seen as significant for the adoption of E-commerce in Tour and Travel Operators business. It can also be emphasized that having tourism related knowledge and know how is crucial for running their travel business giving them an edge over their practical knowledge. However qualification on the other hand doesn't seem to have an impact on the perceptual factors of E-commerce. The main reason though was beyond the study's scope but it could be predicted that for them experience seems to play a major role. With the advancement in the technology equal access to the internet and E-commerce opportunities is evident irrespective of gender or the kind of qualification; no disparity exists any longer. This study adds to the evidence that demographical influence can be seen having partial influence on E-commerce adoption.

LIMITATIONS

- Only TASK members were taken as the respondents for the study.
- The study was limited to J&K state only.

- Few demographic factors were taken into consideration as such there are other influencing factors as well.

REFERENCES

Al-Alawi, A.I., & Al-Ali, F.M. (2015). Factors affecting E-commerce adoption in SMEs in the GCC: An empirical study of Kuwait. *Research Journal of Information Technology*, 7(1): 1–21.

Bagale, G.S. (2014). Determinants of E-commerce in Indian MSME sector: A conceptual research model based on TOE framework. *Universal Journal of Management*, 2(3): 105–115.

Baker, E.W., Al-Gahtani, S.S., & Hubona, G.S. (2007). The effects of gender and age on new technology implementation in a developing country: Testing the Theory of Planned Behavior (TPB). *Information Technology & People*, 20(4): 352–375.

Baldwin, A., Lymer, A., & Johnson, R. (2001). Business impacts of the internet for small and medium-sized enterprises. *E-commerce and V-business*, pp. 103–120.

Barnett, M., & Standing, C. (2001). Repositioning travel agencies on the internet. *Journal of Vacation Marketing*, 7(2): 143–152.

Begin, L., & Boisvert, H. (2002). The internal factors that can make or break E-commerce implementation. *CMA Magazine*, 76(2): 22–22.

Cheung, R., & Lam, P. (2009). How travel agency survive in e-business world. *Communications of the IBIMA*, 10(11): 85–92.

Davis, F.D. (1989). Perceived usefulness, perceived ease of use, and user acceptance of information technology. *MIS Quarterly*, 13(3): 319–340.

Davis, F.D., Bagozzi, R.P., & Warshaw, P.R. (1989). User acceptance of computer technology: A comparison of two theoretical models. *Management Science*, 35(8): 982–1003.

Dolnicar, S., & Laesser, C. (2007). Travel agency marketing strategy: Insights from Switzerland. *Journal of Travel Research*, 46(2): 133–146.

Gibbs, J., Kraemer, K.L., & Dedrick, J. (2003). Environment and policy factors shaping global E-commerce diffusion: A cross-country comparison. *The Information Society*, 19(1): 5–18.

Girish, J., Williams, C.B., & Yates, D.J. (2014). Predictors of on-line services and e-participation: A cross-national comparison. *Government Information Quarterly*, 31(4): 526–533.

Inkpen, G. (1998). *Information Technology for Travel and Tourism* (No. Ed. 2). Addison Wesley Longman Ltd. (book)

Law, R., Leung, K., & Wong, R. (2004). The impact of the internet on travel agencies. *International Journal of Contemporary Hospitality Management*, 16(2): 100–107.

Lawrence, J.E. (2002). The use of the internet in small to medium-sized enterprises (Doctoral Dissertation, University of Salford).

Lee, J.W. (2010). The roles of demographics on the perceptions of electronic commerce adoption. *Academy of Marketing Studies Journal*, 14(1): 71.

Mamaghani, F. (2009). Impact of E-commerce on travel and tourism: An historical analysis. *International Journal of Management*, 26(3): 365.

Nazir, S. (2017). E-commerce Perception and Adoption-A Study of Tour and Travel Operators of J&K State. *Amity Global Business Review*, 12(2).

Poon, S., & Swatman, P.M. (1997). Internet-based small business communication: Seven Australian cases. *Electronic Markets*, 7(2): 15–21.

Rodgers, E.M. (1995). *Diffusion of Innovations*. New *York*.

Rotchanakitumnuai, S., & Speece, M. (2003). Barriers to internet banking adoption: A qualitative study among corporate customers in Thailand. *The International Journal of Bank Marketing*, 21(6): 312–32

Warden, S.C., & Tunzelana, S. (2004). E-commerce: A critical review of SMME organizational barriers in tourism. *In: 6th www Applications conference 2004, Johannesburg South Africa [On line]. Available at.*

Zhu, K., Xu, S., & Dedrick, J. (2003). Assessing drivers of e-business value: Results of a cross-country study. *ICIS 2003 Proceedings*, p. 16.

13

Technology Revolution for Entrepreneurship Promotion with Reference to Jammu and Kashmir

BILAL AHMAD DAR[1]* AND J.K. TANDON[2]

ABSTRACT

This paper focuses on "Technology Revolution and its positive effects on the entrepreneurial promotion especially in Indian context. It will discuss how technology has been an aid to the entrepreneurial process and how start-up and established ventures can be benefitted through the systematic use of technology. The development of Small and Medium Enterprises (SMEs) is vital to create economic prosperity in a nation and Entrepreneurship development can be considered as a reflecting part of SME as well as established venture growth emphasizing on institutional development in the economy. "Technology is the collection of tools, including machinery, modifications, arrangements and procedures used by humans". This tool aids in the entrepreneurship development from beginning to end whether it is the Internet services like Knowledge and awareness sites, Advanced financial transaction technologies, Computers aiding the start-up business, R&D tools and mappings, Machine based operation and production techniques, Advanced marketing through use of modern technology (e.g., new media for advertisement, POS and POP techniques, MIS based on computer data usage etc.) or techno based consumer satisfaction systems. In India, Economic development is structured on entrepreneurial institutional growth and IT revolution and other technological developments (especially in recent times) have paved a path for increased entrepreneurial activities in

[1 2] School of Business and Management, Jaipur National University, Jaipur, Rajasthan.

**Corresponding author:* E-mail: darbilalsultan@gmail.com

the nation building a modern business society. Technology entrepreneurship is gradually being recognized to impact significantly on socio-economic activities of the nation. This paper seeks to examine the importance of technology entrepreneurship as a platform towards industrial development, reducing youth unemployment, and the promotion of socio-economic growth and development in Jammu and Kashmir. Specifically, it also identifies Policy Requirements for Technological Entrepreneurship Development in Jammu and Kashmir.

Key words: Technology, Entrepreneurship promotion, Entrepreneurial ventures.

INTRODUCTION

Uneducated manpower has become one of the most topical and thorny issues in contemporary Jammu and Kashmir. The unemployment situation has changed from previous position marked by prolonged period of unemployment and misemployment, to one in which graduates of tertiary institutions have to normally wait for a long time before getting a first job – if at all (Hassan, 2013) Jammu and Kashmir has 6 lakh youth unemployment. These are mostly young adults that have graduated from universities and polytechnics or institutions of higher learning. In addition to this number, about 3 lakh others are certificate carrying youths that have no formal education, or have completed primary or secondary school, or dropped out from tertiary institutions all of which are annually poured into an already saturated labour. Many of those youths are not productive not because they lack the qualification but because the system has not been able to impact in such individuals technical knowledge and know-how skills required to carry out entrepreneurial activities especially technologically oriented. In recent times, the concept of entrepreneurship has been made prominent by various discussions relating to industrial development. However, it has been observed that while entrepreneurship which is the exploitation of business opportunity would bring about job creation and wealth generation, it has limitation in bringing about accelerated industrial development that will not only expand the job creation and wealth generation phenomena, but also would enable a country to compete in the frontiers of global rapid technological developments. Thus the concept of technological entrepreneurship has gained more and more attention among researchers, policy makers, Government, scholars and firms alike. For instance, we have authors who have discussed the subject of technological entrepreneurship (Mowery & Shane, 2002; Shane & Venkataraman, 2003; Phan & Foo, 2004; Dorf & Byers, 2007). In this body of literature, emphasis seemed to be placed on high-potential technology opportunities, technical systems, innovation, production and commercialization. Within this context, very little technological entrepreneurship can be said to exist in Jammu and Kashmir, and indeed in many developing economies.

Entrepreneurial ventures are considered as the engines for the development of economy and nation. They are the transformation agents and knowledge resource of the nation upon who the responsibility of structured development and radical changes is there. Entrepreneurs need technology for undertaking these responsibilities. Technology as a method, tool, process or modification work as a support element for entrepreneurship development. The process of entrepreneurship involves the use of technology at every step whether it is idea generation, idea selection, resource assemblage, production and services, marketing, customer satisfaction or any other aspect related to development of enterprise.

RESEARCH METHODOLOGY

The data for this paper were originated from secondary sources: Previous research and analysis of scholars, Government documents, magazines as well as journals articles that are related to the subject. This study involved an extensive literature review which critically analyzed the present status, prospects of technology knowledge and technology entrepreneurship as part of the roadmap to wealth creation and reduction of unemployment among Jammu and Kashmir youths.

Concept of Technology Entrepreneurship

Technology entrepreneurship according to Abdullah and Ahcene (2011) is basically the merge of two words from two disciplines:

Technology from the innovation discipline and entrepreneurship from the business discipline. Technology entrepreneurship is referred to the capabilities of a technology entrepreneur, specifically the knowledge and skills required by the entrepreneur to carry out technology based entrepreneurial activities successfully (Abdullah & Ahcene, 2011). Technological entrepreneurship, also referred to as technology based entrepreneurship, can also be defined as the setting up of new enterprises by individuals or corporations to exploit technological innovation (Aderemi *et al.,* 2011). It can also be described as the commercialization of emerging technological discoveries or innovation. Technological entrepreneurship is defined as a style of business leadership that involves identifying high potential, technology intensive commercial opportunities, gathering resources such as talent and capital, and managing rapid growth and significant risk using principled decision making skills (Dorf & Byers, 2007; Aderemi *et al,* 2011). It is also defined the term as the process by which entrepreneurs assemble organizational resources and technical systems, and the strategies by entrepreneurial firms to pursue opportunities (Shane & Venkataraman, 2003; Aderemi *et al.,* 2011). Aderemi *et al.* (2008) positioned technological entrepreneurship as being needed to make full use of the knowledge of science and technology currently available in meeting market needs, thereby making the country in question more productive and more competitive internationally (Aderemi *et al.,* 2008). This suggests the necessary involvement of a process of industrial innovation in the country's area of strength and endowment to generate productivity and competitiveness. According to them, "Technological entrepreneurship is initiated and culminated in design, development, production, engineering and commercialization of innovative new products and processes".

Dimensions of Technology Entrepreneurship

Eight key technology entrepreneurship activities are identified based on the four constituencies of technology entrepreneurship as highlighted by Shane and Venkataraman (2003) in their special issue on technology entrepreneurship, and reviewed by Abdullah and Ahcene (2011) which includes industry, firm, technology and entrepreneur. The 8 key dimensions of technology entrepreneurship are: awareness, search, strategy, core competency, technology paradigm, linkages, learning, and leadership. "Awareness" is referred to the ability to recognize pertinent environmental changes, and the need to improve; "Search" is the ability to explore for opportunities and threat; "Strategy" is the plan of action to achieve the envisioned goals that are significant for the economic growth of the firm; "Core Competency" is the economic strength of the firm that needs to be identified and built upon; "Technology Paradigm" is the ability to understand the existing platform of technology; "Linkages" is any form of collaborative effort established by the firm; "Learning" is the firm's effort to encourage acquisition of codified and tacit knowledge on continuous basis; and finally "Leadership" is the ability of the entrepreneur to lead his firm to achieve competitive advantage and sustain it.

Features of Technology Entrepreneurship

There are certain attributes that characterize technological entrepreneurship. These attributes by (Aderemi *et al.,* 2011) are elaborated below:

High potential opportunity

A new technology-based venture is described as having a high potential opportunity if it is capable of creating new value for its customers, it has a significant level of technology understanding which is difficult to replicate and can often be protected (patented), it has a significant first mover advantage, it has a level of scalability, it creates a barrier to entry, and it also has a high level of initial risk which can be translated into high levels of return.

Technology-intensive opportunity

Technological entrepreneurship is described as a technology-intensive opportunity involving a process of problem solving, raising and safeguarding the quality of life, needing technical skills and applications, identifying potential market, improvement in quality of products in order to improve competitiveness of the firm with expectation of saving in process cost. Furthermore, the sufficient reason for embarking on technological entrepreneurship is borne out of the need to commercialize significant innovations that are expected to guarantee suppliers of materials, long-term stability of firms and increase output.

Unique technology capable of driving a new business

As firms can be viewed as bidding and competing for customers' purchases, and markets can be evaluated based on the extent to which the profitability of a firm hinges on meeting consumers demands if possible, better than its rivals. Consequently, aside from having more share of the market through aesthetic changes, price reduction, and better performance and so on, technological entrepreneurship has the characteristic of being able to advance new technologies that can institutionalize new ventures that adequately meet consumers' need.

The Role of Technological Entrepreneurship in Social and Economic Development

A vast body of research exists on the importance and varied contributions of technological entrepreneurship to job creation, economic and social development, and growth. It was specifically stated as follows (Zahra & Hayton, 2007; Aderemi *et al.,* 2011) technological entrepreneurship is a key source of economic and social progress. It refers to the creation of new firms by independent entrepreneurs and corporations to exploit technological discoveries. These new firms create jobs, contribute to the well-being of their communities and generate wealth for their owners. These firms are also the change makers in their respective.

Industries as they bring in new technological paradigms that alter the dynamics of competition and rules of rivalry. Basically, both incremental and radical innovations are important not only for the positive economic impact they typically create, but also because they fundamentally change the behavior of consumers, often in ways that improve their lives. More specifically, as stated by Aderemi *et al.* (2011) the following are the roles of technological entrepreneurship in socio-economic development:

- Technological entrepreneurship is needed to propel technological innovation efforts into the market. Whenever there is a breakthrough in research and development. It is the place of technological entrepreneurship to commercialize the achievements of technological efforts otherwise; it remains in the laboratory without making any impact. One of the reasons why many research breakthroughs never leave the laboratory is due to short fall of technological entrepreneurs. And unless technological innovation or the output of research and development efforts reaches the market or are commercialized, industrialization would be elusive.
- Technological entrepreneurship has the potential of improving state of technological capability in a country. This is because as technological efforts are being made, learning takes place. This occurs either by doing or observation, thus improving technological capability in the efforts in question.
- Because technological entrepreneurship would necessarily involve the commercialization of a research output, more patents are generated and patents are a well-known indicator and measure of technological development and industrialization in countries all over the world.
- Technological entrepreneurship is the platform that accelerates the diffusion of successful technological innovation in an economy. For instance in Jammu and Kashmir, and in most the states of country, the rate of diffusion of Information Communication Technology (ICT) is on the increase. This is made possible by the private firms that saw an opportunity and decided to market ICT products and services thereby increasing the pace of diffusion. The diffusion in turn has greatly enhanced the quality of life of the citizenries.
- For a technological entrepreneur to be relevant, he must of necessity meet market needs and be a problem solver. In a bid to meet market need, research and development as well as science and technology efforts must be well coordinated. Science and technology as well as industrialization policies are tailored towards meeting the needs of the market. This,

we believe, will invariably bring about socio-economic development.

Policy Requirements for Technological Entrepreneurship Development in Jammu and Kashmir

Many policies covering different sectors of the Jammu and Kashmiri economy have been put in place to guide the development of entrepreneurship but without a concise and effective Science and Technology (S & T) policy, the industrial and other related policies will only promote commerce. It is important to note also, that entrepreneurial interest among J&K students is quite high but the expression of this interest in practice is rather low. The main factors found to be responsible for this are poor funding and inadequate preparation through training. A particularly key institutional weaknesses identified be expressed in the inadequacy of Government support to young and aspiring entrepreneurs. In fact, until Government directed all universities in the J&K to establish entrepreneurship centers, youth entrepreneurship has been left in the domain of agencies and non-governmental organizations. Much has been said about entrepreneurial education and its importance in stimulating and sustaining entrepreneurship, especially among students. In implementing this, however, it is important to note that a uniform curriculum might not yield optimal results across different disciplines or levels. The design of these curriculum should, therefore, consider the peculiarities of each discipline when issues and resource persons are being selected. As a necessity, entrepreneurial training initiatives should include a standardized monitoring and evaluation structure which ensures strict conformance with quality. Besides the strictly formal training, entrepreneurial advocacy is also very beneficial. Institutions, of their own conscious will should seek to organize seminars, workshops, symposia and other similar forums where students could be brought in contact with state-of-the-art knowledge in the practice of entrepreneurship. These forums are also hold the benefit of encouraging the students by bringing them in contact with excelling nascent entrepreneurs. In implementing all of the foregoing recommendations, the place of a stable political atmosphere, strong institutions and sustainable funding cannot be overemphasized. Few, if any, policies and programmes would ever work in situations of chaos and scarcity of resources. It then rests on the government of the day to work sedulously at creating a crime-free and peaceful environment without which entrepreneurship, which is the vehicle of innovation, cannot succeed.

CONCLUSIONS

From all indications, youth unemployment is a menace in Kashmir and constitutes a real danger and a threat to social, economic, political and industrial development. However, career guidance can only be a panacea for reducing the rate of youth unemployment in conjunction with Technical and Vocational Education (TVE) and entrepreneurship. Moreover, the energy, skills and aspirations of young people are invaluable assets that no country can afford to waste and holding them to realize their full potential by gaining access to employment is a precondition for poverty eradication, sustainable development and lasting peace. No amount of career guidance will help if there are no employment opportunities, no entrepreneurial skills to facilitate self-employment and no technical and vocational skills needed for gainful employment.

REFERENCES

Abdullah, S., & Ahcene, L. (2011). "The Understanding of Technology Entrepreneurship According to Shariah Principles". *International Conference on Business and Economics Research IPEDR* Vol. 16, IACSIT Press, Singapore.

Dorf, R.C., Byers, T.H., & Nelson, A.J. (2008). *Technology ventures: From idea to enterprise*. McGraw-Hill Higher Education.

Hassan, O.M. (2013). Curbing the unemployment problem in Nigeria through entrepreneurial development. *African Journal of Business Management*, 7(44): 4429–4444.

Mowery, D.C., & Shane, S. (2002). Introduction to the special issue on university entrepreneurship and technology transfer. *Management Science*, 48(1): V–IX.

Phan, P., & Foo, M. (2004). "Technological Entrepreneurship in Emerging Regions". *Journal of Business Venturing*, 19(1): 1–5.

Shane, S., & Venkataraman, S. (2003). "Guest Editors' *Introduction to the Special Issue: Technology Entrepreneurship*". *Research Policy*, 32(2): 181–184.

Siyanbola, W.O., Aderemi, H.O., Egbetokun, A.A., & Sanni, M. (2011). Framework for technological entrepreneurship development: Key issues and policy directions. *American Journal of Industrial and Business Management*, 1(01): 10.

Zahra, S.A., & Hayton, J.C. (2004). Technological entrepreneurship: Key themes and emerging research directions. *Crossroads of Entrepreneurship*, pp. 185–208.

14

Swachh Bharat Abhiyan and Tourism Industry in India: A Content Analysis

ABID SUHAIL NIKA[1*] AND ADIL AMIN NAZKI[2]

ABSTRACT

The country India (Bharat) is a land of cultural heritage and rich past. The India ranks 101th in natural resources globally but only 1.18% share in Global Foreign Tourist Arrivals (FTA) as on 2016. Tourism industry generates about 9.4% of India's total GDP and employment generation of 41.622 million jobs as on 2017. In addition to employment, tourism industry helps India in earning foreign exchange. India is a country which is rich in every aspect. Almighty has bestowed the country with rich natural as well as manmade attractions and is having highest potential for tourism. It is a country having strong cultural and historical attributes. Tourists from the beginning were lured towards the country not only to visit its attractions but want to get well apprised by the culture of the local people. They don't want to enjoy the services of a five star hotel in India which is already available at their places better than here, but want to visit the remote areas where they get the handy experience about how the people live, what they eat, what are their rituals, beliefs etc. But the biggest limitation for India to promote tourism at the global level is lack of cleanliness. They yet have not been in a position to attract the foreign tourists to that extent as the foreign tourists are very meticulous about hygiene and cleanliness. Swachh Bharat Abhiyan was launched (cleanliness drive) to make India free from waste and dirtiness. The aim was to make it neat and clean. The intention was that Swachh Bharat Mission will increase tourist footfall which will help India in generating more employment through tourism and boost its GDP. The objective of the

[1, 2] Department of Tourism Studies, Central University of Kashmir, Srinagar, J&K.
**Corresponding author:* E-mail: abids157@gmail.com

current study is to analyse the impact of Swachh Bharat Abhiyan on tourism industry of India. The study wants to access whether Swachh Bharat Abhiyan really has been successful in its agenda or not. From the study it has been revealed that there is a positive impact of clean India campaign on tourism development.

Key words: Swachh Bharat Abhiyan, Tourism, Clean India campaign, India.

INTRODUCTION

Swachh Bharat Abhiyan is a gigantic mass movement which was inaugurated on October 2nd, 2014 which was aimed to create a clean and neat India by 2019. Mahatma Gandhi (Father of Nation) through his entire life had put the emphasis on Swachhta which leads to healthy and prosperous life. In order to make the dream of Mahatma Gandhi true, Government of Indian launched the Swachh Bharat Abhiyan. The Abhiyan would cover all rural and urban areas. The urban component of the Abhiyan would be taken by the Ministry of Urban Development, and the rural component by the Ministry of Drinking Water and Sanitation. As the main objective of Swachh Bharat Abhiyan is to eliminate all kinds of pollutions from the country like polyethylene, proper defecation mechanism in trains (Bio-toilets), avoiding open defecation in the fields, conversion of unsanitary toilets to pour flush toilets, proper mechanism to convert biodegradable solid wastes into the manures, proper sanitation, awareness among the masses to keep themselves and environment around them neat and clean, acquaint them about hygiene and good health etc. The concept of 'Smart City' was the outcome of Swachh Bharat Abhiyan in which hundreds of cities in India were given this status. The aim is to have a holistic development of cities like infrastructural development; projects aiming in making the city's waste free, eradication of manual scavenging, management of municipal solid waste and bringing about a behavioural change in people regarding healthy sanitation practices, proper drainage system, health, quality water supply etc. The aim is also to make the tourist sites free from any kind of waste. India's overall focus is on cleanliness, security and better accessibility to tourist areas to boost tourism in the country. The India is not enjoying a good favourable image in the minds of foreign tourists as far as the overall cleanliness is concerned. The Ministry of Tourism Government of India is of the thought that "Swachhta (cleanliness), security and connectivity are the three important pillars of tourism industry. The Government of India is working very hard towards it to attract mass tourists. The Swachh Paryatan (clean tourism) is the "dream" of Ministry of Tourism "which has been inspired by Prime Minister Narendra Modi's cleanliness movement". The Government has given impetus to the cleanliness initiative so that polythene would be banned at all tourist spots.

The other aspect of Swachh Bharat Abhiyan is to focus on cleanliness and hygiene by having full focus towards the use of clean technology *i.e.,* non-polluting in nature. It will definitely involve the use of biodegradable fuel and products. The shift towards clean technology will have dual positive effect on India's entire economy. The use of new technology will bring new employment opportunities like in the case of Information Technology. The new technology will lead to new skill development for innovation which directly helps in generating new employment/ entrepreneurial opportunities for the youth of India. It will make India's entry in the league of skilled economies of the globe. India can become hub of clean technology for entire world. Swachh Bharat Abhiyan is not to be associated only to cleanliness and hygiene but its larger objective is to make India's entry in the League of Nations working towards technological development for future.

Swachh Bharat Abhiyan for Urban Areas

The mission includes exclusion of open defecation, conversion of unsanitary toilets to pour flush toilets, abolition of manual scavenging, management of municipal solid waste and bringing about a behavioural change in masses through awareness programs regarding healthy sanitation practices. The Swachh Bharat Abhiyan aims to cover 1.04 crore households, to provide 2.5 lakh community toilets, 2.6 lakh public toilets, and a proper facility for solid waste management in each town. Under the Mission, community toilets will be constructed in residential areas. The designated locations for the construction of public toilets will be tourist places, markets, bus stations, railway stations, etc. The programme will be implemented over a period of five-years in 4,401 towns.

The ultimate aim of the '*Swachh Bharat Abhiyan for urban areas*' is to keep the all the cities of the country neat and clean and fit for the tourists to come and visit the beautiful tourist spots/ destinations. The objective is to attract foreign tourists to boost tourism in India but we can be successful only when they will experience clean tourism over here.

Swachh Bharat Abhiyan for Rural Areas

The Nirmal Bharat Abhiyan was restructured into the Swachh Bharat Mission (Gramin). The Abhiyan focuses to make India an open defecation free country in Five Years. Its role is to improve the level of cleanliness in rural areas through proper management activities of solid and Liquid wastes and by making Gram Panchayats Open Defecation Free (ODF), clean and sanitized. Under the mission, for the construction of about 11 crore 11 lakh toilets in the country the total expenditure which will be incurred is one lakh thirty four thousand crore rupees. There will be an optimum use of technology on a larger scale for the conversion of *waste into wealth* in rural India in the form of bio-fertilizer and different forms of energy. There will be the involvement of every gram panchayat, panchayat samiti and zila parishad in the country in order to execute the mission on war footing basis, besides roping in large sections of rural population including school teachers and students in this endeavor.

REVIEW OF RELATED LITERATURE

India is not yet in a position to attract large number of tourists to visit beaches, mountains and desert sands and there is utmost need to improve the present branding of Incredible India. There are many issues and challenges faced by tourism industry of India, like lack of infrastructure, hygiene, high tariffs etc. The various clean campaigns are shown in Table 1.

Table 1: Various campaigns launched by different personalities and organizations.

Sl no.	*Author/Organization*	*Campaign/Action plan*
1.	Lee Kuan Yew (1968)	The keep Singapore Clean Campaign.
2.	Greg Duffell (1999)	100% pure New Zealand Campaign.
3.	UNEP and UNDP (2005)	Land use management plan and zoning.
4.	UNEP and UNDP (2005)	National Ecotourism Strategy and Action Plan (Bulgaria), Development of Bulgaria's NESAP.
5.	Zimasa Velaphi (2014)	Waste management and recycling.
6.	Hussain Nasser Lootah (2014)	Clean Up The World.

Clean Campaign's in Various Countries

Singapore

Yew (1968) stated that, "The Keep Singapore Clean Campaign was one of the first campaigns launched by Singapore Government". The most important aim was to make Singapore the clean city, in order to enhance tourism over there and to attract foreign investment.

Bulgaria

As per UNEP and UNDP report (2005), "National Ecotourism Strategy and Action Plan (Bulgaria), Development of Bulgaria's National Ecotourism Strategy and Action Plan (NESAP) was started in 2002 by the Bulgarian Government to create economic growth for communities situated near protected areas, strengthen local support for conservation and contribute to rural sustainable development".

Egypt

UNEP and UNDP report (2005), "Land use management plan and zoning regulations of Egypt, Egypt's Red Sea coast attracts huge number of tourist to experience the marine life over there, including coral reef systems. In 2001, for the Southern Red Sea region the Tourism Development Authority (TDA) started a land use management planning and zoning process, in order to manage future tourism expansion in an area which is having a high concentration of fringe reefs and protected areas".

New Zealand

Duffell (1999), "Commented that the start of 100% Pure New Zealand campaign has been very effective. The campaign is based on a strong proposition, backed by relevant and credible images. Even after ten years, it is relevant campaign for the image of the destination". According to (UNDP) most operators don't have their individual resources to market New Zealand themselves. Because of the consistency and impact of the 100% Pure New Zealand campaign means that operators can go offshore to sell their own product, knowing that the job of laying the groundwork of what New Zealand has to offer has already been done.100% Pure New Zealand has internationally lifted New Zealand's profile and given a strong, clear point of difference in the key visitor markets. Rogers (2008) remarked that "100% Pure New Zealand is accelerating well with other international tourism campaigns". And the meaning of awareness campaign in the communication industry is to make a targeted audience aware of an issue. Pollock (1999) also "Commented that the campaign have been extremely successful for New Zealand. The timing of the campaign was excellent and it did not follow the green consciousness shift. The double meaning of "Pure" worked well in identifying the uniqueness, integrity, authenticity and essence of the overall brand."

South Africa

It has been stated that every South African in spite of age, race, background or economic status has a responsibility to help in keeping the country clean and litter free. Velaphi (2014), "Highlighted the importance of waste management and recycling".

Dubai

Lootah (2014) launched the campaign called 'Clean Up The World' in the Emirate of Dubai under the slogan 'Our Place, Our Planet,

Our Responsibility' with the United Nations Environment Programme (UNEP) in order to extend environmental awareness and education, and maintaining cleanliness through the local participation including individuals, schools, companies and Government departments.

Fiji

FRCS (Fiji Red Cross Society) youth champion deliberated on "Clean Up Campaign" that it is a mode of strengthening nations network and relationship. "The initiative cleaned the streets of Seaqaqa in order to keep area clean and to shun the spread of dengue fever and other diseases".

From the above review of literature we can comprehend that Clean Campaign has been implemented effectively in many countries which has really created a positive impact on tourism development of destinations. It helped in developing a destination image which directly accelerates the scope of tourism promotion, by promoting clean destinations to attract mass tourists.

RESEARCH METHODOLOGY

The study is qualitative in nature and the data has been collected from various reputed journals, national and local newspaper archives. The data has been also encapsulated from online resources like UGC-Inflibnet, EBSCO-Host, and Google-Scholar etc. The various cleaning campaigns as mentioned in the study have been identified through review of related literature.

Critical Analysis

Cleanliness is the condition of being clean and free from dirt, and it is a habit of achieving and maintaining that state. Cleanliness is usually achieved through cleaning. Cleanliness is a moral quality, as reflected by the aphorism. It has been said that "Cleanliness is next to godliness", and should be treated as an important contributing factor towards 'health' and 'beauty'. Cleanliness as observed by Jacob Burckhardt" is indispensable to our modern notion of social perfection". A household or workplace may have good cleanliness, but not purity; cleanliness is a characteristic of the people who maintain cleanness or prevent dirtying at their places. Practically, cleanliness is linked to hygiene and disease prevention.

To critically analyse the impact of Swachh Bharat Abhiyan on tourism industry of India the researcher has evaluated the cleanliness status of various important tourism spots in the country after the launch of the campaign.

The Government of India recognized ten iconic tourist places in 2016 that have undergone cleaning on par in the country in phase I which includes *Taj Mahal, Mata Vaishno Devi temple, Ajmer Sharif Dargah, CST Mumbai, Golden Temple, Kamakhya Temple, Maikarnika Ghat, Meenakshi Temple, Shree Jagannath Temple,* and *Tirupati Temple* as part of a pilot project under the Swachh Bharat mission. Tirupati, a well-known tourist destination was ranked as the 9th cleanest city in India, by Swachh Survekshan 2017.

The Phase II of Swachh tourist iconic places was launched in November 2017 and included *Gangotri, Yamunotri, Mahakaleshwar Temple, Charminar, Convent and Church of St. Francis of Assisi, Kalady, Gommateshwara, Baidyanath Dham, Gaya Tirth and Somnath Temple.*

Ten new iconic sites have been taken up under phase III of the flagship project Swachh Iconic Places (SIP) of the Swachh Bharat Mission namely, *Raghavendra Swamy Temple (Kurnool, Andhra Pradesh), Hazarduari Palace (Murshidabad, West Bengal), Brahma Sarovar Temple (Kurukshetra, Haryana), Vidur Kuti (Bijnor, Uttar Pradesh), Mana village (Chamoli, Uttarakhand), Pangong Lake (Leh-Ladakh, J&K), Nagvasuki Temple (Allahabad, Uttar Pradesh), Ima Keithel / market (Imphal, Manipur), Sabarimala Temple (Kerala)* and *Kanvashram (Uttarakhand)*. The project started by the Prime Minister is being harmonized by Ministry of Drinking Water and Sanitation with due support from the State Governments and Local Administration. These new sites have joined with the 20 iconic places under phase I and II where special sanitation work has been done. SIP (Swachh Iconic Places) is a project run by three central ministries - Ministry of Housing and Urban Affairs, Culture and Tourism. It also involves local administrations in the concerned states and public sector and private companies as sponsoring partners. The tourist sites, which are now the part of SIP, are visited by foreign tourists and pilgrims in large numbers because there has been a proper façade cleaning of the sites. The sites have been renovated where there was a need, proper sanitary facilities, availability of human resource at the spots to keep proper maintenance and other issues have been taken care of.

Swachh Bharat Abhiyan Impact: India Jumps in Top 40 Countries in Travel and Tourism Competitive Index Ranking

As the Ministry of Culture and Tourism took a number of initiatives to put into practice Swachh Bharat's objectives at many tourist destinations from pillar to post in India and which helped India in improving world ranking as a destination for tourists. India is the only third country in the world which improved its Travel and Tourism Competitive Index in a single year by double digits. In 2015 India ranked at 52 but India climbed up by a healthy 12 places to be ranked 40 in 2016. Clarion call given by Prime Minister Narendra Modi's for a Swachh Bharat not only improved India's rural and urban sanitation scenario, but also had a positive effect on India's ranking in the Travel and Tourism Competitive Index. The rankings which are released by the World Economic Forum in the travel and tourism sector maps sustainable developments of countries and how the tourism contributes in the holistic development of the countries. As tweeted Dr. Mahesh Sharma, Minister of State, Culture and Tourism, Swachh Bharat Abhiyan rewarded India in the World Tourism index for cleanliness and safety.

The major objectives of the Swachh Bharat Abhiyan was to improve sanitation and cleanliness of tourist spots and the several initiatives were undertaken to improve the sanitation and cleanliness conditions of India's important tourist spots. It is by dint of Swachh Bharat Abhiyan that in the year 2016, all 3,686 monuments of national importance which are under the shield of the Archaeological Survey of India (ASI) were declared Polythene

Free Zones (PFZ) to reduce waste disposal at such important sites. The Ministry undertook intensive cleaning of Indian monuments. This helped a lot in protecting such vital monuments of national and historical importance. It has been seen that number of tourist arrivals increased and those tourists who had already visited the site in the past praised the country and Swachh Bharat Abhiyan mission in keeping the sites clean when they compared present position of the sites with the past conditions prevailing over there. The Ministry organized 82 programmes during the Swachhata Pakhwada and an audio-visual guide was launched for tourists to follow.

The Swachh Bharat Abhiyan initiatives to create India's premium tourist spots clean and garbage free have already shown their results in the form of better ranking in the Travel and Tourism Competitive Index. India was not enjoying the favourable cleanliness image at the global level, despite the fact of having abundant tourist spots of diverse nature to attract foreign tourists. It has really created a good brand image in the minds of tourists as far as the cleanliness level is concerned, all credit goes to Swachh Bharat Mission. Swachh Paryatan mobile app was launched by the Ministry of Culture and Tourism to make sure that cleanliness around cultural and heritage monuments prevail. The app provides alerts on unclean conditions in different parts of various cities. Efforts of such nature as being undertaken by the ministry to ensure cleaner tourist destinations in India, India hopes to become a frequent destination for the tourists from across the globe.

RESULTS OF SWACHH BHARAT MISSION

(1) As per the report of WHO, Swachh Bharat Abhiyan has shown visible positive results in the country. On 2nd of October 2019, it will be the 150th birth anniversary of Mahatma Gandhi. Swachh Bharat Abhiyan will enable to gift a *"clean and green"* India to him. According to the latest report released by WHO, in between Oct 2014 to Oct 2019 the SBM-G (Swachh Bharat Mission-Gramin) will result in preventing more than 3 lakh deaths due to diarrhea and protein-energy malnutrition. There has been a rapid decrease

in open defecation and an increase in toilet coverage from 45% to 89% from 2014 till August 2018. Large numbers of villages and districts have been declared fully ODF.

(2) WHO also reports that through SBMG there has been a remarkable escalation of rural sanitation coverage of 89.07%.

(3) The report released by Water and Sanitation Programme (WPS) reflected that the inadequate sanitation in India leads tourism-related economic losses. The estimated loss from inadequate sanitation is estimated to be Rs. 12 billion ($266 million), 45% (Rs. 5.5 billion, $121 million) are from loss of tourism earnings, and 55% losses (Rs. 6.6 billion, $145.6 million) are due to gastrointestinal illnesses among international tourists. But due to the Swachh Bharat Abhiyan there has been decline in tourism losses to a higher extent which were earlier caused from bad water and sanitation in India. Now the tourists visiting the country had not to suffer frequently from gastrointestinal illnesses.

(4) The majority of our citizens in rural India, especially the women, no longer have to suffer the indignity of having to go out into the open to defecate. It marks a sea change in the dignity of their daily life. This helped in the overall cleanliness of villages which really helped tour and travel operators to flourish and market rural tourism in the country.

(5) India showed that 32% citizens believe that Swachh Bharat Abhiyan is having a positive impact on children and it really had created a kind of positive mind set-up among them in order to work for the cleanliness of the country. The second big positive of Swachh Bharat Abhiyan is that 32% citizens feel that civic sense has improved in the last 3 years. Neighbourhood and city is cleaner than what it was pre-Swachh Bharat Abhiyan. However, the prime area requiring immediate center of attention according to the citizens is the municipalities.

CONCLUSIONS

The current study has revealed that Swachh Bharat has really shown a positive impact on the cleanliness of the country. It really has leaded the positive approach in the minds of the common people of the country towards it. It not only helped India in minimizing the deaths which earlier were caused due to the poor hygiene and sanitation problems but helped India to gain positive image in the minds of the foreign as well as domestic tourists to visit the place. Swachh Bharat Abhiyan helped India to jump in top 40 countries in Travel and Tourism Competitive Index Ranking. Many historical monuments/places which were taken into loop under different phases of Swachh Bharat Mission got preserved and cleaned. It has been seen that now tourists love to visit these historical places/monuments which earlier were having less tourist footfall because of absence of cleanliness and basic available facilities over there.

LIMITATIONS AND FUTURE RESEARCH

The current research is qualitative in nature and is totally based on content analysis as the data has been collected from various reputed journals, national and local newspaper archives. The data has been also encapsulated from online resources like UGC Inflibnet, EBSCO host, and Google Scholar etc. The future study should be conducted in a sense that the author should take quantitative perspective of the study into the consideration which is very important.

REFERENCES

Duffell, G. (1999). 100% Pure a marketing strategy not an environmental standard [online] Available at: *www.scoop.co.nz/stories/HL1805/S00065/100-pure-a* [Accessed 5 Sep. 2018].

Lootah, H.N. (2014). *Impact of clean India campaign on tourism* [online] Available at: *icrb.international/pdf/papers/Dr.%20Bindu%20V.T.pdf* [Accessed 1 Sep. 2018].

Pollock, A. (1999). Marketing destinations in a digital world. Insights, maj, pp. 149–158.

Rogers, D. (2009). *Monitoring Yellow Sea Migrants in Australia (MYSMA): Northwestern Australian Shorebird Surveys and Workshops, December* 2008.

Tourism in India - Wikipedia [online] Available at: *en.wikipedia.org/wiki/Tourism in India* [Accessed 19 Sep.2018].

UNEP & UNDP (2005). Ecotourism naturally Bulgaria national ecotourism strategy [online] Available at: *docplayer.net/16600527-ecotourism-naturally-bulgaria* [Accessed 6 Aug. 2018].

UNEP & UNDP (2005). Environment Projects - Land Use Planning, Environmental [online] Available at: *www.planning4sd.com/sustainable development/ projects* [Accessed 11 Sep. 2018].

Velaphi, Z. (2014). Zimasa Peteni - HR Intern – Waste Plan - Waste Management [online] Available at: *za.linkedin.com/in/zimasa-peteni-3a18a412* [Accessed 13 Sep. 2018].

Yew, L.K. (1968). *Keep Singapore Clean campaign Infopedia* [online] Available at: *eresources.nlb.gov.sg/infopedia/articles/SIP_1160_2008* [Accessed 16 Sep. 2018].

Subject Index